READ

CW00420514

Hi there, firstly a big thank you for purchasing your copy of Property Investors' Tax Guide.

I hope that this book will in a simple but informative way give you a better understanding of how taxation works in property investing and will help you save thousands along the way.

I have crammed as much knowledge, expert advice, tips and tricks as I can into this book BUT tax legislation moves fast and I constantly have more I want to share with you to keep you one step ahead of the rest.

That's why I have created a bonus online resource for you. This online resource will help keep you up to date with the latest and hottest tax strategies and give you a competitive advantage over other property investors.

To get immediate access to your bonus gift – go here now before you continue reading:

🔍 www.propertytaxguide.co.uk

Shaz Nawaz

This book is dedicated to the community because it is they who inspired and encouraged me to write the book.

FOREWORD
by Mark Homer

Shaz is that rare breed of Accountant who actually invests and develops the type of property upon which he is providing tax advice. This book serves as a mosaic which lays out the legislation with the addition of Shaz's practical experience at the coal face. It comprehensively deals with tax legislation across a broad range of property investment and development strategies and styles.

Written using digestible language it will appeal to most as a simplified guide free of the usual mystifying terminology which many tax books seem to reflect. Very much written with a nod to the "Progressive" culture I have gained much from this guide and will be referring back to it frequently in the future.

CONTENTS

This is not a textbook for Accountants and Tax Advisers: their knowledge will come from reading the legislation, professional articles and textbooks, and from their compulsory Continuing Professional Development.

This is a book for the layperson who is interested in property investment and development. However this book is an overview of basics, not an in-depth, comprehensive guide of all the different taxes. Use it to raise your awareness. A detailed understanding will require a lot more research.

WELCOME
Who is this book for?

Property investment is a huge topic that touches a great many people. But not all of these are landlords building their property portfolios or builders and developers. In fact, some don't even regard themselves as being in any way a property investor, but more of an 'accidental landlord' – maybe the charity with a couple of warehouses for sorting and redistributing donations, the veterinary practice with multiple surgeries across a city or someone who owns a couple of properties. And what about the homeowners paying off their mortgages and beginning to think about what to leave to the children – are they property investors?

By definition, anyone who owns a financial share of a property is in effect a property investor.

So, this includes:

* Property portfolio investors

* Premises-owning businesses

* Serviced accommodation/furnished holiday lets

* Landlords (both residential and commercial)

* Construction and improvement companies

* Home-owners planning their financial future

These are all property investors of one kind or another; and for all of them, tax legislation can have a significant impact on their business or financial decisions. However, particularly for those who own property but don't see themselves as investors, it can be hard to make the connection between their property and their tax affairs.

I know from my own clients and their experience in real life that tax planning and management is a *holistic* concept. The amount of tax we pay can be influenced by a wide range of things, often seemingly unconnected. In reality it is very difficult to make an isolated tax planning decision without impacting on something else down the line. A decision you might make as a company director on behalf of the company may also affect your own personal tax situation or that of your employees. Equally, as a homeowner, the way you organise the property within your wealth portfolio can have direct ramifications on your nearest and dearest.

So that's why I wrote this book, to give anyone with an investment in property an introduction to the full spectrum of potential tax-planning strategies and rules that might affect them. I was also influenced by the following considerations:

The frustration of property investors at the constantly changing tax landscape and the difficulty of keeping up to date

Unfair and inequitable tax impositions, such as the restriction on mortgage interest relief phased in from 5 April 2017 by s.24 Finance (No.2) Act 2015

There is no single book that covers the very wide scope of property investors and developers in language that is straightforward and easy to read

And none of the tax books that do exist are written by full-time investors, or those tax advisers who concentrate on property investors, who also have significant experiences themselves of using different property strategies. I have that experience as I spend most of my time either investing in property development or advising clients.

Why choose THIS book?

Unlike some books, this is not a DIY tax guide - reading a book so that you can do it all yourself can be a dangerous shortcut. As a property tax specialist, I want you to be making the right decisions for your business or your inheritance. So my book gives you a foundation of knowledge that will help you enjoy a more productive partnership with your own tax expert.

Recent research has shown that anyone with financial or business interests tied up in property benefits hugely from working with a *property-invested accountant*. As this book will show, the tax landscape relating to property is complicated and an expert with first-hand experience is the best guide. I am delighted to offer myself as that guide as you work through this book.

Anyone whose business, at some point, involves buying or selling property(s) stands to gain or lose depending on how they manage their tax affairs. And this book isn't just for established formal businesses; a private homeowner planning an inheritance for their children or grandchildren can have just as much to gain or lose. That's why I have included a comprehensive section specifically for those wishing to plan strategically for their financial legacy.

The tax code is an evolving beast

I know that some readers will come to this with plenty of experience and knowledge while others may be taking their first steps. It's difficult to cater for everyone, but I've done my best to keep it balanced. I hope it will be read in the spirit in which it is written: a guide for any investor, but by no means a conclusive and comprehensive tax book (which would result in certain investors being isolated and ignored).

This is an overview of the current tax environment and nothing else. You'll soon see how complex tax is - so please always seek expert guidance from a specialist property accountant. I can't possibly cover everything without writing 'War and Peace' - and that would be way too much information for most people!

If there is one message above all to take from the book it is this: nothing stays the same forever. Taxation is governed by Parliamentary legislation, but this is not always the final word on the matter. When a dispute goes to court, new case law may be established that is based on an interpretation of the legislation. As a result, the opportunities for managing your tax efficiently whilst staying within the letter of the law can change, and so any book can only be a guide.

What you ultimately need is the opportunity to sit down with an expert and examine your own unique circumstances in the light of the most recent case law. It is my job to keep myself completely up to date with the very latest legislative changes and legal cases that colour the interpretation of tax legislation. However, I find that the most productive discussions are with those clients who have found the time to learn a little themselves – a small investment for potentially very big returns. You didn't become an investor in order to become a tax expert - but I didn't become an investor in order to become a builder! However, I've had to learn how building work is done. The same applies to you and your relationship with tax. Get acquainted and learn to feel comfortable with it - this will serve you well.

So, this book is both an introduction and a topical reference manual. It cannot possibly contain everything there is to know but it will give you sufficient insight, whatever your topic of interest, to know what questions to ask next.

How the book works

Clearly, with a book written for a potentially wide audience, some sections may be more relevant to you than others. The Contents List should help you to find your areas of particular interest.

The main book falls into four parts:

Sections 1 and 2: This is background information to help you decide what kind of investment interest you have in property, along with an important section devoted to the legal aspects of property taxation.

Sections 3 to 9: Here is the meat of the book, covering everything from VAT to insolvency. All but the last two sections apply to most types of property investor (sections 8 and 9 relating to very specific types), but by the time you reach these you may already be rethinking your own property profile, perhaps with a view to expanding your operation, and so I hope you find these helpful to read too.

Section 10 to 12: This covers the core issues to consider when planning for inheritance. Not concerned solely with wills (or with the consequences of dying intestate – without having made a will), we also consider the benefits of gifting and of using trusts. The chief gains are reductions in Inheritance Tax and Capital Gains Tax but, of course, there is also the all-important question for many of us of how to plan efficiently for our spouse/partner and our family.

Section 13, the Appendix and the Glossary: The final part provides a variety of useful additional information, beginning with a section to help you select your own team of property investment experts, based on my own extensive experience of being an investor. It's there to be a helpful guide, although I appreciate that your experience may be different or better.

The Appendix mostly provides further reading on some very specific points referenced in the book, and the Glossary is a useful resource if you feel overwhelmed by the acronyms and taxation terminology.

Gender references

Please note that throughout this book any terms noting gender, such as 'he', 'she', 'his' or 'hers', apply equally to male and female unless I state to the contrary. Similarly, in order to avoid gender-specific terminology, I have used 'them' and 'themselves' when, strictly speaking, it refers to individuals in the singular. This may also creep in when I'm referring to a limited company which should, strictly speaking, be 'it'. I've done this simply to make the text easier to read.

There are very few situations in modern taxation where a rule or case applies only to one gender but, should this be the case, I will certainly clarify it. For example, in the case law examples I've given it is possible that, without necessarily infringing the Equality Act, the gender, ethnicity, marital status, age, level of disability and other characteristics of a taxpayer *may* have had an effect on the outcome - this is usually in cases where the personal circumstances of the individual give rise to a claim that the legislation should not apply or should be applied in a particular way. I think it will be obvious where this is the case.

Disclaimer

The topics I'll be considering in this book are in many cases quite complex, and it's virtually impossible to give more than a general overview. Although every care has been taken to ensure the information is accurate and up-to-date at the time of publication of this edition, I do need to make it clear that you should take specific advice prior to making any decisions, and therefore no liability is accepted by me or by my practice for the outcome of taking or refraining from taking action based on the contents of this book unless you have first consulted me on a formal basis.

Acknowledgements

Where deemed helpful I have taken simple explanations directly from the government's websites.

This can be a good place to start for a statement of Parliamentary legislation. Do remember though that although the government sets the parameters it is HMRC who police the system and interpret the rules. So although it can be helpful to see what the HMRC view is, their interpretation isn't the law i.e. don't rely on it without question. And if your tax adviser is always sending you links to HMRC's website (without further comment), then you may want to question this.

SECTION 1: PROPERTY – WHY, WHO AND HOW?

This section will help you to identify your current interest in property (or to make the decision to begin investing in property) – and in turn this will help you navigate your way around the more detailed parts of the book.

#01. Four great reasons to invest in property

On the back of recent financial crises there has been much talk of whether property remains a solid investment. I'm here to give you information on tax (in a general sense, not guidance specific to you), and not investment advice, but I can state with complete confidence that property remains a very realistic business proposition and shows no signs of becoming a dangerous place to invest your money, unless you're very reckless.

I say this not as a tax adviser but as a very active and busy investor. I'm there at the coalface, doing deals on a regular basis and at the time of writing I have five on-going developments deals with a collective Gross Development Value (GDV) of £13.6million, with another one that has already reached the conveyancing stage, and a couple more in the pipeline.

Here are the four great reasons - but you'll find more reasons in other books relating to Property Investing.

1. Cashflow and capital growth

has risen by 50% since January 2005, fairly impressive in terms of capital growth. Even better, while you wait for this capital growth you also enjoy superior cash flow if you choose to invest in rental property - and a steady cash flow is a must with capital growth as the bonus, not the other way around.

Of course, running a rental property business (residential, commercial, serviced accommodation, etc) is like any other business – you need to manage the cash flow carefully. You might be showing profitability in your accounts, and hence be liable for tax, but also be cash-strapped because you didn't monitor receipts inwards against expenses outwards. I can't stress enough how easy it is for a business to fail in this way simply because they run out of cash, but at least with property investment (unlike some types of business) it's fairly easy to see where you are.

Development eats cash, fast. I know this through firsthand experience. So, keep an eye on it and factor in all costs plus a contingency element. You can go broke very, very quickly!

2. Property is tangible with an ascertainable value

With property you can see what you've got, and, more importantly, judge its worth on the current market. This also makes things a lot simpler when you're trying to raise finance to expand your property business.

There is a transparency and an honesty about property. This is not something you are always guaranteed in more complex financial investment products. And it exists on two levels, both of them equally reassuring to the investor:

1) you can see and touch a property – it exists in bricks and mortar; and

2) the value of property is easy to ascertain, as is any movement in value over time, since in most cases the market is well-known (dilapidated properties being something of an exception). You can also do simple things to increase that material value (home-improvement etc).

3. Property is a flexible investment

One property? Ten? Fifty? The choice is yours.

The simplest type of buy-to-let business can expand as much or as little as it wishes so long as your income or the property itself can guarantee loan or investor repayments, plus a positive cash flow.

4. It's not rocket science!

Property investment is a well-trodden road. Unlike many other businesses, it does not require a vast amount of specialist knowledge, and you don't need to sit exams or have a formally-recognised qualification. But you must seek education in the field of property as it is comprises specialist areas with many variants. It also has a degree of risk, owing to the big amounts involved and the general economic cycles. So, don't go blind, and remember that ignorance is more expensive than knowledge. I can tell you that from my own experience!

The main attributes are a positive mindset and a 'can do' attitude - but do bear in mind that the more you get into property the more specialist knowledge you are likely to need (see 'Property development' below). In my experience the most successful property investors are those who undertake training and are lifelong learners.

What about the risks?

Rental property cash flow and changes

If you're running a property rental business, your cash flow isn't just dependent on matching receipts with bills; you need to factor in dead periods when the property(s) is empty. You may also face late payments from tenants. Wise landlords always maintain a contingency fund for these voids as well as for unforeseen expenditure, including tax changes and changes in the law, such as the recently-introduced cap on fees charged to tenants.

Selling off property

You might at some point want to change the profile of your portfolio by replacing some properties. Although it's easy to acquire property, it isn't always easy to sell at the right price as soon as you want to. So you must embrace it as an investment for the medium to long term (unless you're a property developer, in which case you'll already be working to a more detailed strategy for acquisition, funding and disposal).

Managing property

Property investment is not something you can just leave to its own devices. You do need to exercise a management strategy (or pay someone to do so).

Property development

Property development – buying, improving and selling on properties – involves much more than just the two rental parties, landlord and tenant; unless you are skilled in all aspects of building and improving (and, in some cases, legal considerations) you will need to buy in the relevant expertise and knowledge. This can be expensive and means you'll need your finger on the pulse for costs and expenses.

However it's a false economy to skimp on the cost of appointing advisers. Good quality ones are worth their weight in gold. Better to splash out and get someone really good than to underpay and lose the deal or the maximum profit.

* Now, it's possible that you haven't yet seen yourself in the section above. That's fine. Property investors come in all kinds of guises. The next section simply identifies the mainstream types of investor and touches on why property tax matters to them.

#02. What type of property investor are YOU?

I keep emphasising that this book is for a full range of property investors, from billionaire entrepreneurs to single property homeowners. This is because the rules apply equally (apart from different tax bands and thresholds), so everyone can learn from this book. Sometimes, however, it is useful and reassuring to identify *yourself* when reading a book like this one, which inevitably deals with some technicalities, especially when trying to work out what is or is not relevant to you.

That said, my experience is that it's usually the really successful and knowledgeable people who have an on-going thirst to learn more - and that's one of the clues to their success.

So below I'm simply going to present some of the types of property investor and just touch on the tax landscape each might experience.

Buy-to-let landlords

This is the largest single group – people who own property and rent it out – but it breaks down into three subgroups with important differences in the way they run their businesses and in the tax rules that affect them.

1. Residential

In 2017 (the latest government statistics available at the time of writing) the number of homes being rented in the UK had reached 4.5 million , rising from 2.8 million in 2007. Every single one of these has a landlord. And that landlord might be anything from a single person with just one rental property to a large limited company with hundreds, or indeed a housing association, charitable organisation, pension fund or mutual investors.

Every single one of them must observe tax laws but these, along with the tax breaks and incentives available, will be defined by the organisational structure of the business.

2. Commercial

Walk down any high street and many of the shops you see are owned by landlords and rented to a commercial tenant. It is the same in a large shopping centre or on an industrial estate; many businesses rent their premises rather than owning them, preferring to use cash to invest in the business as working capital.

Just as for residential landlords, the tax landscape is principally governed by the structural organisation the landlord has set up (sole trader, limited company, etc). Of course the current downturn of our towns' high streets might suggest that this is not an easy investment route – that has to be a carefully considered business decision.

3. Serviced Accommodation

A furnished holiday lets business might be a single seaside cottage or several blocks of holiday apartments. Serviced Apartments/Accommodation is also very popular and works well both in holiday destinations and city centre locations. My experience is that the term of choice these days is 'Serviced Accommodation' and so that's the term I'll be using for the remainder of the book. Once again, the business taxation issues are all governed by the way the business is set up and run. Failure to meet certain requirements (for example about the number of days per year a holiday let is made available) may mean you are no longer eligible for specific tax breaks.

Whichever type of Buy-to-Let landlord you are, you can find out how your operating model relates to taxation in Section 3: 'Organisational Structure: What Does Your Business Look Like?'

Businesses operating from their own premises

Any type of business or other organisation that owns the property from which it operates is a property investor; and so the same umbrella of tax issues and laws affects them just as for other genres of property owner.

However, for these owners, more perhaps than for portfolio builders, their property tax decisions may be deeply entwined with their business decisions. Having an asset(s) of this significant value impacts directly on the balance sheet,and bearing the sole financial burden for maintenance impacts directly on profit. It is important to have a good understanding of tax laws and of potential tax breaks that come from how you may handle your property as an asset.

It's worth mentioning here that a trading business (as opposed to an investment business) could structure its property-owning to take advantage of a different tax relief (ie Entrepreneurs' Relief) on sale of the property, or on the cessation or transfer of the business. This depends largely on the organizational structure and also on whether the property is owned by the business-owner himself and on whether it is rented to the business. I'll be talking about the difference between trading and investment in Section 3 and about Entrepreneurs' Relief in Section 5.

Developers, builders and improvers

From single-operator 'property flippers' to large development and building companies, there are many businesses whose buying and selling of property generates specific property tax issues. As well as the decisions about how to structure the business (and the tax implications that follow) there are some tax-efficient opportunities and structures and some allowances specific to the construction industry to possibly benefit from too. Clearly, with properties passing through the business relatively frequently, Stamp Duty Land Tax is also a major concern, one given a large section later in the book.

Homeowners and inheritance planning

Inheritance law and related taxation are extremely complicated, but if you put in the effort to plan properly the gains can be considerable. And, of course, when planning legacies, your main residence may be one of the largest single items.

The chief concern is in retaining as much of the property's value as possible when it passes to your children or grandchildren (although you may also be planning for your spouse should he/she survive you). But, as with financial legacies, property inheritance needs careful and timely planning if you are to gain the most (or lose the least) by making best use of opportunities such as trusts, nil-rate tax bands and so on. We look at this in depth in *Section 10 – Managing Your Property For Inheritance.*

Finally a reminder about the holistic nature of tax planning

We must not forget that the decisions you will make in relation to property tax, strategies, reliefs and benefits are only one part of the picture. In all of these examples, personal income tax may also be affected by how you manage your property tax. And of course VAT may be a huge consideration too. Both of these and much more are discussed in depth later in the book.

SECTION 2: PROPERTY TAX AND THE LAW – A MUST-READ

This entire book is all about helping you to manage your tax – not how to avoid it or cut corners but how to work *within* the system as efficiently as you can. By getting this right you can reduce your tax bill through the wise business choices you make as a property investor.

So, it's really important to work carefully through this opening chapter. It is not dynamic reading, but it gives a flavour of the taxation hurdles and regulations you will face – and *without* this you may struggle to make sense of what then follows and how to use your planning to minimise your tax liabilities legally and profitably.

#03. Tax evasion, tax avoidance and tax planning – what's the difference?

People often find these terms confusing – just what is legal and what isn't? Fortunately, clarification is available and it all stems from one basic principle:

A taxpayer is fully entitled to arrange his affairs so that the result is advantageous to him from a tax point of view – as long as the transactions, strategies and procedures are within the law.

This principle is also articulated powerfully by Lord Clyde with reference to the 1929 Ayrshire Pullman case:

"No man in the country is under the smallest obligation, moral or other, so to arrange his legal relations to his business or property as to enable the Inland Revenue to put the largest possible shovel in his stores."

Now, right from the outset I want to reassure you that I will not encourage you to do anything at all that would be remotely illegal. And for this reason we need to be as clear as possible about the distinction between 'evasion' and 'avoidance' as this is what often confuses people.

Tax evasion

This one is simple - the deliberate misrepresentation of business activity in order to pay *less tax than is actually due*. Tax evasion involves breaking the rules, and can relate to income, expenses, taxable periods and so on. Anyone who commits tax evasion has broken the law and may be punished accordingly.

Tax avoidance

This one is a grey area that the courts have attempted for years to define but without complete success. The Institute of Chartered Accountants in England and Wales (ICAEW) explains the difficulty like this:

> *'The definition of 'avoidance' is an evolving area that can depend on the tax legislation, the intention of Parliament, interpretations in case law, the view of HMRC and the varying perceptions of different stakeholders.*
>
> *'Publicly, the term 'avoidance' is used in the context of a wide range of activities, be it multinational structuring or entering contrived tax-motivated schemes. The application of one word to a range of activities and behaviours oversimplifies the concept and has led to confusion.'*

You may think that this is not much help by itself, so to clarify matters let's look at the third category:

Tax planning

Her Majesty's Revenue and Customs (HMRC) distinguishes between avoidance and planning is this way:

'Tax **avoidance** involves bending the rules of the tax system to gain a tax advantage that Parliament never intended. It often involves contrived, artificial transactions that serve little or no purpose other than to produce this advantage. It involves operating within the letter – but not the spirit – of the law.

'Tax **planning** involves using tax reliefs for the purpose for which they were intended, for example, claiming tax relief on capital investment, or saving via ISAs or for retirement by making contributions to a pension scheme.'

This definition then goes on to explain where planning tips over into avoidance or evasion:

'However, tax reliefs can be used excessively or aggressively, by others than those intended to benefit from them or in ways that clearly go beyond the intention of Parliament'.

So, there you have it – evasion is definitely illegal, avoidance is frowned upon even if not strictly against the law – but planning is the way HMRC always intended us to manage our tax affairs.

#04. When does naïve or mistaken interpretation of tax law become dishonest?

This is an important question; after all, many of us learned in the school playground that claiming ignorance - "But I didn't know it was forbidden" - can be a good way to avoid punishment. So, might an unintended error in tax accounting similarly avoid punishment?

Let me be absolutely clear - tax evasion is a crime. Thus, if HMRC suspects criminal intent, it has the option to prosecute via the courts. There have of course been many high-profile cases of tax evasion, and, being a criminal offence, the usual principle of 'innocent until proved guilty' applies. The Crown therefore, in prosecuting for a crime, must prove their case 'beyond reasonable doubt' and that's a very high standard. So, in many cases HMRC instead adopts a penalty system (in addition to demanding payment of any due taxes) rather than pursuing a criminal case. This means that, if you genuinely make a mistake rather than setting out to deceive HMRC, the degree of your 'naivety' may be pertinent in determining the severity of any penalty.

How does this work?

The way that HMRC assesses and applies penalties is quite different from the normal process of a criminal case. This is how it works when you mistakenly submit inaccurate figures. Below are the stages you may go through, from initial tax calculation right through to a tribunal as the final step if you wish to appeal against an HMRC penalty:

1. HMRC will have issued a tax assessment based on the information you have supplied. Unless you have reason to contest the calculation you will then have paid the tax. However, if HMRC later discovers factors that you unwittingly did not disclose, then:

2. It will open an enquiry and the outcome may lead to another assessment being issued which may also include penalties. If you are unhappy about HMRC's new assessment, then:

3. You may choose to appeal against it. Your appeal may be against the tax assessed, or it may be that you accept this but want to appeal against the penalty. If you are unable through this to reach agreement with HMRC, then:

4. You can proceed to the First Tier Tribunal. The Tribunal will decide whether the penalty is properly levied and, if so, whether at an appropriate level.

There is an important difference between this and a criminal case. The Tribunal claim is a civil matter and the burden of proof is now on you, the taxpayer; HMRC does not have to prove anything. The standard of proof however is 'the balance of probabilities' i.e. 51% - much lower than 'beyond reasonable doubt'.

With regard to the HMRC system of penalties, this can run from a nominal amount up to 100% of the tax which should have been paid, and operates on a sliding scale taking into account whether the error is innocent, careless or deliberate, and also whether it was brought to light voluntarily or only upon prompting by HMRC, and whether there was a deliberate attempt to conceal. HMRC are at liberty to impose whatever penalty they feel is appropriate (subject to their code of fair practice), leaving it up to you to appeal this.

Of course in a number of cases the argument with HMRC never reaches the Tribunal stage, not least because of the costs involved. Many cases are settled at enquiry stage without the necessity of involving the judicial system. This depends partly on how deep your pockets are, because professional advice on full tax enquiries and representation before the Tribunal is expensive, and you cannot usually recover your costs from HMRC even if you are successful. So you may decide to accept the HMRC decision rather than spend money in challenging it.

It's worthwhile mentioning here however that most accountants and tax advisers are able to offer you insurance against the expense of tax enquiries. Whilst you can never insure against the consequences of what amounts to dishonesty (tax evasion), the insurance will cover the additional fees incurred if HMRC commences an investigation, and also the representation at the Tribunal. You will need to check exactly what is covered.

How can you avoid penalties?

Something my radar is always looking out for is a sign that distinguishes between an honest (but possibly misguided decision) and one that deliberately sets out to bend the tax rules. Sometimes the client can't really be blamed as it comes down to a simple interpretation of the English language and a flexible use of general terminology. In that case, it is likely to be accepted that there was no dishonest motive.

In a tax enquiry, or in taxation litigation, the HMRC approach is likely to be that of 'strict interpretation' which usually emerges as a black and white case that you failed to comply with the tax rules. However, business and tax law are considerably more complex than that, and the skill of your tax adviser will be to demonstrate why the course of action you adopted is indeed within the law. Your motives may well be relevant, not just because there was no dishonest intention, but because in many cases the reasons for your actions have an impact. The problem is that proving your intentions can be difficult, and this is why I always help my own clients to think through their strategy carefully and especially to document their reasons for choosing a particular option, with a view to being able to demonstrate this as a later date.

It's quite an art, as any barrister (and some tax advisers!) will tell you, to find a way of demonstrating not only that you had no dishonest motive, but also that your actions and in some cases your intentions result in compliance with particular legislation. This is not helped by the fragmented nature of our tax system, where different rules and tests apply to different taxes, but we have to work with what we have. There are areas of tax law where there is little room for manoeuvre - either you meet the test or you don't - but in most cases skilled representation to HMRC will at least avoid the more severe penalties.

#05. Tax mitigation – using tax law for better tax planning

In my work I make use of all the tax reliefs, allowances and exemptions that are either laid down in statutes by the government of the day or which HMRC have listed as being in line with their own interpretation of fiscal legislation. This is called tax mitigation and is the acceptable and wholly legal and ethical attitude towards tax.

I help you achieve your objectives by formulating bespoke strategies based on the tax legislation and case law, and tailored to your unique circumstances.

Result: you pay the right amount of tax and no more.

To do this I keep bang up to date with evolving tax law. I use my understanding and interpretation of tax law and HMRC practice to ensure that you take full advantage of the tax reliefs, allowances and exemptions made available to you by the government. Keeping up to date is essential – from time to time HMRC seeks to close this or that tax window, and ignorance is no defence.

However, in law the distinction between avoidance and mitigation remains open to interpretation, hence the court cases where HMRC disagrees with what you may have regarded as a wholly legitimate tax decision. Here is an example – not the full case history but just enough to show you how HMRC is not always right in the eyes of the law. In this case the defendants' claim to have used legal tax mitigation was being challenged by HMRC, but the judge found in their favour.

In the 1997 House of Lords decision in the case IRC v Willoughby, the Commissioners of Inland Revenue sought to assess one Professor Willoughby on the benefits of offshore investments he and his wife had taken out whilst resident outside the UK during Professor Willoughby's employment as Professor of Law at the University of Hong Kong.

Leaving aside the complexities of taxation on offshore investments, Lord Nolan, in giving judgement (in favour of Professor Willoughby) made the following distinction:

"Tax avoidance is to be distinguished from tax mitigation. The hallmark of tax avoidance is that the taxpayer reduces his liability to tax without incurring the economic consequences that Parliament intended to be suffered by any taxpayer qualifying for such reduction in his tax liability. The hallmark of tax mitigation, on the other hand, is that the taxpayer takes advantage of a fiscally attractive option afforded to him by the tax legislation, and genuinely suffers the economic consequences that Parliament intended to be suffered by those taking advantage of the option. Where the tax payer's chosen course is seen upon examination to involve tax avoidance (as opposed to tax mitigation), it follows that tax avoidance must be at least one of the taxpayer's purposes in adopting that course, whether or not the taxpayer has formed the subjective motive of avoiding tax"

If the learned judge means what I think he means, then tax avoidance occurs where a reduction of tax is obtained by actions that do not deliver an opposite and equivalent economic disadvantage (such as a drop in profit). By contrast, tax mitigation would be where, for example, a taxpayer gains a tax advantage but also, in relation to this, deprives himself of control of an asset (the economic 'hit') by putting it into a trust.

It is important to note that the judge touches on 'motive' something I mentioned earlier. It may not be enough to show that you didn't take any action to avoid tax – you may need to prove that you had no strategy (motive) to avoid it either.

As a footnote, and following the logic of the example above, you may now be asking the question: *"Why bother making a tax saving if it means at the same time I incur an economic penalty?"* The answer is that you do this all the time in your financial planning, accepting a loss here to enable a gain there. No business can run without any expenses eating into the cash; it all comes down to how you choose which expenses are worth making to sustain or grow your business.

You can find out more about the relationship between businesses, HMRC and the law in the *Appendix: Understanding HMRC's perspective.*

#06. Anti-abuse rules – GAAR and TAAR

I describe these in detail in the *Appendix* but will touch on them briefly here as they are tools by which HMRC challenges tax violation.

General Anti-Abuse Rules (GAAR) and Targeted Anti-Abuse Rules (TAAR) were introduced by the Finance Bill of 2013 as part of the tax code that aims to ensure fair taxes are levied and collected to finance the state's services and facilities provided for its citizens.

Put simply, General Anti-Abuse Rules aim to deter taxpayers from entering into arrangements designed deliberately to abuse the tax system (and to deter those who offer those arrangements). The complexities of business and tax mean that loopholes in apparently watertight legislation are inevitable. Where there's a loophole there's someone who will devise a scheme to get through it: you may be the innocent victim by agreeing to such a scheme without realising. So the anti-abuse rules are there to protect you as much as the government coffers themselves. There are other tax avoidance strategies that can be challenged under the tax code, but they only fall within the scope of GAAR if they are abusive.

Targeted Anti-Abuse Rules are a form of GAAR that cover very specific anti-avoidance rules – for example 'phoenixism', a process where solvent companies are liquidated so that shareholders dispose of their shares to realise a Capital Gains Tax charge rather than paying income tax on the profits that would otherwise by distributed. This TAAR prevents people who have liquidated from going back in the same or a similar business for two years.

* Before moving on to Section 3, can I draw your attention to an item in Section 13 – How To Get The Best From Your Property Expert; there I briefly explain the ethical backbone to my professional approach in more detail. Whoever you appoint as your specialist property tax adviser, I recommend you use this as a benchmark.

SECTION 3: ORGANISATIONAL STRUCTURE – WHAT DOES YOUR BUSINESS LOOK LIKE?

When you're setting up a business there are many excellent books that take you through the different options and the ways they might impact on your subsequent experience of actually running and funding your business. They all will (or should) mention that there are tax implications depending on how you do it. They rarely, however, offer much depth into this important topic.

So in this section we take time to consider the structural differences from a taxation-orientated perspective. But, because you still have to run the business, we also tackle a few organisational issues that you may well face at some time in the future, if not right away. This is relevant both to start-ups and to established businesses that may be looking for an opportunity to change their overall organisational structure. And it provides an important foundation for the detailed sections that follow later in the book.

#07. How tax relates to your business style

I just want to run through some of the basic choices you make when first starting up (or growing) a business, and show you how many of them will have accompanying tax implications – implications we don't always consider when wearing an entrepreneurial hat.

All good business advisors recommend using Key Performance Indicators (KPIs) when running your business. This is because profit alone is not the only barometer of business success, not by a long way. You should always be measuring performance against pre-set goals in a *variety* of dimensions relevant to your operation. The simple way to establish those KPIs is to think of the 'key numbers' – what is key in terms of income and of expenditure.

In property-related businesses, those key numbers are derived from three drivers – income, costs and success:

Income drivers

The measurable goals you might set include (but are not limited to):

- Rental income;
- Number of properties rented out;
- Voids – the number of unrented properties;
- Sales and leases;
- Development opportunities.

You might also include time and resources (expert consultations, etc.) spent researching available properties.

And here is a small selection of taxation issues you might have to consider as you decide where to set your KPIs:

- Rules affecting taxation relating to portfolios in both the UK and the EEA;
- Restriction of tax relief on loan interest
- Capital Gains Tax when offloading property;
- Remaining viable for tax breaks as a serviced accommodation business.

Costs drivers

Below are KPI topics you might use for monitoring your costs:

- Salaries, employers' NI and workplace pensions;

- Notional salary for your time if not included under general salaries;

- Staff recruitment and retention costs;

- Acquisition costs (including SDLT);

- Development costs;

- Sale costs;

- General professional costs;

- Debtor days;

- Average credit period from suppliers;

- Repairs and maintenance costs;

- Finance costs;

- Fluctuating interest rates.

Just a few of the related tax issues that may arise in connection with some of these include Stamp Duty Land Tax, tax-beneficial incentive schemes for employers and for construction companies, capital allowances on your assets, interest on personal loans to the company, and so on.

Success drivers

These are the KPIs that matter to you personally, reflecting what you want to get out of the business; this is by no means an exhaustive list but some examples include:

- Return on investment;

- Return on tied-up capital;

- Personal wealth;

- Your inheritance plans;

- Personal growth and fulfilment.

The last item may have little to do with taxation unless maximising your mitigation is a personal goal, but overall your personal wealth goals are very dependent on the tax choices you make during the life of your business.

Of course in all of this there is the fundamental difference between, say, being taxed solely on your income (as a sole-operator business) or, as a limited company, through corporation tax, *and* on your own income tax on any salary and dividends you draw. The decisions you make about your business structure may deliver very different tax outcomes.

In other words, when you are making purely business decisions, perhaps in relation to cash flow or to funding an expansion plan, you're also making taxation decisions. **But without some expert guidance you may not realise this until it is too late to take full advantage of what is legally allowable as tax mitigation.**

So, let's move on to the basic organisational choices – from a tax perspective.

#08. The basic choices, from sole trader to limited company

We have already established that your business interest in property could be anything from running a small serviced accommodation property to building a letting empire, or from improving and selling on houses to extracting the most inheritable wealth from your own home.

The one thing these all have in common is that to benefit from legitimate tax mitigation they are (or must be treated as) businesses. This means making some fundamental choices about the business structure that best suits your needs.

The four basic business structures to choose from are:

1. Sole trader;

2. Ordinary partnership;

3. Limited liability partnership (' LLP'); and

4. Limited company.

Needless to say, there are advantages and disadvantages to each of these. But before we delve into those, let's consider some criteria that will help you to assess what might be best for your business model.

Just as there are four basic business structures, so there are four leading criteria – but, as you'll see shortly, they all impact on each of the four structures.

1. **Your personal liability:** As a business owner you need to think carefully about how much or little you want your own assets to be separate (protected) from the business – especially if things go badly or the business runs out of cash.

2. **Management style and work/life balance:** In essence, how much involvement in – and responsibility for – the business do you want personally? Factors governing your choice may include lifestyle (now or in the future) and your strategy for how you want your business to grow.

3. **The burden of compliance:** Between HMRC and the law you may be required to stick to very important rules when running and reporting on your business – but the extent of these vary depending on the structure you choose.

4. **Taxation:** Different structures bring different tax regimes, and it's not always just about minimising tax from your business; which will suit your circumstances?

And I'm going to add a fifth – **legal status**. This refers to any legal requirements that come with the organisational structures.

The above are just some of the considerations when deciding on your business organisational structure, and are by no means exhaustive.

Now, with these in mind, let's take a closer look at the pros and cons of the four main business structures – but as everyone's priorities are different I won't attempt to give them any weighting.

Sole trader

Liability

You have personal liability for your business - so if you incur debts, all of your assets, not just your business assets, are at risk.

Management

The management style is entirely down to you – essentially, in every aspect of your business and the way you run it you have freedom but the buck stops with you.

Compliance

There are no statutory requirements for the way you format your accounts, just the same need to account for your income and expenditure as for any other self-employed person.

Taxation

Any profits from your business are added to the rest of your personal income, and you are then taxed on the total (after deducting your tax-free personal allowance). *N.B. You can read more about personal Income Tax in the Appendix.*

Legal

The only consideration (from the point of view of choice of structure) is if you bring someone in to help you. You can still be a sole trader if the person is an employee, but otherwise you are may effectively be running a partnership (see below).

Ordinary partnership

Liability

As with a sole trader there is personal liability for all the debts in the business, but in an ordinary partnership this risk is not shared out amongst partners; instead each individual partner can be pursued for the entire debt (leaving that partner to claim the appropriate contribution from the other partners).

Management

Management style depends upon the partnership agreement - differing roles may be allocated to individual partners. Bringing in another party depends on the terms of the partnership agreement (and consent between partners).

Compliance

As with sole traders, there is no statutory requirement for the format of your accounts, and your share of the resulting profit will be included on your personal tax return.

Taxation

The partnership as a single entity needs to file its own Self-Assessment tax return, (showing the profit and loss account of the partnership business for the tax year, any capital allowances and the ratio in which the partners are entitled to share the profits). However, your income from the partnership is still added to the rest of your personal income and you are personally taxed on the total.

You yourself are treated for tax purposes as being self-employed, so the responsibility for paying any tax due (and self-employed National Insurance contributions) is yours, not that of the partnership. However, if you are what is often referred to as a 'salaried partner', you take a fixed income (instead of a share that fluctuates with the profits and losses) and will usually be paid and taxed under PAYE.

Legal

The partnership is governed by and must adhere to its partnership agreement, and by the Partnership Act 1890.

Limited liability partnership (LLP)

Liability

You are **not** personally liable for the debts of the LLP; instead only the LLP assets are liable for business debts.

Management

Management style depends upon the LLP agreement. There must be at least 2 'designated members' who will have greater management responsibilities plus any number of 'ordinary' members. Bringing in another party depends upon the terms of the LLP agreement and upon agreement with the other partners.

Unlike an ordinary partnership, an LLP can have corporate partners. A corporate partner will carry out its functions (as a member of the LLP) via its directors. There are however additional tax rules if there is a corporate partner, relating to the taxation of profit shares.

Regarding the division of profit in an LLP, if there is no written agreement of the profit-sharing ratio then the members are deemed to receive the profits in equal shares. Annual accounts will constitute a written agreement as to profit-sharing provided that these are signed by all members.

Compliance

Your accountant will need to prepare LLP accounts and these will be submitted to HMRC and also filed at Companies House. A statutory format for accounts applies but it is possible to file an abbreviated form of accounts to go into the public domain.

Taxation

An LLP is treated for tax purposes in the same way as an ordinary partnership – see above. It is transparent for taxation purposes.

Legal

An LLP partnership must be 'incorporated' and registered at Companies House and there must be a written LLP agreement. There are a number of registration and reporting requirements that must be observed

An LLP is a separate legal entity - in other words it counts as a separate 'person', albeit an artificial one, operating via its members.

Limited company

Liability

You are **not** personally liable for the debts of the company - only the company assets are liable for business debts. However, you will be personally liable if you have given a personal guarantee or possibly if you allow the company to trade whilst insolvent.

You can also be made personally liable as a director if you are fraudulent or allow the company to trade with the intention of defrauding its creditors, if you intentionally make a false representation on behalf of the company, or if you misapply company funds. Recent developments in the law also make it possible for directors to be held personally liable for the consequences of negligence as a director e.g. corporate manslaughter or compliance failures.

Management

Management style depends upon agreement between the directors. All directors are individually responsible for the management of the company, whatever their individual roles. Bringing in another party depends upon the terms of the Articles (which may restrict the transfer of shares) and also any other agreement such as a shareholders' agreement.

A shareholders' agreement is one whereby some or all of the shareholders in the company agree with each other in terms which are not covered by the Articles. This might relate to the decision-making process (with shareholders' consent being required for certain directors' decisions, or for certain decisions to be unanimous) or to declaration of dividends. Such an agreement binds the company if the company is a party to it but avoids a possibly complex alteration of the Articles themselves. Similar agreements can be used for other purposes, such as an agreement relating to investment in the company, either by a shareholder or by a third party.

Compliance

Your accountant will need to prepare company accounts and these will be submitted to HMRC and also filed at Companies House. Statutory format for accounts applies but it is possible to file an abbreviated form of accounts to go into the public domain.

A limited company is a creature of statute (as is an LLP), and the accountancy fees are likely to be higher for a limited company than for an unincorporated organization of a similar size, owing to the burden of compliance and regulation. A further consideration is that it is usual (but not obligatory) for the accountants to also prepare the tax computations and returns for the directors' personal affairs, which is an additional task, whereas for a sole trader, the income from the business is his personal income anyway, taxable on him personally together with any other source of income.

Taxation

The company files its own Corporation Tax return and pays its own tax. You will pay income tax on any salary, dividends or distributions from the company.

Legal

A company is a separate legal entity - in other words it counts as a separate 'person', albeit an artificial one, operating via its board of directors. The company must be 'incorporated' and registered at Companies House and there must be written Memorandum and Articles. There are a number of registration and reporting requirements that must be observed.

#09. The benefits of running a limited company

From a tax perspective, it may seem that the sole trader option is the simplest, but this overlooks the potential tax advantages of the other models. For someone running a business on their own, however, the idea of becoming a limited company may seem daunting. **It needn't be.** Indeed, it is fair to say that in many ways it is the limited company that gets the best taxation, financial and security advantages. Here are just a few examples (some of which we will explore later in the book):

- Protection via limited liability (compare with the exposure of the sole trader or ordinary partnership);

- The ability to raise outside funds via the Enterprise Investment Scheme (EIS) subject to qualification;

- The (at present) low Corporation Tax rate advantage for profitable companies;

- The ability to 'spread' ownership through share capital for different shareholders in a range of shareholdings;

- A clearly defined separate business for subsequent sale, separate from personal assets and money;

- The advantage of placing a risky diversification project within the protection of a limited company;

- The availability of tax reliefs which can only be claimed by a limited company, not by a partnership, LLP or sole trader. These include Research & Development Relief and Land Remediation Relief (both of which we will look at in some detail later on);

- The ability to plan for the shareholders' possible 45% income tax rate via the use and timing of dividends.

To put some flesh on the bones, here is a simple illustration of the tax savings for a sole trader who converts to a limited company.

Dave runs a property trading business (flipping property) and his business model indicates that he will make profits of £65,000 in the current year. He has no other income.

As a sole trader his tax for 2019/20 will be as follows:

Income tax	£	£
Profits	65,000	
Personal allowance	(12,500)	
Taxable income	52,500	
Tax at basic rate	37,500	7,500.00
Tax at higher rate	15,000	6,000.00
Total tax		**13,500.00**
National Insurance	**£**	**£**
Class 2		156.00
Class 4 – 9% on £8,633 to £50,000		3,723.12
Excess - 2% on £50,001 to £65,000		300.00
Total NI		**4,179.12**
Total tax and NI		**17,679.12 (26.95% of profits)**

So, what changes if Dave decides to convert to a limited company? You may find it helpful first to read the section below that clarifies how the calculations work, but otherwise you can jump straight to the table that follows this.

Personal Allowance

Every individual has a Personal Allowance for Income Tax which he sets against his income for the tax year. For 2019/20 this figure is £12,500 and historically the amount of the Personal Allowance has risen in most tax years. This means that the first £12,500 of the individual's income is exempt from Income Tax. If you don't use up this amount of tax-exempt income then the unused surplus allowance is lost. It is possible to transfer this between married couples (the Marriage Allowance) and I will be explaining later on how this works.

In the example above, I've assumed that the income from the business is Dave's sole income and so all the exempt amount is set against this. However, if Dave has other sources of income, then the exempt amount is only allowed once, so, if the whole of this is set against his sole trader income, any other income would bear tax (without any exempt amount).

Please note that if your total income from all sources exceeds £100,000 then the amount of the Personal Allowance is reduced by 50p for every £1 income in excess of £100,000.

Income Tax Rates

Income Tax is charged on individuals in a series of bands. In the tax year 2019/20 the first £37,500 of taxable income (after deducting the personal allowance) is taxed at 20% (known as 'basic rate').

As stated, this applies to your total income, not to each individual source of income, and in the example I've assumed that the sole trader business is Dave's only source of income.

Taxable Income from £37,501 to £150,000 is taxed at the higher rate which for tax year 2019/20 is at 40%. If you are fortunate enough to have taxable income above £150,000 then this will be taxed at the additional rate which is 45%.

Please note: if you have dividend income, either from investing in other companies or because you run your own business as a limited company, then there are separate rates of Income Tax for that income. I've explained how this works in the next example.

Other exemptions

You may of course be entitled to other exemptions if you meet the criteria and I'll be discussing these later.

For the purposes of calculating your Income Tax generally, if a source of income is exempt, then this is ignored for the purposes of calculating your taxable income and the rate of tax which applies. If on the other hand there are special rates of tax, such as for dividend income, this comes into the whole calculation (see below).

Capital Gains Tax and the Higher Rate Taxpayer

The standard rate of CGT is 18%. However, if you are a higher rate taxpayer, then at least part of your chargeable gain on the disposal of residential property will suffer CGT at the rate of 28%.

Disposal of your main residence is usually exempt for CGT (under Private Residence Relief), and if you are disposing of all or part of your trading business, or shares in a trading company, or of a property which you have used in your trading business, then you may qualify for Entrepreneurs' Relief, which will reduce the CGT to a flat rate of 10%. Both of these topics are discussed later in the book.

National Insurance

Unlike Income Tax, National Insurance Contributions (NICs) are not calculated on your income as a whole but on different sources of income. If you have been employed, you will recall that your NICs were calculated on your remuneration package from that employment only. If you had another employed job, that would have its own NIC calculation. What governs your liability (and that of the employer for the employers' NIC) is whether you are paid weekly or monthly and whether your remuneration reached the relevant level in the period. So it was quite possible to have more than one job and for there to be no NIC liability for the lower paid one (or in theory for either or any of them).

Just a point about how your NICs affect your ultimate entitlement to the State Pension. If you have earnings in any particular job less than the Lower Earnings Limit (LEL) (£118 per week or £512 per month in 2019/20) then you do not pay any National Insurance. However, you will not accrue a qualifying year towards the basic State Pension. If you have two or more jobs and earn less than the LEL is each of them, then again you are not liable to pay NI contributions. You do not accrue a qualifying year towards the State Pension even if, when combined, your earnings from all your jobs are above the LEL

I recommend that you consider this if you, or your dependents, are working part-time in one on more employments, as the entitlement to a basic State Pension can be an important factor in your future plans.

For the self-employed, (sole traders or partners) NICs are calculated differently and are based on your total self-employed business income. First of all you are liable to pay a flat rate Class 2 contribution which for tax year 2019/20 is £3 per week, so that's £156 per year. If your income is not more than £6,365 then there is an exemption. (There is also a voluntary Class 3 contribution, and you might want to consider that if you are not paying obligatory Class 2 or Class 4 NIC-because the obligatory Class 2 NIC only covers you for certain benefits).

Then Class 4 NIC, for which you are also liable, is based on your profit, so this can only be calculated after the year end and you pay the Class 4 NIC together with your Income Tax payments. The rates for Class 4 are

- 0% for profit up to £8,632

- 9% on profits from £8,633 to £50,000

- 2% on profits over £50,000

Remember, for this purpose the whole of the taxable profit is taken into account (£65,000 in the above example). You don't deduct the Personal Allowance first.

Now let's compare this to the position if Dave traded as or via a limited company and made the same pre-tax profit. I'll explain the calculations in detail shortly, but let's start with the overall picture.

The point to remember here is that it is the **company's** profit we are concerned with now, not Dave's personal income. So we have to look first at the tax on the company's profit, which is calculated differently and then at the income Dave draws from the company by way of director's salary and dividends as a shareholder. As you can see below he stands to walk away with more disposable income as a result – and it is all entirely legitimate.

N.B. For simplicity, Dave decides to pay himself a salary identical to his pre-tax personal allowance so that this element of his income is free of tax.

	£	£
Company position		
Profits (before director's salary)		65,000
Less: salary	12,500	
and employer's NI (a)	562.48(1)	(13,062.48)
Profit before tax		52,937.52
Corporation tax (at 19%) (b)		(9.868.12)
Profits available for distribution		43,069.40

	£	£
Dave's position		
Income tax		
Salary	12,500	
Dividend	43,069.40	55,569.40
Personal allowance		(12,500)
Taxable income		43,069.40
Tax at basic rate	Nil	Nil
Dividend allowance	2,000	Nil
Less Tax at dividend ordinary rate 7.5%	35,500	2,662.50
Less Tax at dividend higher-rate 32.5%	7569.40	2460.05
Income tax (c)		5,122.55
National Insurance (d)		489.12(2)
Total tax and NI (a+b+c+d)		**16,042.27**
	(24.68% of profits)	
Saving on incorporation		**1.480.85**

Notes

- 1 £12,500 – £8,424 (threshold) at 13.8%.

- 2 £12,500 – £8,424 (primary threshold at) 12.0%. (secondary threshold is £46,384 – 2%)

- See Appendix for more information on NI rates.

This is just one possible scenario. Different figures will give a different outcome. So before deciding whether incorporation if for you, you need to run the numbers and consider all points.

Here is a more detailed examination of these calculations:

Director's Salary

As a director, Dave is an employee of the company. He's entitled to draw a salary for his services and this will be an expense of the company which will reduce the amount of profit. See below for how this works for Income Tax and National Insurance.

The amount of a director's salary is up to the company, (or rather, it's a matter of agreement between the company and the director). Clearly the director is providing services to the company in respect of the administration and running of the company. However, it could also be the case that the director is providing services which would otherwise have to be provided by someone else. For example if a self-employed plumber decides to run his business as a limited company, presumably he is still carrying out at least some of the plumbing work.

For the purposes of taxation, there is no distinction. A director is deemed to be employed by the company 365 days of the year and his salary is deemed to accrue evenly over the course of the year. There are areas of the law outside the scope of this book (for example employment law and benefits law) where a distinction may be made between services performed as a director and services performed as a result of the individual's profession or trade, but for taxation and company law there's no difference. The only exceptions are the use of a management company for remuneration purposes and also what are termed 'service companies' where the sole activity of the company is the offering of the professional services of an individual, the leading case on this being the Arctic Systems case (which I refer to later on).

Corporation Tax

This is fairly straightforward. The taxable profit is computed by deducting the expenses of the company from its income. Some expenses may not be deductible for tax purposes (more on this later) and these are added back into the computation. The resulting net taxable profit suffers Corporation Tax (payable by the company) at the rate (for the tax year 2019/20) of 19%.

National Insurance (NI)

This relates solely to the director's total remuneration package. I use that term because it's quite common for the director to receive benefits in addition to his salary. To keep things simple, in the above illustration I've shown Dave as taking a straightforward salary of £12,500, but he could of course have other benefits, which may be treated as benefits-in-kind.

Just as with any other employee, the limited company, as employer, is liable to pay Employer's NICs on the salary paid (not including any benefits-in-kind) where this exceeds the threshold which for 2019/20 is £8,424 annually.

Now the salary, in Dave's hands as an individual, is also subject to Class 1 NICs where this is in excess of the threshold. Remember that a director's salary is deemed to accrue annually (even if it is paid weekly or monthly), so we're only concerned with the annual threshold. However, the company will generally need to run a Pay As You Earn (PAYE) scheme if it makes any payment to employees (even if the only employee is the director), so in reality the NIC (both employers' and employees' NIC) will be paid to HMRC on the same frequency as salary payments.

Just on the point of the need to run a PAYE scheme, you don't have to run one if the only payments are for casual labour (as defined by the PAYE legislation) or to employees who have only one job and whose earnings are below the Lower Earnings Limit for National Insurance. If however any employee has another job then you do need to run a PAYE scheme.

As an employer, once you have more than one employee where you are liable to pay employers' NI, then there is any Annual Allowance against this of £3,000. If your total employers' NI for the year is £5,000, you will only pay £2,000. The way this works is that it is set against your employers' NI on a month by month basis. If your total employers' NI for the year is under £3,000 then the rest of the relief is lost.

If Dave does receive any benefits-in-kind, then the company must file a P11d return of these at the end of every tax year and Dave will be liable for Class1A NIC on the value of the benefit. But, as I say, in the example given, Dave is not receiving any benefits-in-kind. There is no employers' NIC on benefits-in-kind.

Dave has chosen to take a salary at a level that renders both himself and the company liable for NI. Many directors decide to take a salary that is just below the NI threshold. By doing so, they extract money from the company but also safeguard their personal entitlement to social security benefits.

Workplace Pension

You may have noticed that there's no mention of this in the example. The general rule for auto-enrolment is that any qualifying employee earning above the trigger threshold (on an annual basis this is £10,000 for 2019/20) must be automatically enrolled in a qualifying workplace pension scheme. The individual is then at liberty to opt out.

So obviously Dave could have been auto-enrolled and could then have opted out. However, where a director does not have a contract of employment with the company, then, as long as the company does not employ any other staff (or other directors who do have a contract of employment), the director(s) is exempt as he is not technically a worker.

A contract of employment does not have to be written down; it could be verbal or implied. However, if there is no written contract or other evidence of creating an employer/worker relationship, HMRC will not seek to argue that there is an implied contract.

Income Tax

Dave's salary as a director is subject to personal Income Tax. However, as this does not exceed the Income Tax Personal Allowance, no tax will be deducted by the company under the PAYE scheme.

What about the dividends that Dave receives from the company as a shareholder?

Dividend income, whether from your personal company or from any other company in which you invest as a shareholder, is subject to personal Income Tax, but at different rates.

First of all, the first £2,000 of dividend income in each year is taxed at a nil rate. The rest is taxed according to the same bands as for ordinary Income Tax, which I set out in the previous section.

The basic rate band is £37,500 (after first deducting your annual Personal Allowance for Income Tax which is £12,500 for tax year 2019/20). The initial £2,000 is taken off this, leaving £35,500 to be taxed and this will be at the rate of 7.5% (as opposed to 20% for other income). Then the next band is £37,501 to £150,000 and any dividends falling into this band will be taxed at 32.5% (as opposed to 40%). If you have dividend income in the band over £150,000 then this is taxed at 38.1% as opposed to 45%. All these rates are for tax year 2019/20.

There used to be a system of the company paying dividends net of basic rate tax but this is no longer the case. So, irrespective of whether Dave's dividend income falls into the basic rate band or the higher rate or additional rate, he must still complete a Self-Assessment Tax Return and pay the Income Tax due.

Interaction with Personal Allowance

In the example above, Dave has chosen to take £12,500 as salary which uses up his Personal Allowance, so all his dividend income falls into one or more of the tax brackets (except the £2,000 which is tax-free under any circumstances).

If however he had decided to take less salary, for example £10,500, then he would still get the first £2,000 of dividend income tax-free, but in addition another £2,000 of income would also be tax-free, because this would take up the £2,000 (£12,500 less £10,000) which is not being utilised by the salary.

Level of Dividends

As you will see, in the example, Dave is taking all the surplus profit (after payment of Corporation Tax) as dividends. He is quite entitled to do so, but there may be circumstances where it would be prudent to allow some of these funds to remain in the company. This decision will be governed by factors such as order level, planned expansion and cashflow (although cashflow does not necessarily correspond to the profit and loss account!).

The point is that, once the dividend has been declared, this counts as income in Dave's hands, even if he has not yet received payment, and tax must be paid on it.

You may also want to bear in mind the relationship between income and your entitlement to Child Benefit. I will be looking at this later on, but if you or your partner have more than £50,000 income, you will either have to cease claiming Child Benefit or pay the High-Income Child Benefit Tax Charge. If one of you has over £60,000 income then you lose your entitlement altogether.

In making the decision about what dividends should be declared, you should consider the company's needs, your own position and of course the taxation consequences. All of these are points that your accountant should help you with.

> * So, you can see how the two models deliver different final outcomes. Of course, Dave may still think that all the extra work involved in meeting the compliance requirements of a limited company is not worth the extra £1,480.85 he keeps. However, I think we can convince Dave by going through some of the other benefits he will enjoy.

The advantages of running a property trading business as a limited company

Dave only ever handles one or two properties at a time before selling them on; so he may feel his operation is too simple to be a limited company. serviced accommodation businesses with just one or two properties may feel the same.

However, have a look at the benefits:

- As director/shareholder you're still in control;

- You have *ongoing access to the income* (but of course subject to personal Income Tax on any withdrawals you make);

- If you want to share the benefits of ownership with married or civil partners it is much easier (and more tax efficient) to do this through transfer of shares rather than ownership of the actual properties;

- Transferring a property portfolio *into* a limited company can be done in a tax efficient manner, (providing that this is done properly and you meet the rules), including statutory reliefs that avoid triggering a Capital Gains Tax (CGT) charge;

- Loan interest on money raised to buy property carries *full relief* against the income at the Corporation Tax (CT) rate (within the company). This is 19% for 2019/20;

- Income is charged at CT rate rather than at the usual personal tax rates (20%/40%/45%);

- When you transfer your properties to the company, they are *acquired at the current market value*, crystalising any increase but without CGT being incurred by the transfer (subject to s.162 Incorporation Relief being applicable to your situation). Then, if you sell a property in the future, tax only relates to the uplift in value between that transfer into limited company and the subsequent property sale;

- Stamp Duty Land Tax (SDLT) should *not* be payable on transfer (subject to very specific circumstances relating to partnerships) but will be payable if you have a sole trader business;

- Please note Entrepreneurs' Relief is available on sale of shares irrespective of whether or not you are retiring from the business, but only if the company is classed as a trading company and not an investment company. Please remember that renting property is an investment activity and Entrepreneurs' Relief is not available;

- Your *personal assets* are protected as only the company's assets are liable for the company's debts.

But of course nothing is perfect, so here are some of the possible downsides:

- The cost of *renegotiating property loans* (as company loans) with the lender; there will be an arrangement fee and you may also have to provide a personal guarantee;

- The *legal fees* arising from legal transfer of properties;

- Stamp Duty Land Tax (SDLT) on the transfer of the properties to the limited company; there is no relief from SDLT on incorporation and SDLT will be charged on the market value of the property. However, you may be able to avoid this if the property is first held by a partnership; this has an element of risk and I recommend that you take specialist advice;

- You will lose the annual personal allowance for Capital Gains Tax (CGT) which is available for chargeable gains made by an individual only;

- The risk of an immediate charge for CGT if the rules for incorporation relief are not met (your accountant should advise); s.162 Taxation of Capital Gains Act 1992 rolls over the gain until you dispose of the shares;

- The *initial cost of setting up* the limited company;

- *Compliance obligations* as a limited company (but the cost of this is likely to be minimal); however, you are likely to incur increased accountancy fees, as indicated earlier;

- Any income losses not yet used against your sole trader income *will be lost* when the business is transferred to a limited company. The same goes for *unused interest relief*.

So, from this second list, please note that if you incorporate your business with outstanding losses you then lose these as they can't be transferred and used in your corporation tax returns.

Extracting value when you have incorporated your business

One of the benefits of becoming a limited company is the range of ways for extracting value (money or financial savings). The company's income is taxed under Corporation Tax but any money left over as surplus to the company's requirements can then be paid out (or the amount of money available to shareholders increased) in various ways:

- **Directors' remuneration** (subject to NIC if above the threshold);

- **Dividends** (but the tax-free threshold introduced in April 2016 is falling – for the tax year 2019/20 it is down from £5,000 to only £2,000);

- **A full deduction of interest** paid via the limited company;

- **A lower rate of CGT** (the Corporation Tax rate is 19% at the time of writing, as opposed to Income Tax at rates of up to 45%);

- **A lower rate of personal tax** (depending on the profit extracted if done via dividends).

I need to make a couple of important points here about Capital Gains Tax (CGT), incurred when a property is sold.

1. As a limited company, when a property is sold there will be Corporation Tax to pay on the capital gain (unless your company is classed as a trading company - more below). Unlike capital gains for private individuals there is an indexation allowance for gains by companies (but only for gains up to 31 December 2017). This enhances the amount you can set against your capital gain.

2. If you die, properties held personally (e.g. as a sole trader) will benefit from the tax-free uplift in value for CGT as at the date of death. However, if held by a limited company, this tax-free uplift does not apply to the value of your shares in the company.

3. If properties are sold out of the limited company then you will pay personal Income Tax on the profit extracted: you could end up paying more in Income Tax than you would have paid in CGT (if you still owned the properties personally) at a maximum rate of 28% on the gain less the amount of the annual CGT exemption.

#10. Compliance and penalties - what can go wrong?

Whichever organisational structure you choose, you must comply with rules and regulations about how you report your business activity to HMRC (and, if relevant, Companies House). Whichever model you use, the penalties for getting these wrong can be severe. So in this section I will list the main penalties you may incur – in the *Appendix* you can find a really useful table listing all the various deadlines for submitting returns and accounts to HMRC. Please note that once you have registered with HMRC and, if relevant, with Companies House (see below) the relevant forms should usually be triggered and sent to you in good time. But if not, it is your *responsibility* to chase them up – non-receipt is not a defence for late reporting or payment!

Self-employed/sole trader compliance

The first penalty will come if you fail to register with HMRC in time. You should register with HMRC as soon as you can and have *up to six months after the end of the tax year ie 5 October*. However, since the tax year 2018/19 this requirement only applies once you have reached £1,000 profit from your business. You must also pay any tax bill within the specified time limit or face the following penalties:

Late filing:

For filing tax return up to three months late – automatic penalty of £100

PLUS: If 3-6 months late - £10 a day up to maximum of £900

PLUS: If 6-12 months late - £300 or 5% of tax owing

PLUS: If 12 months late filing - £300 or 5% of tax owing

Late payment:

Up to 30 days late payment - 5% of tax owing

PLUS: If 1-6 months late payment – addition of 5% of tax still owing

PLUS: If 6-12 months late payment – further addition of 5% of tax still owing

Interest on unpaid tax:

Interest on tax due runs at 3%

Maybe these penalties don't seem harsh but just look at the knock-on effect:

If you owe tax of say £500 on 31 January but don't file your return until 15 May and then don't pay for a further 6 months, the additional cost will be:

- £100 automatic late-filing penalty PLUS £10/day for 15 days in the 3-6 month period – total £250 for late filing

- £50 for late payment

- £11.84 interest

So you incur a total of £311.84 in penalties – adding more than 50% of the original tax debt.

Limited companies' compliance

With **Corporation Tax** the penalties get tougher! Also, you have to file your accounts and returns with *both* HMRC *and* Companies House.

Late filing penalties from HMRC:

Late filing - £100 automatic penalty even if late only by one day

If late by 3 months – a further £100

After 6 months - the additional penalty is 10% of whatever HMRC estimates to be your tax liability (and you can't challenge this estimate)

After 12 months – an additional 10% of due and unpaid tax

If your tax return is late 3 times in a row, the £100 penalties become £500.

N.B Where HMRC has estimated your tax, once you have filed your return the tax due is recalculated using the actual figures.

Late payment and interest:

Although there are no late payment penalties for Corporation Tax, there is a charge of 'failure to notify' if you don't tell HMRC that you owe them Corporation Tax (and this can also apply to individuals). Penalties range from 15% to 100% of the tax due, depending on whether the error was careless or deliberate and whether you disclosed it unprompted or not. Interest will also be charged for late payment.

Late filing with Companies House:

If you're late filing your accounts and returns at Companies House, a separate system of penalties applies.

Late filing by:

Up to 1 month - £150   Up to 3 months - £375

Up to 6 months - £750   More than 6 months - £1,500

N.B. If a company files late in two successive years, the penalties for the second year are automatically doubled.

There is no penalty for late filing of the confirmation statement (which replaces the annual return) but Companies House may seek to prosecute the directors and also have the company struck off. In addition, the lack of filing and the lateness of filing will all be on the public record and this will be bad for the company's credit rating and credibility. Compliance with this requirement is not a major issue, so why risk it? So many do!

However, any well-run business will have a system for logging and flagging up deadlines for all kinds of things, including filing accounts and returns, and of course paying any tax bills. The table in the *Appendix* shows how easy it should be to input these deadlines into your system.

#11. Investment business or trading business?

This distinction is a vital part of the tax treatment of the profits from property management. Some tax reliefs are only available to trades. But although all trades are businesses, *not all businesses are trades*.

At its simplest, a business that owns properties simply to let them out is an *investment business*. By contrast one that buys, improves and then sells property is a *trading business*. However, nothing is ever quite so black and white in the world of tax; nuanced judgment is involved (along with scope for dispute) in designating a business as investment or trading.

To make sense of it, let's begin by looking at the 'badges of trade'; the established indicators by which HMRC decide whether or not an activity can be classed as trading:

- Profit-seeking motive;

- The number of transactions;

- The nature of the asset;

- Existence of similar trading transactions or interests;

- Changes to the asset;

- The way the sale was carried out;

- The source of finance;

- Interval of time between purchase and sale;

- Method of acquisition.

The more of the badges you can demonstrate, the better your chance of being classed as a trade.

Now, much of this list appears to relate to buying and selling property. So what if your business is renting out your property? Here are two relevant facts:

1. Income Tax (Trading and Other Income) Act 2005 refers to the activity of acquiring and letting properties as a 'property rental business' - and that doesn't make it a trade. It depends on exactly what you (or your company) does.

2. A business of serviced accommodation will qualify as a trade for certain tax purposes if it is carried on as a business and meets the rules, no Class 4 National Insurance contributions payable (for the business owner – NI would, of course, be payable if you have employees) and Inheritance Tax (where Business Relief is not available for businesses which only generate investment income, serviced accommodation being a grey area depending on the level of service you provide). There are other tax issues covered elsewhere in the book on serviced accommodation.

But this still doesn't clarify which is better – to be an investment or a trading business.

So let's now consider the pros and cons of investment vs trading:

Some disadvantages of being classified as an **investment** activity include:

*   No sideways loss relief against other income for Income Tax purposes, and restrictions on carry-back relief;

*   No carry-back for loss relief for Corporation Tax;

*   No relief for Corporation Tax on disposal of a substantial shareholding;

*   No Enterprise Investment Scheme (EIS) relief;

*   No capital allowances for plant and machinery used in a dwelling house (unless it's serviced accommodation);

*   Only limited Capital Gains Tax relief (roll-over generally not available and no Entrepreneurs' Relief). For a trading business you will generally get CGT relief on disposal;

*   No Investors' Relief (which we will look at later);

- No Inheritance Tax Business Relief (unless it's a serviced accommodation with a high level of service, which can be very difficult to demonstrate).

But there are some **advantages** to being an investment business:

- There is no National Insurance Contribution (NIC) for income from an investment business;

- You are eligible for s.162 incorporation relief if you incorporate and can demonstrate you have a business;

- Lettings relief - the present position is that if you let out a property previously occupied by you as your residence, you may be able to claim relief for the period of the let against the computation of the capital gain when you sell. However the Chancellor proposed in the Autumn 2018 Budget to restrict this so that it only applies where the landlord shares accommodation with the tenant. On this occasion the budget proposal did not make it into the Finance Act 2019 - but at the time of writing we are expecting this to be implemented in April 2020.

As with all things tax, cases of dispute are referred to the courts. This can be a complex issue to weigh as the following examples show:

Some more case law

In the 1974 case of Ransom v Higgs, several learned judges attempted to define what is meant by 'trade'. The HMRC view remains that whether or not a trade exists is primarily a question of fact. Hence the decision as to whether there is a trade in any particular case will depend on an interpretation of all the facts and circumstances of that case, including the weighting to be given to each of those facts and circumstances.

In the later case of Marson v Morton & Others, the judge cemented this by saying (in nice judicial language):

'It is clear that the question of whether or not there has been an adventure in the nature of trade depends on all the facts and circumstances of each particular case and depends on the interaction between the various factors that are present in any given case'.

In the case of Town Investments v Dept of Environment (1978) Lord Diplock stated *"the word "business" is an etymological chameleon; it suits its meaning to the context in which it is found"*.

Clearly the best outcome is to avoid a dispute by ensuring as best as you can that you treat your business correctly. So let's look at how all of this impacts specifically on a property business.

How does investment vs trading impact on property business taxation?

Broadly speaking, if an **investor** acquires property with the intention of holding it **long term** with a view to deriving an income from lettings, coupled with capital growth over a period of time, then it's investment.

So if all you are doing is acquiring properties that you then let out, HMRC will see this as an investment activity only.

A property **trader** is likely to seek a much **shorter-term profit** by buying, refurbishing and then selling on, with lettings being either short-term or non-existent. This constitutes activity that goes beyond incidental management of rental property.

So how does all of this impact on your tax bills? The answers to this will crop up throughout the book. Here I'll just mention a few examples.

1. Capital Gains Tax: This applies only when selling properties from an investment portfolio, not to property bought, improved and sold as a trading business. However, as we have already seen, agreeing what is and is not an investment or a trading business is not always easy.

I mentioned earlier that the Income Tax (Trading and Other Income) Act 2005 uses the term 'Property Rental Business' in relation to what it regards as an *investment* business operation – but I feel this can be misleadingly simplistic. Sometimes defining a business comes down to how the 'business activity' is regarded, as the legal case below illustrates:

An interesting landmark case

Terrace Hill (Berkeley) Ltd v. HMRC (2015)

The company had acquired and refurbished a property which was then disposed of but only *after* it has been let as offices to various tenants. This had all the hallmarks of a trading activity, as it is a common strategy for developers to establish good quality tenants before selling on. However, the company claimed it should be treated as an investment activity – and the judge agreed. Why?

The company was deemed to have entered into a legitimate tax avoidance scheme that incurred tax on capital gains but not on trading profits. The First Tier Tribunal accepted the evidence of the directors that the *original intention* had been to retain the property as an investment and the plan had only changed when the returns from letting proved disappointing and they received a good offer from a purchaser. The outcome might well have been different had the directors not been able to demonstrate their original intention.

This is a good illustration of the 'badges of trade' measure mentioned earlier. You can see from the case that the reality of how the business is run and with what motive is really important. There are few hard and fast rules.

2. **Property developers:** If your business is developing property, including refurbishment and renovation, you are evidently a trading company, but you are also eligible for construction-related tax breaks – but only if you comply with the Construction Industry Scheme for tax purposes. We will discuss this in *Section 9. Property Construction and Development.*

What if there's an economic downturn which means that you can't sell your development properties, at least without suffering a loss, so you let them out on a short-term basis? Does this automatically cause these properties to be treated as an investment? This very much depends upon the facts.

Provided you keep on marketing the properties, even if no acceptable offers are made, this demonstrates your intentions and motives, which you will remember is one of the 'badges of trade'. If this continues for more than a couple of years, then there could be a risk that the activity will be classified as investment. I'm afraid I can't tell you a specific length of time for this, as this itself is something that HMRC will consider on a case-by-case basis.

It's really important that you document and record your decisions, for example by board minutes and letters to the agents instructing them to keep on marketing. As you will see from the Terrace Hill case above the key factor was that the directors could demonstrate their original intentions and a plausible reason for the change of plan.

3. Incorporation relief: If you're letting property as an individual **and** you meet the criteria as set out in the Ramsay case (above), then you will be a treated as having a business. sole trader. If you then want to incorporate your business, property rental does count as a business activity for the purposes of *incorporation relief*. It does not, however, help you to get the new limited company classified as a trading company, should that be your aim.

Later in this section we take a careful look at Holding Companies, one of the additional types of organisational structure you can consider. This option can offer convenient ways to rearrange how the property or business premises are held and taxed. First, however, I want to take a quick look at a simpler choice you might face as a trading business – keeping your property in your own name, not as an asset of the company.

Keeping property outside a trading company

Let's say you have a trading company – there are definite advantages to owning the business premises personally rather than putting them into the business. Why?

- This avoids the potential charges to SDLT that would apply where premises are transferred into the company but are not part of trading stock. It is possible to avoid SDLT if the premises are held by a partnership *(more in Section 7. All About Stamp Duty Land Tax)*;

- It is a useful choice if you anticipate a future sale of the business but not of the premises. If the premises were held by the company and then sold, any gain in value would be subject to Corporation Tax, and there would also be an additional charge to you if you then received the proceeds of the sale from the company;

- Entrepreneurs' Relief is still available on the chargeable gain if you sell the property within three years of the disposal of your shares in the company, provided that the premises are used by the trading company for the purposes of its trading activity. However, if the company is paying you a full commercial rent for the property, it will be treated as an investment, so no ER will be available. Charging less than a full commercial rent means that only a proportion of the gain on sale will qualify for ER, based on the difference between actual rent and full commercial rent, and also any period of ownership for which a full commercial rent was not charged;

- Holding the business premises outside the company may be more tax-efficient if the company pays you, the owner, a commercial rent rather than the profits of the company being artificially inflated by not having to pay for business premises;

- Also, if the company fails, the premises will be protected as your personal asset, rather than being swallowed up by the company's debts;

- New measures introduced from April 2016 (and further restrictions in the March 2017 Budget) mean that extraction of profits from a company via dividends is no longer as tax-efficient. If the company owns the property outright then the company's profitability may be greater and you will then need to extract that profit from the company. By keeping it in your own name, you retain the capital asset and in due course should be able to claim Entrepreneurs' Relief on any gain on disposal (see above) as long as you have not charged a rent. But if you have a mortgage on the property then not charging rent may not be a viable option.

However, it may be very difficult not to effectively charge a rent if the property is subject to a mortgage in your personal name (unless of course you are able to discharge the mortgage payments from your other personal assets);

- As there is no interest relief *restriction* on commercial premises, if the property is subject to a mortgage then full relief for the interest paid is allowable either through the company or for the owner. So, this being tax-neutral, you need instead to consider the other advantages listed above.

How do you manage the expense of the premises when not held within the company?

There are two options – 1) the business paying you, the owner, a commercial rent, or 2) having artificially inflated profits through not incurring a premises expense. Option 1 may be more tax-efficient from the owners' point of view, depending on the personal tax position. This is because your extraction of profits from a company via dividends is no longer as tax-efficient since April 2016.

#12. Other organisational options

Even for sole traders there are benefits to incorporating the business. But there are of course some additional organisational options to consider – holding companies, joint ventures and special purpose vehicles (SPV).

Holding Companies

This topic relates to the trading vs investment debate above.

The term 'parent company' is used to mean a company that controls subsidiary companies by holding at least 51% of the shares and the voting rights. This means that a parent company could be a trading company. A 'holding company', however, is effectively a parent company that usually exists solely for the holding of assets (and shares) of subsidiaries. As such, a holding company is not a trading company (unless of course it is carrying on trading activities).

Typically a holding company simply controls a group of related companies to manage legal liabilities and, sometimes, benefit from consolidating tax obligations. It principally deals specifically with assets, investments and management rather than providing goods and services with a view to making a profit from production and sales. A further advantage to the holding company structure is that, provided of course that the holding company has not given a guarantee, it is not liable for any of the subsidiary company's debts and consequently the assets in the name of the holding company are protected. This enables the holding company to manage risk for the group.

To qualify as a 'holding company', s.1159 Companies Act 2016 states that:

- The parent company must hold greater than 50% of the voting rights in the subsidiary;

- The parent company must be member of the subsidiary and have the right to appoint or remove a majority of its board of directors;

- The parent company must be a member of the subsidiary and, in accordance with an agreement with other shareholders, alone controls a majority of the voting rights in the subsidiary.

- The section deals with the definitions of 'subsidiary' and 'holding' companies only, not with the issue of whether the holding or parent company is carrying on a trade.

A **holding company** is not seen as carrying on a trade or business if all the following apply:

- It has no assets other than shares in companies which are its 51% (or more) subsidiaries;

- It is not entitled to a deduction, as charges or management expenses, in respect of any outgoings;

- It has no income or gains other than dividends which it has distributed in full to its shareholders and which are, or could be, franked investment income received by that company.

There are also many *intra-group tax* reliefs available where a group structure exists. However to benefit from these, in many cases (notably relief for SDLT), the holding company must own at least 75% of the shares and control at least 75% of the voting rights in the subsidiary.

Other definitions

An **investment company** is a company carrying on a business of making investments, and not a trade, and so is not dormant.

A **dormant company** is not treated as an associate of another company under common control.

Any clearer?

Case study: an example of how a holding company can be beneficial

One of our clients was the majority (66%) shareholder in a well-established wholesale food warehousing and distribution business, run from large warehouse-type premises that were owned by the company.

Our client wanted to hive off the premises (which were of considerable value) from the company and create a structure whereby the existing shareholders became shareholders of a new company that in turn held all the shares of the trading company. The premises would then be transferred to the holding company. However, to comply with General Anti-Avoidance Rules (GAAR), it was important that the client had a bona fide commercial reason for doing this – and that we could argue the case for this. But first we needed to examine the tax implications.

On the face of it, these transactions would result in a number of taxation liabilities. So, it was necessary not only to structure the transactions in such a way that either the tax burden would be alleviated or, at least, there would be a tax-neutral situation. We also needed to obtain HMRC clearance that the proposed transactions would not trigger a charge to tax (CGT on a share exchange, Income Tax on transactions in securities, and Stamp Duty Land Tax on the transfer of the premises).

This is how we presented the case for the client:

'The underlying bona fide commercial reasons for this decision are as follows:

a)   to create a group structure;

b)   to allow the premises to be held separately from the goodwill and stock of the trading business so that this can operate as a separate entity and can, if required, be disposed of with the benefit of the lease;

c)   to permit incentivisation of employees of xx Limited (the trading company) which relates solely to the performance of that business;

d)   *to permit flexibility;*

e)   *to bring other business enterprises owned by the current shareholders into the group structure.'*

To achieve this, the transactions were ordered as follows:

1.   The creation of NewCo Ltd with identical shareholding and directors as trading company

2.   The exchange of shares by shareholders in trading company for shares in NewCo, with NewCo. This was achieved by NewCo issuing new shares the consideration for which was the shareholders' existing shares in the trading company, with the result that the trading company became a wholly-owned subsidiary of NewCo

3.   The transfer of the premises by the trading company to NewCo, at open market value with vacant possession

4.   The premises leased back to trading company on commercial terms.

We were successful in obtaining the clearance and the transactions went ahead. In this particular case, the transfer of the premises to NewCo also involved re-financing, with the new loan to the holding company being used to redeem the existing borrowing. It could therefore be argued that the consideration for the transfer to Newco was not nil (which would not attract SDLT) but the value of the redemption (which would attract SDLT). We believed that intra-group relief could be claimed and separate clearance was obtained for this, both on the transfer of the freehold and on the subsequent lease back *(see Section 5. Getting To Know Capital Taxes, Reliefs And Schemes for more information on SDLT and Reliefs).*

I'd just like to point out that strategies of this type are very complex as there are many different aspects to consider. So if you are looking at implementing something like this, please do contact me.

Joint Ventures vs Limited Liability Partnerships

As its name suggests, a Joint Venture is a form of common enterprise, but with some very important distinctions from a partnership. Let's start with the definition of a partnership as set out in section 1 of the Partnership Act 1890 (which, despite the passage of 100 years or so, remains unaltered):

'Partnership is the relation which subsists between persons carrying on a business in common with a view of profit'

However, section 2 (as amended) goes on to say that any association formed under the Companies Act 2006 or any other Act of Parliament, letters patent or royal charter is not governed by the 1890 Act.

So where does this leave Limited Liability Partnerships (LLP)?

For this you have to go to the Limited Liability Partnership Act 2000, because LLPs, like limited companies, are entirely a creature of statute. This states that an LLP is:

'A body corporate (with legal personality separate from that of its members) and created under the 2000 Act.'

In section 2 of the LLP Act 2000 it states that (amongst other requirements) for an LLP to be incorporated:

'Two or more persons associated for carrying on a lawful business with a view to profit must have subscribed their names to an incorporation document'

So, what is a Joint Venture and how is it different? After all it certainly looks quite similar, especially with regard to the profit motive.

A joint venture is a contractual business undertaking between two or more parties. So far, so good; however, whereas both the Partnership Act and the LLP Act refer to carrying on a business, which suggests an ongoing, long-term business relationship, a joint venture is often based on *a single business transaction*. Sadly however this is not conclusive: nor can the title you give to the undertaking be decisive one way or the other.

Whether or not a relationship is a joint venture or a partnership is a matter of fact – but one that is inferred from all the circumstances.

Why does this matter?

It's because the liability and tax treatment may differ between the two models.

In a joint venture the parties pool their resources and expertise to achieve a particular goal, sharing the risks and rewards. However, there is no obligation to share risks and rewards *equally*, only as agreed by the participants. This is the key difference between a joint venture, and both an ordinary partnership and an LLP. An ordinary partnership will be governed either by written agreement or in its absence by the 1890 Act, but the agreement is only between the partners who, as is fairly well-known, are jointly and severally liable personally for the debts of the partnership to third parties. In an LLP this liability is limited (just as with a limited company). In a partnership or LLP the partners take as their profit the agreed partnership share, but in a joint venture the benefits are according to the JV agreement.

So, it can be vital to establish whether you are in a partnership or a joint venture. There is no rule as to how finite a JV should be so this alone cannot be your deciding factor. Instead, in my view, the best distinction is whether the purpose is a single defined goal (or set of goals) making it a joint venture, or to create and manage an ongoing business which may evolve and change, which is more likely to be a partnership.

Special Purpose Vehicles (SPV)

An SPV is a limited company *formed for a specific purpose* rather than, as many companies are, for general commercial purposes. Why would you choose to form one?

General company law indicates that a company can undertake any role that is permitted by the Articles of Association, or not prohibited by them. Many company Articles contain a 'catch all' provision allowing the company to carry on any activity which the directors agree would be to the benefit of the company alongside its stated activities.

The reason for an SPV lies in the realities, especially financial, of the commercial world. Many commercial lenders prefer to (or will only) lend to a limited company that is restricted to a specific purpose (and also some lenders dislike the 'holding company' structure). This is particularly the case in the buy-to-let market. With an SPV, as opposed to a general trading company, it is easier for the lender to understand how it will operate and, crucially, easier to underwrite the risks. Such a company will generally be restricted to holding and letting property and nothing else, The Standard Industrial Classification of Economic Activities (SIC) Code used when filing the company's annual (or other) confirmation statement will be the one for letting property and the lender will need to see that there is no sign of any revenue passing through the company's accounts other than from letting.

I must be clear that being an SPV is *not* essential to being in the property-letting business, but you may well find that your borrowing options are severely restricted.

Alphabet share structures

There are a number of ways in which shareholdings can be structured to get the required result, for example when transferring shares to your minority-aged child but wanting to restrict income (and grow the capital value instead) until they reach a certain age. They usually involve the creation of alphabet shares, so called because they are typically designated Class A shares, Class B shares and so on. The various classes can have different rights attached and when dividends are declared (a decision of the directors) then different dividends can be declared on different classes.

Other reasons why you might want to structure the shareholdings include:

- To 'reward' different classes of shareholders at different levels;

- To provide shares with a fixed rate of income (fixed rate shares);

- To give investors a preference when it comes to dividing profits or in a sale or winding up (preference shares);

- To include someone in the profit-sharing of the company but restrict their power to interfere in the management;

- To attract investors by planning for the return on investment to be only at a specified time. These are known as flowering, growth or hurdle shares because they are designed to receive a dividend only once a 'hurdle' in terms of profitability or growth is reached.

Generally speaking the issue of shares is a directors' decision although there may be restrictions in the Articles or in a shareholders' agreement.

However one point to watch is share dilution or 'value-shifting' which may arise where new shares or classes of shares are issued without being offered to existing shareholders pro-rata.

s 29 Taxation of Capital Gains Act 1992 provides that where a person, or persons, who controls a company uses that control so that value or valuable rights pass out of shares which they own (or are owned by persons connected with them) into other shares in, or rights over, the company, then this is a disposal or part disposal for CGT.

An example:

- X Ltd was set up in April 2010 by A and B (his son). A held 900 £1 ordinary shares, and B held 100 £1 ordinary shares.

- In 2016 A (using his majority voting powers of at least 75%) arranged for the company to amend the rights for the existing share capital

- A's shares became preference shares with a 5% dividend (which would be paid before any other dividends were declared

- B's shares 'A' ordinary £1 shares, with all other rights of voting, profits, and on liquidation.

- So although A had the advantage of a 'preference' dividend, his shares no longer had any other entitlement to share in the company's profits or assets or to vote.

- It is a question of fact how the changes affected the value of what are now two different classes of share, and this is something that would need to be agreed with HMRC Shares and Assets Valuation Division.

- Let's assume that it was agreed that the value of A's shares immediately prior to the change was 9,000, and that afterwards it was no more than the face value of the shares (£900).

- This must mean that the value passing to B's shares is £8,100 (£9,000 less £900)

- So the value-shifting rules mean that A is treated as having made a part disposal of his shares and the proportion disposed of is

  £8,100/(£8,100 + £900)   = 90%

Even though A has not in fact actually transferred his shares, only had them re-classified, A will be liable for CGT on any capital gain resulting from that deemed part disposal

The key point here is that the arrangement was only possible because it was A who (as a shareholder with more than 75%) controlled the amendment to the Articles by being able to ensure that the appropriate shareholders' resolution was passed. Had the value-shifting occurred the other way (with value passing from B's share to A) then on the face of it the rule would not apply because B did not control the control the company.

However, you will have noted that B is actually A's son - so he is a person connected with A. This means that the rule will apply in any event because it also catches situations where value passes out of the shares of someone who is connected to the person with control of the company.

The value of the disposal is governed by the circumstances. I recommend that HMRC clearance be obtained beforehand.

#13. Other organisation-related issues

Purchase of own shares by the company

It's often the case that a company needs to re-organise its shareholdings. This could be because shareholders who are employees are leaving the company, or because a shareholder or all the shareholders are retiring, perhaps in connection with handing the business on, or making arrangement with another entity.

A private limited company may repurchase its own shares out of capital, distributable reserves or the proceeds of a fresh issue of shares made for the purpose of financing the repurchase. Additionally, in 2015 the law around share buy-backs was amended to permit private companies to make so-called 'de minimis' repurchases out of capital without having to identify available distributable reserves.

There is however a trap for the unwary which relates to the 'connection test'.

s.1042 Corporation Tax Act 2010 requires the exiting shareholder to have no connection with the company after the buyback has taken place. 'Connection' means an interest of less than 30%.

Section 1062(2) of the same Act defines 'connection' as follows:

'A person is connected with a company if the person directly or indirectly possesses, or is entitled to acquire, more than 30% of –

(a)   the issued ordinary share capital of the company, or

(b)   the loan capital and the issued share capital of the company, or

(c)   the voting power in the company.

'Loan capital' effectively means any money borrowed by the company. 'Issued share capital' means the nominal value and includes preference shares.

So, as you can see, it would be very easy to allow the company to purchase back the shares of someone who left outstanding a loan to the company (including a credit balance on their director's loan account), or who retained some preference shares with no voting rights. If these breach the 30% rule, then the outgoing shareholder will not be treated as having made a disposal for Capital Gains Tax (which, with Entrepreneurs' Relief, will be at a rate of 10%).

Instead the payment will be taxed as an income distribution and dividend rates of up to 38.1% will apply.

In summary a private company can buy back shares:

- **Out of capital.** This requires quite a complex procedure under the Companies Act 2006 and is not very much used as, in many cases, the same result can be achieved by a reduction in share capital.

- **Out of capital up to an aggregate purchase price** in a financial year of the lower of (i) £15,000 or (ii) the nominal value of 5% of its fully paid share capital as at the beginning of the financial year. This option is very useful for buying back small parcels of shares.

- **Out of distributable profits** (or the proceeds of a fresh issue of shares made for the purpose of financing the purchase). This is the most popular route but it does depend upon the company having sufficient distributable profit. If it doesn't, and a reduction of share capital doesn't meet the shareholders' requirements, one solution may be a management buy-out.

Management Buy-Outs

A management buyout (MBO) is a deal that allows the management team of a company to acquire the business they work in from its owner. This clearly means that the buyers will need to have considerable available funds up-front if the selling owners are not to be exposed to risk. So in a large number of cases the bulk of the finance to acquire the business is provided by banks and private equity groups.

The benefits to the owners is the realising in financial terms of what may well amount to many years of effort. There may also be circumstances which are forcing the owners to sell e.g. poor health, death or adverse economic conditions in which the owners no longer wish to continue. You might think this would make the company an unattractive purchase, but the management team can make significant gains on their investment in the business – even if the business does not grow significantly.

This is a good alternative to Purchase of Own Shares, if the company can't meet the rules set out above. Please contact me for help in structuring one or both of these.

An example:

The company is acquired by the MBO team for £15m, financed by £10m from a bank loan and £4.25m of private equity loan, with the balance of £0.75m provided by the MBO team. The private equity lender puts up risk capital for a 30% stake. As the equity lender has paid more for its equity than the management team this is offset by agreeing that its loan stock will be repaid before the equity shareholders.

On Day One the value of the business is equal to the value of cash paid for the shares, £0.75m. Deal costs will be paid out of this.

After five years, let's assume the business is now worth £20m having grown steadily over the period and has also reduced the bank debt to £4m. The

Equity Value is now £20m less bank and private equity debts of £4m and £4.25m respectively – thus £11.75m. Shareholding percentages have not changed and management's stake is therefore now worth £8.23m.

There are other benefits to the MBO team and/or the owner, for example when:

- The sellers want a quick sale (management know the business and can act quickly);

- They may not want to sell to a competitor;

- The management team is rewarded and the workforce secured;

- The MBO team know the business so will require fewer legal warranties than a third-party buyer;

- The MBO team's knowledge gives them a very good idea of how likely the business is to succeed under their direction.

Insolvency

This is a term that strikes fear into the hearts of most businesspeople. So let's start by understanding what the term actually means.

The usual definition is that an individual or company can't meet its financial obligations as they fall due – but this is actually quite a loose definition. Many businesses might point the finger of blame at their customers failing to meet their obligations to pay on time and in full.

Looking first at limited companies and LLPs, we have already stated that only the company's assets are liable for the company's debts (except of course where a personal guarantee has been given). In the strict legal sense this is true, but the 'corporate veil' is not quite as opaque as it used to be. There is such a thing as 'insolvent trading', when the directors allow the company to go on trading even though they know, or ought to have known, that the company was insolvent. However, bearing in mind the definition of insolvency given above, how do you know exactly when that stage has been reached? This ambiguity may be why it is hard to find many cases of insolvent trading.

However, more recently there have been a few cases where directors have been prosecuted for 'reckless trading' and this appears to mean that they have gone on trading without any regard for their obligations, usually to their staff and also to HMRC. This can result in a fine or in a ban on acting as a director. It's interesting to note that many instances of non-compliance in company law are in fact ' offences' rather than civil wrongs.

Turning now to sole traders and partners (not LLPs), there is no escaping the fact that they are personally liable for the debts of the business. Partners may well have an agreement as to how losses are borne but that is only applicable between themselves. Creditors are at liberty to *pursue all or any of the partners personally*, leaving it to the partners to sort out how they claim a contribution from each other.

Personal bankruptcy is no joke. Admittedly you can nowadays expect to be discharged from the bankruptcy within a reasonable period (one year), but the effects can be far-reaching. Also, if you inherit anything before you are discharged it will go to your creditors. Worse still, let's say your assets include a house that is still mortgaged (and thus not worth the Official Receiver's effort to force a sale). Then, long after being discharged, you pay off the mortgage. You may well think that the house is now safe, but you'd be wrong. Way down the line, with no mortgage attached, the house could still go to your creditors (unless you've paid them off in full) because it was an asset of the bankrupt estate.

Many people look at putting assets in a relative's name. That's fine but the Official Receiver can overturn any transaction made less than two years beforehand and can go back five years in the event of a sale at an undervalue. In fact there is no time limit if it can be shown that it was a 'transaction defrauding creditors' (S.423 Insolvency Act 1986), in other words seeking to put the asset beyond the reach of creditors.

So what do you do if you find yourself facing insolvency? First of all, get some advice from a licensed insolvency practitioner. There are a number of strategies other than winding up or bankruptcy and key to all of them is facing the difficulties, being realistic and, above all, staying in communication with your creditors. Most creditors don't want you to go bust (unless there are unencumbered assets they can get their hands on) - they just want you to pay

Investing and trading in a group structure

In principle I feel you should avoid mixing trading and investing in this way. However, there is a small amount of leeway if a trading entity also has investment properties.

If yours is a trading business, section 165A Taxation of Capital Gains Act 1992 states (in connection with Entrepreneurs' Relief) that in order to retain trading status, non-trading activities must not be substantial. HMRC interpret this as being not more than 20%. How is this measured? There is no simple formula but the following are some of the indicators that might be taken into account (not an exhaustive list):

- Turnover from trading and non-trading activities

- Profit from trading and non-trading activities

- Asset base

- Time spent and expenditure incurred on different activities

- Company's history e.g. looking at receipts over a longer time-scale, or at seasonal variation

None of these indicators are conclusive taken in isolation but will build up a picture of whether, overall, the non-trading activities amount to more than 20%. The indicators, now adopted for the purposes of Entrepreneurs' Relief, are the same as those previously used in connection with other tax reliefs so have been in use by HMRC for some time.

My advice is that you should try to avoid investments building up.

If you do lose trading status, then a disposal of the shares can still qualify for Entrepreneurs' Relief if the date at which trading status was lost is no earlier than three years before the date of disposal **and**, at that date, trading and other conditions had then been satisfied throughout the previous two years (the usual 'qualifying period').

So, in the case that investments have accumulated, an alternative is to look at a **demerger** within a group structure.

There are two types of demerger, discussed further below:

- Statutory demerger exempt under Corporation Tax Act 2010;

- Non-statutory demerger under S.110 of the Insolvency Act 1985.

Demergers and reconstructions

These events usually occur either a) when one or more of the directors or shareholders decide they want to go their own way, or b) it is decided that it would be more efficient for different parts of the business to be carried on by different companies. The usual route is for one or more new companies to be created and the business or assets to be divided, usually in exchange for shares. Another instance is where it is desired to create a group structure, possibly so that major assets such as the business premises can be held by the parent company, or different types of assets held by different companies, or to have a structure involving both investment and trading companies. These can also be known as 'hive-ups' or 'hive-downs'.

In all these cases, the idea is to achieve the objective without incurring onerous CGT or other taxation liabilities, or at least to defer them. However, a bona fide *commercial* reason will be required in order to obtain advance tax clearance.

Demergers are complex, but let's take a look at a couple of different types.

1. Statutory demerger

There are a number of conditions that must be satisfied, and the original company must remain a trading company with the intention of retaining the demerged or successor company and not selling. There is also a need for sufficient distributable reserves to affect the demerger (which may be a stumbling block).

No income tax implications should arise for the shareholders as the 'exempt' demerger will be deemed to have been made at asset market value. There may be a chargeable gain, as there will be a receipt of shares, but the transaction should be covered by the 'tax exempt distribution' provisions in s.192 TCGA 1992.

The company will have disposed of part of its business to the new company and to ensure no chargeable gain, but the demerger will need to fall within the 'scheme of reconstruction' provisions s.139 TCGA 1992. This means that, under the scheme of reconstruction involving the transfer of the whole or part of a company's business to another company, the transfer is at a 'no gain, no loss' value. In addition the transfer must be effected for bona fide commercial reasons with no consideration made other than the assumption of its liabilities by the transferee company.

There may be stamp duty implications as the transaction involves a transfer of shares. There is no obligation for the shareholdings in the new companies to be a precise reflection of the shareholdings in the old company as long as pro rata values are maintained.

One other important feature is that both the demerged business **and** the remaining business must both be trading businesses. This rules out the statutory demerger if the businesses are wholly or partly investment businesses.

A statutory demerger cannot be made if the intention is that one or more of the demerged business is to be sold. If a de-merged business is sold within five years then clearance has to be sought from HMRC to avoid the demerger proceeds being taxed as income.

2. Non-statutory demerger

If you can't satisfy the statutory demerger conditions, the alternative is the 'non-statutory' procedure under s.110 Insolvency Act 1986. This involves the voluntary liquidation of the original company and distribution by the liquidator of the relevant assets to the new companies owned by the shareholders.

This would normally be regarded as an income distribution for the shareholders. However, this depends on the disposing company being liquidated before the reconstruction exercise is undertaken. Also, amounts received during the course of liquidation are generally not income distributions.

Unlike the statutory demerger, a non-statutory liquidation demerger requires at least two transfers of the business unit. The original company will cease to exist, being replaced by other companies into which assets of the original company are transferred.

This is a specialist area and it is advisable to seek HMRC clearance first.

The demerger may involve 'share for share' exchanges and this may be possible without adverse tax implications where the intention is for the owners of one business to exchange their interests and receive shares in the new company as consideration. As long as no actual consideration is received and values are the same in that there is no additional value transferred, the transaction is effectively just a swap of shares and, as such, will not generally attract an income tax charge; nor would CGT implications generally arise as long as what are known as the 'stand in shoes' provisions apply.

There are other alternatives for disposing of businesses or of shareholdings without incurring a large charge to Capital Gains Tax. These include using the Substantial Shareholding Exemption, but only if the business is to be sold, which is often the simplest way forward.

Alternatively, you can carry out a reduction in capital by setting up a new holding company using a share for share exchange, with separate classes of shares relating to the two businesses to be demerged. You then hive up once of the businesses to the new holding company and the remaining business (or shares) will then be transferred to a new company in exchange for the issue of new shares to the shareholders in the holding company. Prior clearance from HMRC is a must.

These are all very complex strategies and I recommend that you do not consider them without first taking specialist advice.

Employees, workers and self-employed

You might think it easy to tell if you are employing someone or not – but it's not always so simple. With Income Tax and National Insurance, you can get a nasty surprise if someone you thought of as self-employed is deemed to be your employee. The trouble is that it is not just a choice you make; you have to meet set criteria too.

The attraction of having self-employed workers, especially for smaller businesses, is very real: Income Tax and National Insurance are the worker's responsibility, not yours; you don't have to pay employer's NI either or offer a workplace pension, nor do you have to pay the National Minimum Wage (not that I advocate you should not pay minimum wage!); and you don't have to worry about the usual protections against unlawful or unfair dismissal or an entitlement to redundancy.

So what happens if HMRC decides you are wrong – that your self-employed worker is in fact an employee?

You will be liable for the accumulated employers' NI that you should have paid *plus* interest and penalties, and you'll also be primarily liable for the PAYE and NI you should have deducted, leaving it to you to try and recover this from the employee.

How does HMRC decide whether an engagement is employment or self-employment?

It is not a case of how your contract or terms of engagement are worded; it's about what is *actually happening* in your working relationship. Even then you can't claim that features of your worker's arrangements are necessarily evidence of self-employment status. For example, you would not get far arguing that simply because you don't deduct PAYE and NI from your worker's pay or offer 5.6 paid weeks of annual holiday, your worker is therefore self-employed.

If challenged, the circumstances of employment can ultimately only be decided by the First Tier Tribunal (considering tax liability and/or employment rights) using various criteria. Let's say *you* are the worker whose status is being challenged. Here are some of the criteria the Tribunal will look at:

- Are you required to work regularly - either set days or set hours?

- Are you required to do a minimum number of hours?

- Can the business stipulate the hours you work?

- Do you expect to be paid for the time worked, either by a regular salary or per hour worked?

- If you work additional hours do you expect to be paid for these or given Time Off in Lieu?

- Are you responsible to a manager or supervisor who directs how the work should be done?

- Are you required to carry out the work personally (i.e. you are not able to send a substitute to do the work)?

- Does the business provide the necessary materials, tools and equipment for your work?

This is not an exhaustive list but if you can answer 'yes' to the majority of the above points, you will probably be judged to be an employee.

Let's look at the other side of the coin:

- Are you in business for yourself, and responsible for its success making either a loss or a profit?.

- Are you free to decide what work you do, and when, where and how you do it?

- Could you subcontract the work, if you wanted to? (including using a substitute)

- If there was a problem with your work, would you be responsible for fixing it in your own time and at your own expense?

- Do you agree a fixed price for your work, regardless of how long the job takes to finish?

- Do you use your own money or funding to buy what's necessary to run the business and deliver the work?

- Are you free to work for more than one client?

- Do you put in bids or give quotes for work?

- Are you generally responsible for supervising the work?

- Do you invoice for the work you've done?

If you answer 'yes' to the majority of the above points then you will probably be regarded as self-employed.

However there is a third category. If you answer 'yes' to most of these questions then you are a 'worker' but not necessarily an 'employee':

- Do you have a contract or arrangement to do work for a 'reward'? This can be written or verbal.

- Is this reward either money or a benefit in kind? E.g. promise of future work, perks or a loan.

- Do you have a limited right to subcontract the work?

- Do you have to report for work, even if you don't want to?

- Is the business owner obliged to have work for you to do as long as the contract or arrangement lasts?

In addition, you must not be doing the work through your own limited company where the 'employer' is actually the client/customer of the company.

Finally, if you're a sole trader or a partner (including in an LLP) then you will be self-employed, but of course you may well have employees. If you are a limited company director (but not a shareholder unless also an actual employee), you are an employee of the company.

Paying children

If you employ your children (or anyone else's children) in your business, then there are rules to be observed, some relating to Income Tax and NI:

- The youngest age that a child can work is usually 13 and they cannot work full-time until they reach the school-leaving age. There are restrictions relating to working during school holidays as well as during term-time. A few hours a week on light duties (e.g. answering the telephone, stuffing envelopes, sending out emails or taking messages) will not usually infringe this rule;

- If a child under the school-leaving age (whether or not 13 or over) is to take part in films, plays, concerts or other public performances that the audience pays to see, or that take place on licensed premises or in any sporting events or modelling assignments where the child is paid, then the person running the event musts apply to the child's local council for a performance licence

- Children may not work in factories or industrial sites or in places like pubs and betting offices. Local byelaws may place additional restrictions on the places and times at which children may work and may require an employment permit to be issued

- Children of school age are not entitled to National Minimum Wage;

- Children under 16 don't pay NI so you only need to include them on payroll if their earnings exceed the Personal Allowance for income tax;

- Children aged 16-17 are entitled to the National Minimum Wage.

- The legislation on 'settlements' is aimed at preventing parents from gaining an Income Tax advantage by transferring income-producing assets to their minor children; any income from assets gifted by the parents will, as long as the child is a minor, be treated as income of the parent and taxed accordingly. So any employment of your own minor children must be 'genuine' in the sense that the child is actually performing the tasks and receiving an appropriate level or remuneration - not just a sham job devised as a way of passing some of what would be the parent's income to the child. A good test is to look at whether, if the child was not available, someone else would be employed to do that task and what they would be paid.

- The payment must be for work actually done - and obviously there is a limit to how much work a younger child can do, both in practice and permitted by law; Payment must be commensurate with the work carried out;

- The salary must actually be paid to them, not just a paper exercise;

- You must comply with all PAYE procedures in the same way as with ordinary staff.

NB – the last four points above also apply to employing your spouse. As always, when employing family in this way it is sensible to check your proposals with your accountant.

SECTION 4: UNDERSTANDING VAT AND 'MAKING TAX DIGITAL' (MTD)

The essence of VAT registration is not complicated: when your business turnover reaches a threshold you are required to register and account for VAT, passing on to HMRC any surplus after deducting the VAT you've been charged from the VAT you have levied on your own invoices. However, there are some special pointers relating to property businesses and the recent implementation of mandatory digital VAT records to consider. Also, certain smaller businesses not reaching the VAT threshold are still allowed to register for the VAT scheme, and it may be in their interests to do so. However this doesn't apply to buy-to-let property businesses (excluding serviced accommodation, letting agents, rent to rent, etc) and that means you cannot register for VAT.

We'll try to unravel it all in this section, starting with this last point.

Some terminology:

When discussing VAT it is common to use words like 'chargeable', 'charge', 'supply' and so on. Most of the time they make sense, but to clarify one usage: a 'supply for VAT' refers to the sale or transfer of something (goods or services) that must have VAT added to it if the supplier is VAT-registered, even if the rate of VAT is zero.

#14. Electing to register for VAT

If you own and let out commercial property, your rental income is not chargeable to VAT, but you could be making supplies that are not exempt, such as commission on letting as an agent. If your non-exempt income is below the compulsory threshold for registering (currently £85,000), you should still consider registering for VAT. If you decide to, you then opt to tax for each of your commercial properties and can add VAT to the rent. But if this makes your property a more expensive prospect to your tenant and yet you don't get to keep the VAT, why would you do this? You also have to charge VAT on disposal of property if you opt to tax.

The answer is that you also get to reclaim all the VAT that is charged to you for the property costs, such as the fees when buying it, the improvement work and any maintenance.

However, your target tenants will be disadvantaged if they are not registered for VAT, or are VAT-exempt (as opposed to zero-rated), as they can't claim back the VAT you're charging to them. So you need to weigh this up carefully based on the type of property you're letting out and the tenant profile.

Once you have opted to tax (which only applies to commercial property, not residential), the option remains in force on the property (see VAT opt to tax on property below) for 20 years (although there are some exceptions). Despite this, however, if you then sell the property, the new owner needs to make his own 'opt to tax' in order to continue to charge and reclaim VAT.

VAT opt to tax on land

There are two interesting aspects of this VAT election (which is for commercial property only).

First, although VAT will relate to the income and expenses from running your property, the opt to tax for VAT (explained above) is made on the property itself. This means that if a VAT-opted property changes hands, it remains VAT-opted for the remainder of the 20-year period unless the new owner doesn't opt or is able to dis-apply the option. Secondly, when you opt to tax for VAT on your property, you are actually opting on the *land* itself, not just the buildings – more on this in a moment.

The process of exercising an option to tax is twofold. First you must decide to exercise the option (for a limited company this would be at a board meeting of directors) and you should keep a record of when the decision was taken. Then you must notify HMRC, usually within 30 days of the decision, although HMRC may accept belated notification.

Although I've said that the option to tax, once made, usually lasts for 20 years, it doesn't automatically lapse. You must notify HMRC in order to revoke and, in some cases, seek permission to revoke. You can also disapply the option to tax in certain circumstances such as upon converting a commercial building to residential.

Back to VAT being on the land, not just the buildings: this means that any buildings on the land at the time of opting or constructed *afterwards* will be subject to the option (unless excluded by notice to HMRC after construction begins), and even if you specify a building in your option (because it is the prominent feature on the land) then the land will still be subject to the option if the building is demolished. But if you opted to tax before 1 June 2008 and it's clear from your notification that the option was made on that specific building only (for example by stating the exact address) then you can, if you wish, treat the option as revoked once the building is demolished

Finally, you do not have to own the freehold in order to opt to tax, as long as you own an 'interest' in it. This means any interest in, right over or licence to occupy the land. It follows that if you grant a lease or a sub-lease of opted land, the tenant or sub-tenant can decide whether or not to opt to tax, in the same way as if he had purchased the freehold.

The opt to tax regime is all about allowing an owner of land or of an interest in land to decide whether or not it is beneficial to be able to claim back VAT on supplies. The rules surrounding this area are complex with many exceptions and exemptions, so these need to be approached with care.

#15. MTD – digital business records and VAT

If you are registered for VAT, do your VAT-able supplies (in broad terms, your business turnover) exceed the VAT threshold? If so, you need to comply with this new mandatory system.

Making Tax Digital (MTD) is a new scheme running from April 2019 that requires any business that reaches or exceeds the VAT threshold to maintain all records relating to VAT digitally (it will eventually be extended to all accounting records, not just VAT). It does not affect a business below the threshold that has chosen to register for VAT. Its purpose is to generate VAT returns digitally via software for HMRC, and eventually it will extend to cover all financial returns.

What does Making Tax Digital mean?

- VAT- registered businesses and organisations (including sole traders, partnerships, limited companies, non-UK businesses registered for UK VAT, trusts and charities) whose supplies reach the VAT threshold must maintain digital accounting records. Paper records will cease to meet the legal requirements.

- These businesses and organisations will be required to use a functional compatible software product to maintain their accounting records and submit their returns to HMRC. The software will use HMRC's API (Application Program Interfaces) platform to submit information to HMRC. The current HMRC online tax return services will be withdrawn for those within the scope of the MTD rules.

- The requirement applies for your first VAT return period beginning on or after 1 April 2019, but there is a 6-month deferral for some businesses such as those required to make payments on account and those using the annual accounting scheme.

- HMRC's online VAT return will remain available only to businesses that are *voluntarily* registered for VAT (i.e. those whose supplies are below the £85,000 threshold).

"How will I comply?"

While some businesses may be able to develop their own compliant software which they can register with HMRC, most will need to acquire a suitable commercial software product or appoint an agent with access to this to submit returns to HMRC on their behalf.

No changes are being made to:

- The underlying VAT rules;

- The amount of information required to be submitted to HMRC; the VAT return will contain the same nine boxes that it does currently though the regulations do allow for additional information to be submitted on a voluntary basis;

- The current filing and payment deadlines for VAT.

The current rules apply when working out taxable turnover i.e. standard-rated, reduced-rated and zero-rated supplies are all included but you exclude outside-the-scope and exempt supplies.

"When might the requirements kick in for me?"

Deciding when you meet the criteria for compulsory VAT registration uses the same rolling 12-month system as before. There is no rule requiring you to look forward and estimate reaching the VAT threshold. However once you do reach the threshold you will only have a very limited period to consider how you are going to meet the MTD requirements and to implement these.

Voluntarily registered businesses will need to continue to monitor their turnover to establish when they need to start complying with the MTD for VAT requirements.

Please note: MTD is a one-way street and there's no going back. In other words, once your business is required to comply with the MTD for VAT, that obligation continues even if the turnover of the business subsequently drops below the VAT threshold.

Exemptions

There are some exemptions – but be careful how you rely on these! In general they apply to those who are regarded as 'digitally excluded' – i.e. are unable to comply for reasons such as of age, disability, religious objection or location.

Existing exemptions from online filing for VAT should carry over automatically to MTD for VAT. However, difficult new cases will arise in interpreting a barrier to using digital records, for example where an individual has some basic skills such as being able to send emails, but would not be able to cope with accounting software or a spreadsheet. Location exemption covers those who cannot obtain access to broadband because of where they are located. It does not include those who could sign up for broadband but choose not to.

The current process to apply for exemption is to phone the VAT Helpline or make a written request, but while MDT is being rolled out HMRC recommends that applications not be made until further guidance is published.

Businesses in specific insolvency procedures are exempt from the MTD for VAT requirements. The current paper-based processes are expected to continue, for both pre- and post appointment returns.

Software

HMRC is working closely with software providers to ensure that a range of suitable products will be available at a variety of price points. It is unlikely that a free software product with MTD for VAT functionality will become available.

The software will be designed for you to:

- Keep records in a digital form;

- Preserve records in a digital form;

- Create a VAT return from the digital records;

- Provide HMRC with VAT returns and voluntary information by using the API (application program interface) platform;

- Receive information from HMRC using the API platform. This will include messages about a requirement to file and confirmation of successful filing and will allow HMRC to send 'nudge' messages to the business/agent.

I currently advise my clients to use the Xero or QuickBooks system, for the following reasons:

- It's quick and efficient;

- It is easy to use;

- The Real Time Information results in better decision-making;

- As our own system of choice it means we can extend our support more easily to include enhanced management expertise;

- It provides secure and accessible cloud-based storage;

- The useful add-ons can help you manage cashflow, finance, KPI reporting, property management and much, much more.

Digital record keeping requirements

You can still keep documents in paper form if you prefer, but with MTD each individual transaction (not just summaries) must also be recorded and stored digitally. HMRC wants to encourage records to be kept in as near to real time as possible, but it will still be possible to create the digital records at quarterly intervals using a bookkeeper or other agent if required, so long as the information is entered into a digital record keeping system at that stage.

The regulations require the following records to be kept digitally:

Designatory data:

- The name of the business or organization;

- The address of the principle place of business;

- The VAT registration number;

- Details of any VAT accounting schemes used.

For supplies made:

- The time of supply;

- The value of the supply;

- The rate of VAT charged.

If multiple supplies subject to the same rate of VAT are made at the same time these do not have to be recorded separately. You can record the total value of supplies on each invoice that has the same time of supply and rate of VAT charged.

If an invoice has supplies at different rates of VAT (e.g. adults' and children's shoes) there must be a separate digital record for each rate of VAT charged. You must split the total value of supplies on the invoice and make a separate entry in the digital records for each rate of VAT charged.

This is necessary to meet the requirement to have a record of outputs value for the period split between standard rate, reduced rate, zero rate, exempt and outside-the-scope outputs. There is a relaxation for mixed rate supplies at a single inclusive price (e.g. meal deals).

For supplies received:

- The time of supply;

- The value of the supply including any VAT that is not claimable by the business;

- The amount of input tax to be claimed.

If there is more than one supply on an invoice the business can record the totals from the invoice.

VAT account

The VAT account is the link - *the audit trail* - between the business records and the VAT return. Known as the "electronic account", this is where the data, required to be input digitally, is used by functional compatible software to calculate and fill in the VAT return.

To create the audit trail between the **output** tax in the records and the output tax on the return, the business must have a record of:

- The output tax it owes HMRC on sales;

- The output tax it owes on acquisitions from other EU member states;

- The tax it is required to pay on behalf of its suppliers under the reverse charge procedure;

- The tax that needs to be paid following a correction or error adjustment;

- Any other adjustment required by VAT rules.

For the audit trail between the **input** tax in the accounting records and the input tax on the VAT return, the business must have a record of:

- The input tax it is entitled to claim from business purchases;

- The input tax allowable on acquisitions from other EU member states;

- The tax that it is entitled to reclaim following a correction or error adjustment;

- Any other necessary adjustment.

There are certain records, such as fuel scale charge calculations, partial exemption calculations and capital goods scheme adjustments, that you don't have to keep digitally – instead you calculate these outside the digital records with a journal entry being made for each type of adjustment.

Records must be kept for six years (or 10 years if the business uses VATMOSS). If you deregister for VAT, digital records will need to be maintained for six years but may be kept in alternative formats rather than in functional compatible software.

Digital record keeping requirements in particular situations

Although the MTD regulations generally require a digital record of each and every transaction, there are some exceptions to this, including:

Retail schemes: Retailers can record gross daily takings (not weekly, monthly or quarterly) rather than each individual transaction. This means that you don't need a digital link between tills and the accounting records; it is sufficient to record the daily totals in the digital accounting records. N.B. Many businesses use a retail scheme without realising it, so you may need to consult your accountant.

Flat rate schemes: The flat rate scheme will continue and digital records of supplies received will not be required (unless they relate to capital items which cost more than £2,000 including VAT).

Margin schemes: The additional records required for margin schemes and the calculation of the marginal VAT charged do not need to be kept in digital form. These records must still be maintained in some format.

Records maintained by third parties: The regulations allow HMRC to relax the digital record-keeping requirements where it would be impossible, impractical or unduly onerous to comply. HMRC is using this power to allow supplies made by third parties to fall outside the digital record-keeping requirements until the point at which the agent supplies the information. This allows a summary received from an agent to be treated as a single invoice to create the digital record, for example from a letting agent. This relaxation does *not* apply to employees or to others such as charity volunteers who are not third-party agents.

There is a similar relaxation for supplies received by third party agents and for employee expenses.

#16. MTD for income tax

So far we have talked only about MTD for VAT. It will eventually apply to income tax as well.

Although not coming into effect until at least April 2021, this will apply to you if you are self-employed or in a partnership and also if you receive income from property. Not much detail is known yet, but here are some pointers:

- Businesses/taxpayers within scope must maintain digital accounting records as paper records will cease to meet the legal requirements;

- Businesses and organisations will be required to use a functional compatible software product to submit their returns to HMRC. The software will use HMRC's API (Application Program Interfaces) platform to submit information to HMRC (see reference above under MTD for VAT);

- There will be no changes to current income tax rules regarding the level of detail of information required and the filing and payment deadlines;

- There will be an exemption for those with an annual turnover below a threshold. This is still to be set, but the threshold is likely to apply to the *total* turnover from all self-employment and income from property;

- There is also likely to be an exemption for the largest partnerships (i.e. turnover in excess of £10 million);

- MTD is likely to come into effect for the first accounting period after 5 April in the year in which MTD for income tax becomes mandatory;

- Other exemptions (e.g. lack of internet ability or facility) will be similar to those for VAT (see above);

- Businesses will be able to choose their periods of account and their update periods. The basic requirement will be for four quarterly updates a year. The legislation does not allow HMRC to require returns more often, but a business will be able to submit extra updates mid-cycle if it wants to. The time window for submission will be from 10 days before the quarter end to one month after.

MTD Income Tax Pilot

This started in April 2017 on a small scale and any business that meets the eligibility criteria and has MTD-compatible software can now join the pilot. The eligibility criteria for joining the pilot are:

- sole traders with income from one business; and/or

- income from letting UK property (excluding furnished holiday lettings).

Digital record-keeping requirements

As with MTD for VAT (above), you can still keep documents in paper form if you prefer. However each individual transaction (not summaries) will need to be recorded and stored digitally. HMRC will encourage records to be kept in as near to real time as possible, but it will still be possible to create the digital records at quarterly intervals, using a bookkeeper or other agent if required, provided the information is entered into a digital record keeping system at that stage.

The following records will need to be maintained digitally:

- the amount of the transaction;

- the date of the transaction, according to the basis used (cash or traditional accruals basis for accounting); and

- the categories of transactions into which the transactions fall, to the extent those categories are specified. The categories are expected to be those that are currently used for the full self-employment and property pages on the self-assessment return (SA103F and SA105).

- The indications are that, as with VAT, retailers will be able to elect to record their gross daily takings rather than individual transactions. At the moment there is no draft exemption for situations where it would be impractical, impossible or unduly onerous to maintain digital records for each transaction, but this is likely to be included.

As you can see, MTD for income tax is likely to affect most property investors and developers if you are operating as an individual or partnership.

#17. MTD for Corporation Tax

As with MTD for income tax, eventually it will encompass Corporation Tax as well, the earliest date for mandatory requirements being April 2021, but little further information has been released.

Just a reminder: LLPs do not pay Corporation Tax. The legal status of an LLP is a separate legal entity for statutory, legal capacity and liability purposes, but not for taxation. Essentially the members of an LLP are taxed in the same way as an ordinary partnership and therefore pay income tax, so will come under the MTD for income tax provisions set out above.

#18. Additional VAT issues

Below is a selection of other VAT-related schemes or regulations. They only apply to very specific circumstances, which I highlight at the start of each section so that you can skim through and see what may be relevant to you.

Tour Operators Margin Scheme (TOMS)

How this relates to Serviced Accommodation businesses.

This is a special scheme for businesses that buy in and resell travel, accommodation and certain other services as a principal or undisclosed agent (that is, acting in your own name).

It can apply to anyone who is making these types of supplies even if this is not your main business activity or you do not view yourself as a 'traditional' tour operator. So, for example, it could apply if you are providing serviced accommodation, hence its application to a property business.

In order for a transaction to fall within TOMS, the services sold to the end-customer must not be 'materially altered'. Unfortunately there isn't a legal definition of this, but if what the end-customer receives is substantially different from what you bought in, then TOMS will not apply.

How it works

Normally, when you are registered for VAT, you must account for tax on the full selling price of your supplies, and you can then reclaim the VAT charged on purchases (subject to the normal rules).

However, imagine you buy in and sell on tourist attractions (entry to venues, bus rides, etc). Under TOMS, you cannot reclaim any UK or EU VAT charged on the travel services and goods you buy in and resupply, as the tax on such goods or services is accounted for (in the relevant member state) by the providers of those services (hotels, airlines and so on).

That seems a disadvantage, but also under TOMS, as a tour operator based in the UK, you don't have to account for the full VAT you may charge your customers but only on the *margin* you make on your margin scheme supplies – i.e. the difference between the margin you receive from your customer (including any amounts paid on behalf of your customer by third parties) and the amount you pay your suppliers.

There's a special rule for long-stay guests. If a guest stays for more than 28 days (or, more precisely, nights) then 100% of the VAT on sleeping accommodation (but not other charges) is relived. This doesn't make this part of the supply VAT-exempt. You still have to account for the supply, but at a zero rate.

This only applies to accommodation in a hotel, inn, boarding house or similar establishment. If you're charging an inclusive amount for bed and board you must apportion it reasonably and charge VAT on the full amount that is not for the accommodation. To do this, you calculate the amount of your charge that is for meals, drinks and other services, and also treat at least 20% of the remainder as being for facilities. But if the true value of the facilities is more than this, you must charge VAT on the true amount.

At the end of this section you can find a useful flow chart showing whether or not TOMS applies to a particular transaction. Meanwhile here are some other points to note about TOMS:

- If you sell a package including one or more supplies that qualify for TOMS, then you can include the whole package in TOMS.

- If your supply is part bought-in and part in-house supply, then the transaction is within TOMS but with special rules for in-house supplies.

- It TOMS applies to one or more of your transactions, then you must do an annual calculation of all the TOMS transactions in the year and calculate the total TOMS liability (as opposed to transaction by transaction).

- Under TOMS it is your margin that determines whether you are liable to register for VAT, not your gross sales (turnover) as with mainstream VAT.

- If you are currently not using TOMS, once you've determined whether or not you're liable to register for VAT (i.e. your total turnover has reached, or your TOMS margin would have reached, £85,000) you don't have to seek permission or register separately to use TOMS. However, it's always a good idea to check this with HMRC and obtain clearance.

Do you *have* to use TOMS? Well, why wouldn't you if your business is serviced accommodation? It is also invaluable if you are operating in the EU and outside the UK as otherwise you would have to consider registering for the equivalent of VAT in every EU country in which you provide the supply. But in fact, if you meet the criteria, registering for TOMS is **mandatory** once your margin from TOMS activity has reached the threshold. VAT is essentially a European tax, but will doubtless be with us regardless of what happens with the legacy of Brexit!

To clarify, you are obliged to use TOMS if you are either a principal or an undisclosed agent (see above) making a 'Margin Scheme supply' of a designated travel service. This is where you supply goods or services which are either:

a. bought in from another person and re-supplied without material alteration or further processing; or

b. supplied by a tour operator from an establishment in the UK for the direct benefit of a traveller.

The definition can also cover other types of supply if these are packaged with Margin Scheme supplies.

As you can see, it can be quite difficult to work out whether or not you are actually obliged to use TOMS! On the other hand, you can structure your business to use TOMS and gain the tax advantages from this. We can help you with this.

Below is the table mentioned earlier:

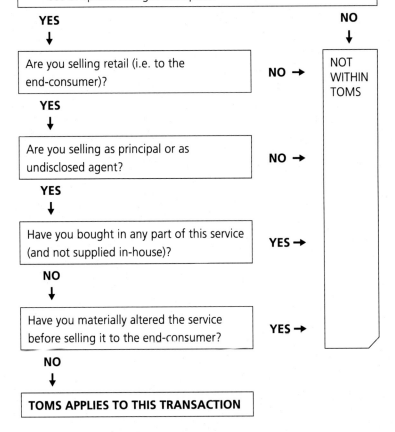

Does the transaction include **any** of the following?

- Serviced Accommodation (i.e. not simply a short-term tenancy
- Passenger transport
- Hire of means of transport (e.g. car hire)
- Trips or excursions
- Services of tour guides
- Use of special lounges at airports

YES ↓   **NO** ↓

Are you selling retail (i.e. to the end-consumer)?   **NO →**   NOT WITHIN TOMS

YES ↓

Are you selling as principal or as undisclosed agent?   **NO →**

YES ↓

Have you bought in any part of this service (and not supplied in-house)?   **YES →**

NO ↓

Have you materially altered the service before selling it to the end-consumer?   **YES →**

NO ↓

TOMS APPLIES TO THIS TRANSACTION

Transfer of a going concern (TOGC)

This also relates to Stamp Duty Land Tax (SDLT). See also Transfer of Interests in Land under TOGC (below).

This is a complex topic, so first I'll explain the concept of TOGC and then we'll see how it applies to property businesses.

A transfer of a business and its assets (which may include property) as a TOGC (by a seller who is VAT-registered) is *not a supply for VAT* provided that the purchaser is also registered for VAT and has the intention of using those assets to carry on the same kind of business as the seller and provided that the other conditions are met.

TOGC is principally an advantage for VAT purposes but it can also achieve SDLT savings. *In Section 7. All About Stamp Duty Land Tax*, I explain how, when buying property, SDLT is calculated when buying property on the whole consideration which includes the VAT (at 20%). Clearly this can be a substantial increase in the total consideration, whether it's a freehold or a leasehold. Now, if the business (or property business) you are buying includes premises, you'll want the freehold title or lease to be transferred to you, and this is what gives rise to the SDLT charge. So under the TOGC terms, there is no VAT on the purchase price for the premises and happily the SDLT will also be less than it would have been.

For example, if you sold a business for £500,000 which included business premises with a value of £200,000, the VAT on the whole consideration would be £100,000. The proportion of VAT applicable to the premises would be £40,000. If you are VAT- registered then you will of course be able to claim back the VAT paid of £100,000. However the consideration for SDLT on the transfer of the premises will still be £240,000 (resulting in SDLT of £1,800, which you cannot claim back.

However, if the transaction qualifies as a TOGC, then there is no VAT charged or claimed back. Not only does this save you the outlay of

£100,000 at the time of the purchase, but your consideration for SDLT on the premises is only £200,000, resulting in SDLT of £1,000 - £800 saved.

Where TOGC applies then VAT is neither charged by the seller nor reclaimed by the buyer. The TOGC rules are mandatory and not optional and the qualifying conditions are:

- The assets must be sold as part of the transfer of a 'business' as a 'going concern' ;

- The assets are to be used by the buyer with the intention of carrying on the same kind of 'business' as the seller (but not necessarily identical);

- Where the seller is a taxable person, the buyer must be a taxable person already or become one as the result of the transfer;

- In respect of land which would be standard-rated if it were supplied, the buyer must notify HMRC that they have opted to tax the land by the relevant date (usually the date of contract), and must notify the seller that their option has not been dis-applied by the same date;

- Where only part of the 'business' is sold it must be capable of operating separately;

- There must not be a series of immediately consecutive transfers of 'business'.

There can be a TOGC where the seller is not registered for VAT - for example, because the seller is trading below the registration limit or making wholly exempt supplies. A TOGC is still possible in both these circumstances. So the sale of a non-VAT registered business that includes trading stock that might otherwise take the trader over the registration limit will not do so because if it is treated as a TOGC and therefore not a supply.

There must be no significant break in the normal trading pattern before or immediately after the transfer, taken in the context of the business concerned.

If the transfer is of only part of the business, that part must be able to operate alone. It does not matter whether it will be operated separately from any other businesses the buyer carries on.

What kind of property businesses are classed as TOGCs?

The transfer of a property rental business will not attract VAT unless you are a, for example property letting agent and registered for VAT. This type of business can be a TOGC as long as the relevant conditions are met, mostly in relation to the nature of the letting or letting agreement. In addition to meeting the general conditions, here are some examples that meet the TOGC criteria. Bear in mind that in general there is no VAT on residential property so the examples in general apply only to commercial (non-residential) property which has opted to tax...

- If you own the freehold of a property that you let to a tenant and sell the freehold with the benefit of the existing lease, you are transferring a business of property rental to the buyer. This is a business transferred as a TOGC even if the property is only partly tenanted. Similarly, if you own the lease of a property (which is subject to a sub-lease) and you assign your lease with the benefit of the sub-lease, this is a business transferred as a TOGC.

- If you own a building where there's a contract to pay rent in the future but where the tenants are enjoying an initial rent-free period, even if the building is sold during the rent-free period, you're carrying on a business of property rental.

- If you granted a lease in respect of a building but the tenants are not yet in occupation, you're carrying on a property rental business.

- If you own a property and have found a tenant but not actually entered into a lease agreement at the point when you transfer the freehold to a third party (with the benefit of a contractual agreement for a lease but before the lease has been signed), there is still enough evidence of intended economic activity for there to be a property rental business capable of being transferred.

- If you are a property developer selling a site as a package (to a single buyer) which is a mixture of let and unlet, finished or unfinished properties and the sale of the site would otherwise have been standard-rated, then subject to the buyer opting to tax for the whole site, the whole site can be regarded as a business transferred as a going concern

- If you own a number of let freehold properties, and you sell one of them, the sale of this single let or partly let property can be a TOGC of a property rental business.

- If you have a partially-let building, this is capable of being a property rental business, providing that the letting constitutes economic activity. This may include electricity sub-stations or space for advertising hoardings providing that there is a lease in place.

- If you purchase the freehold and leasehold of a property from separate sellers without the interests merging and the lease has not been extinguished, providing you continue to exploit the asset by receiving rent from the tenant, then such a transaction can be a TOGC.

  Freehold and leasehold interests merge when the landlord and the tenant are the same person or entity, so if the same person or entity acquired both the freehold and the tenant's lease, the lease would disappear.

And here are some examples that would **not** be classed as TOGCs:

- If you are a property developer and have built a building that you allow someone to occupy temporarily (without any right to occupy after any proposed sale) or you're 'actively marketing' it in search of a tenant, there is no property rental business being carried on.

- If you own the freehold of a property and grant a lease, even a 999-year lease, you are not transferring a business as a going concern, you're creating a new asset (the lease) and selling it while retaining your original asset (the freehold). This is true regardless of the length of the lease. Similarly, if you own a head-lease and grant a sub-lease you are not transferring your business as a going concern.

- If you sell a property where the lease you granted is surrendered immediately before the sale, your property rental business ceases and so cannot be transferred as a going concern. Even if tenants under a sublease remain in occupation, when the lease is brought to an end the property rental business carried on by the former freeholder has ceased and cannot be transferred.

- If you sell a property freehold to the existing tenant who leases the whole premises from you, this cannot be a transfer of a going concern because the tenant cannot carry on the same business of property rental. This would remain the case even if the new freeholder vacated the property on acquisition and found a new tenant as, when the lease is brought to an end, the property rental business carried on by the former freeholder has ceased.

- You grant a lease in respect of a building to a tenant who is running a business from the premises, and the tenant then sells the assets of their business as a going concern and surrenders their lease to you. You then grant the new owner of the business a lease in respect of the building - this is not a transfer by you of a property rental business.

The transfer of a number of sites or buildings where some of the sites or buildings are let, or partially let and some are unlet, needs to be considered on a case by case basis. The nature of the sites or building and their use are all factors for consideration. It's important to look at whether the assets can be identified as a single business or an identifiable part of a business.

Transfer of interests in land under TOGC

Originally, it was held that when a TOGC involved the transfer of an interest in land, this only qualified for relief if it was the *same* interest as that used by the transferor in his business. So for example, if the seller owned the freehold but, in the TOGC negotiations, decided to grant a 999 year lease to the buyer (instead of transferring the freehold) the freeholder's business was not transferred as a going concern because what had happened was that a new asset has been created.

However in the case of Robinson Family Limited v HMRC [2012], the First Tier Tribunal disagreed with that interpretation. Robinson Family Limited (RFL) was a developer that purchased a 125-year interest in a site owned by Belfast Harbour Commissioners. The terms of the lease were that the site could only be divided up by sub-leases, so RFL granted an interest of 125 years less three days to a purchaser, subject to, and with the benefit of the proposed letting. HMRC did not treat the grant of the sub-leases as TOGCs, because RFL did not assign the full term of its lease to the purchaser.

The First Tier Tribunal found that, although RFL retained the head-lease, that distinct interest in a three-day reversion and the small economic interest which it represented in no way altered the substance of the transaction. Therefore, the transaction put the transferee business in a position where it was able to continue the previous lettings business of RFL.

The HMRC Guidance is now that, for a valid TOGC, any interest in land and property retained by the seller has to be shown to be small enough not to disturb the substance of the transaction. It will be accepted that where a reversion is retained by the transferor, this is sufficiently small for TOGC treatment to be applicable provided that the value of the interest retained is no more than one per cent of the value of the property immediately before the transfer (disregarding any mortgage or charge).

Where more than one property is transferred at one time, this test should be applied on a property-by-property basis rather than on the entire portfolio.

If the interest retained by the transferor represents more than one per cent of the value of the property, HMRC will regard that as strongly indicative that the transaction is too complex to be a TOGC.

There may be scope for some businesses to claim a repayment of VAT retrospectively in similar cases, both in connection with the VAT and where the fact that VAT has been charged may have also lead to an overpayment of Stamp Duty Land Tax.

Dis-applying the option to tax on conversions

This relates to paying (or not paying) VAT when converting a building.

First some background: I mentioned that when you opt to charge VAT it generally remains in force for 20 years. However, if you buy a building where the option to tax has been exercised, you also need to make an election as new owner – i.e. both the building and the taxpayer must be subject to the option. In the same context, simply ceasing to be VAT-registered (e.g. because you de-register) does not mean that the building itself ceases to be subject to the option. These really are two halves of the same whole.

So, say you buy a building to convert it into flats, and it has an option to tax in force. To remove the option to tax, you must 'dis-apply the option' using Form VAT1614D. And if you make the application before you buy there will be no VAT on the purchase price (but you must give the VAT1641D certificate to the seller before the price is legally fixed i.e. before exchange of contracts).

If you're not doing a conversion, then there are other 'supplies' where VAT is not payable even if an option to tax is in force. These include:

* Buildings designed or adapted and intended for use as dwellings (for example existing houses and flats);

* Buildings designed or adapted and intended for use for relevant residential purpose (e.g. a nursing home).

In both these cases you do not need the VAT 1614D certificate but it is a good idea to have evidence of intended use and in the second case the buyer must inform the supplier (preferably in writing) of the intended use.

VAT recovery on site acquisition and exit

This also relates to property development

VAT recovery on development of residential property can be done via the zero-rating regime. If a developer constructs a residential building and either sells the freehold or grants a lease of over 21 years, this will be zero-rated, so the developer can then recover most of the VAT.

But what if you are planning to rent out the building? The granting of short leases to tenants is not zero-rated and although you will not have paid much VAT on the construction costs, because the building of new residential property is itself zero-rated, you may still have had to pay VAT on the purchase price for the site if it has opted to tax ie buying land with planning permission. You may be able to recover the VAT incurred by transferring or granting a 21+ years lease to a group entity, which would then grant assured short-hold tenancies to tenants. The transfer or lease must take place after the foundations are above ground level (the "Golden Brick" stage) and will qualify for zero-rating.

However, you do need to be careful in order to avoid claw-back later on. This could occur if an inter-group lease has been granted and the lease is 'collapsed' (by the free hold and leasehold interests merging) within 10 years. The lease needs to remain in place for at least 10 years and if you sell during that period then both the freehold and leasehold interests must be sold. From the buyer's point of view, the acquisition would need to be by separate entities, to avoid the freehold and leasehold interests merging as a matter of law.

Please note however that this could have adverse SDLT consequences for the buyer if the result is that the buyer is unable to apply Multiple Dwellings Relief to the whole transaction *(see Section 7: All About Stamp Duty Land Tax)*.

N.B. VAT incurred by the developer on 'white goods' such as fitted kitchens and bathrooms is never recoverable and will always represent an additional cost to the developer. However, a Design and Build Contract helps you overcome this problem.

SECTION 5: GETTING TO KNOW CAPITAL TAXES, ALLOWANCES, RELIEFS AND SCHEMES

In some ways this is the heart of the book where we make the connection between a major tax on selling assets, Capital Gains Tax, and the reliefs and schemes that can help to reduce it – i.e. tax mitigation. Much of this section relates to limited companies so…

…is THIS section relevant to YOU?

Yes. If your property business is a limited company, you should certainly read this section very carefully to learn what may or may not be applicable in your circumstances. And if you're a sole trader or a partnership, you should definitely dip into each topic. Some are directly relevant to you, while others will reveal even more about the potential benefits of incorporating your business.

There are of course other major taxes to consider such as Stamp Duty Land Tax and Inheritance Tax but these have their own sections in the book. Here we're concerned principally with Capital Gains Tax.

#19. Capital Gains Tax (CGT) and how it relates to a property business

"Capital Gains Tax is a tax on the profit when you sell (or 'dispose of') something (an 'asset') that has increased in value. It is the gain you make that is taxed, not the amount of money you receive." www.gov.uk

This seems straightforward – and clearly the process of selling off property may fall right into the CGT net. But what sort of business organisation is exposed to CGT? Here are some pointers:

- CGT applies to the sale of property by an **investment** business, and not only to trading businesses or companies. It also applies to the sale or disposal of a business itself, or to the sale or disposal of shares.

- In a **trading** business, the proceeds of a property sale are treated as part of profit and subject to Income Tax or Corporation Tax.

- However, if you sell your **trading** business itself (rather than just assets from within it) CGT will apply.

- And if, as an **investment** business, you hold and maintain an unchanging portfolio for many years, it will still at some point be sold or change hands and, unless it has lost value, will incur CGT. However, if there is a capital loss on disposal, this is available to set against other capital gains (unless the disposal is to a connected party).

- Meanwhile, if you are a **limited company which is a trading business** and you sell off some property you will not be charged CGT, but the company will pay Corporation Tax on the profit (as taxable profits of a trading business)..

- But if you are an incorporated investment business you will pay Corporation Tax on the **gain** on disposal of the property. There is indexation relief for companies (frozen as at 31 December 2017) but not for individuals.

There is also the question of the date of disposal – when you sold or transferred the property asset from a taxation perspective. The operative date for the disposal is the date on which you enter into a binding contract (or, if the contract is conditional in any way, the date upon which it becomes unconditional). This is an important distinction, especially in property transactions where legal completion may take place sometime after date of binding contract.

So you see, CGT is a complicated area requiring expert guidance. On the plus side, there are various tax reliefs and schemes that you can apply in order to reduce your CGT liability – for example, Entrepreneurs' Relief when you are selling part of your sole trader business or shares in a partnership. These are discussed under Reliefs and Schemes, further below.

#20. Annual Tax on Enveloped Dwellings (ATED)

This is the other major tax specifically affecting businesses that own property, in this case exclusively concerning *enveloped dwellings*, residential properties owned by a company (or by a partnership which has corporate members) rather than by private individuals.

For any 'non-natural person' in the UK owning a residential property valued at £500,000 or over on 1st April 2016 there is an annual charge. However, if the properties are buy-to-let properties let on a commercial basis to third parties, then relief can be claimed to set against the annual rental tax due.

You'll need to complete an ATED return if your property meets the following criteria:

- It is a dwelling;

- It is in the UK;

- It was valued at more than:

    o £2 million on 1 April 2012, or at acquisition if later, for returns from 2013 to 2014 onwards;

    o £1 million on 1 April 2012, or at acquisition if later, for returns from 2015 to 2016 onwards;

    o £500,000 on 1 April 2012, or at acquisition if later, for returns from 2016 to 2017 onwards;

- It is owned completely or partly by:

  o A company;

  o A partnership where one of the partners is a company;

  o A collective investment scheme - for example a unit trust or an open ended investment vehicle

ATED returns must be submitted on or after 1 April in any chargeable period in which you own qualifying properties (whether or not any tax is due). There are however reliefs and exemptions from this tax, which may mean you don't have to pay ATED.

The amount you'll need to pay is worked out using a banding system based on the value of your property.

Chargeable amounts for 1 April 2017 to 31 March 2018

Property value	Annual charge
More than £500,000 but not more than £1 million	£3,500
More than £1 million but not more than £2 million	£7,050
More than £2 million but not more than £5 million	£23,550
More than £5 million but not more than £10 million	£54,950
More than £10 million but not more than £20 million	£110,100
More than £20 million	£220,350

Please note that these rates were set to rise, announced in the Autumn 2018 Budget, from 1 April 2019 by 2.4%, in line with the September 2018 Consumer Prices Index. It is of course entirely possible that there will be further similar increases in future years.

ATED Reliefs you can claim

You may be able to claim relief for your property if it is:

- let to a third party on a commercial basis and isn't, at any time, occupied (or available for occupation) by anyone connected with the owner;

- open to the public for at least 28 days a year;

- being developed for resale by a property developer;

- owned by a property trader as the stock of the business for the sole purpose of resale;

- repossessed by a financial institution as a result of its business of lending money;

- being used by a trading business to provide living accommodation to certain qualifying employees;

- a farmhouse occupied by a farm worker or a former long-serving farm worker;

- owned by a registered provider of social housing.

How to claim reliefs: If you have a claim to relief that reduces your ATED charge to nil, you can make a claim using a Relief Declaration Return for each relief you claim. You then need to complete an ATED return for each of your qualifying properties.

Exemptions: These relate to charitable companies, certain public bodies and bodies established for national purposes, so are not applicable to the average landlord.

De-enveloping: Removing the envelope is an attractive proposition for both onshore and offshore owners. This is because ATED-related CGT, and non-resident CGT now apply to sales of residential property by offshore companies as well as individuals. From 6 April 2017 Inheritance Tax (IHT) applies to offshore companies, and higher rates of Stamp Duty Land Tax

(SDLT) apply to purchases by companies of residential property (see section below).

So, how do you take the property outside the scope of future ATED charges, and what impact might this have in terms of Stamp Duty Land Tax?

If the owning company has no debts or liabilities, then the usual route is to pass a resolution to put the UK or offshore company into voluntary liquidation and carry out a distribution *in specie* (in kind) of the property and then transfer into the names of individuals or trustees. There should not be any Stamp Duty Land Tax (SDLT) on the transfer.

If the company does have a debt or liability to a *shareholder*, such as a loan made by the shareholder to the company, then one way is to cancel the debt and transfer the property to the shareholder. Again this should not give rise to SDLT.

What if there is a debt due to a third party and the shareholder takes over the liability? Or suppose the shareholder provides finance to clear the debt before the transfer of the property? This will render the transfer liable to SDLT (read more about this in *Section 7. All About Stamp Duty Land Tax*) and the consideration upon which the SDLT is calculated will be the amount of the debt.

The way in which companies transfer properties to their shareholders is likely to be a distribution *in specie*. This will usually be exempt from SDLT provided that it is a voluntary transfer for no 'chargeable consideration' (e.g. the assumption of a debt by the transferee or the provision of finance to clear the debt).

It is essential to check the company's Articles of Association to ensure that the company has the authority to pay a dividend *in specie*, and of course the company should have sufficient distributable reserves for it to declare the distribution in specie. The key to mitigating SDLT is that the transfer is voluntary and that there is no chargeable consideration, so there must be no obligation to pay a dividend; if there is, then there will be liability to SDLT.

Documentation must be prepared in line with the above. In particular:

- If the shareholder takes on a mortgage or debt over the property, the assumption of such mortgage or debt is a chargeable consideration that will result in SDLT being payable.

- The wording of the resolution approving the dividend must be clear. It should provide for a distribution of assets by way of a dividend *in specie*. It should not say it is a cash value dividend equivalent to the market value of the property to be settled by way of a transfer of assets, to avoid the later transfer of the property being deemed to be in settlement of such cash dividend.

#21. Allowances

I am going to discuss two contrasting allowances – capital allowances that a company can claim against sizeable costs, and the £1,000 trading and property allowances, of interest to individuals.

#22. Capital Allowances

This is the flip side to CGT in so far as it is a cost that a business can usually 'write off' when it *buys* assets such as plant and machinery, including:

- Equipment;

- Plant and machinery;

- Integral features of a building e.g. air-conditioning ducts

- Business vehicles.

Capital allowances and property businesses

How does all this relate to a property business?

First, sadly, capital allowances do not necessarily apply to the purchase of an investment property itself as an asset (unless it's a commercial property). Capital allowances are not available for a dwelling, unless it is serviced accommodation (see paragraph below); but they are allowed for qualifying commercial property such as shops, offices, hotels, restaurants, care homes, factories, etc. When it comes to improving a qualifying property, you can claim for improvements such as fixtures and fittings, and for items in the common areas of a residential building, such as a table in the hallway of a block of flats, and for the communal areas of a House in Multiple Occupation (HMO).

Secondly, capital allowances do not apply to trading activities as such. However, an investment property that is serviced accommodation, and therefore in effect a trading business can qualify, providing the property is:

- available for letting for 210 days, and

- let for 105 days or more.

In calculating the period of days for which the accommodation is actually let, you ignore any lets which are for periods of more than 31 days each, unless this happens as a result of an unforeseen occurrence, such as the occupant having an illness or accident, or being obliged to delay their departure due to a cancelled flight. However, apart from these exceptional circumstances, if the total of all the lettings of more than 31 days each add up to more than 155 days in the same tax year, then your property will not qualify as serviced accommodation.

What if you don't meet the letting requirements? There are two options:

a. If you have more than one serviced accommodation property, you can use the averaging election, to average out the total qualifying days of occupancy over the total number of properties. Please note that you can't use the averaging election over a mix of UK and EEA properties.

b. You can use the 'period of grace election' if your lettings don't meet the criteria in some tax years but do so in others. To use this, you must be able to show a genuine intention to let during the tax year. Provided the property has satisfied the criteria in the previous year (either alone or as the result of an averaging election), you can make the period of grace election if it doesn't do so the next year. Provided you have made the election, then if the property still doesn't meet the criteria the following year (we're now in Year 3), you may make a further period of grace election.

So, in simple terms, in order to use this election, you must meet the criteria once, then you get two years in which you can elect for a period of grace. But if, after making this election in two consecutive years, you fail to meet the criteria in the fourth year, then no further election can be made (at least until you have a year in which you successfully meet the criteria).

One point to watch is the 'apportionment' in a contract for purchase of a building (if you think capital allowances can be claimed). The legal contract should show how the price is made up of the value of the leasehold or freehold, the value of the 'fixtures and fittings' and the value of the goodwill (if any). The key point here is that anything classed as fixtures and fittings is potentially 'plant' (or possibly as 'integral features') and therefore may be eligible for capital allowances, so it is important to have this clarity. Although the apportionment of price should be shown in the contract, apportionments are an accountancy and taxation point, not a legal point -so please speak to your accountant about this at an early stage or at least make sure that your solicitor is liaising with your accountant about this.

If this doesn't happen, then it is possible to deal with this post-contract or even post-completion by making an election under s.198 Capital Allowances Act 2001. However, for a s.198 election there *must* be formal agreement on the apportionment and the election must be made *jointly* by the seller and the buyer (apart from where this relates to integral features, where capital allowances may still be claimed by the purchaser). So you can see why it really is best to agree this at contract stage – otherwise you might find the seller not agreeing to the apportionment or, worse, disappearing with your money after completion without signing the s.198 election!

The enquiries your solicitor will raise before contract (usually in a standard format known as Commercial Property Standard Enquiries or CPSEs) will also provide useful information on points such as whether capital allowances have already been claimed on any assets, so do share these with your accountant.

Claiming capital allowances

This is achieved by using the Annual Investment Allowance ('AIA'), or the writing down allowances for different parts of the qualifying assets. Let's just go through each of the categories of allowances as they might apply to property:

Plant, machinery and equipment includes:

- items that you keep to use in your business, including cars;

- costs of demolishing plant and machinery;

- parts of a building considered integral, known as 'integral features' (see below);

- some fixtures, e.g .fitted kitchens or bathroom suites (see below);

- alterations to a building to install other plant and machinery - this doesn't include repairs.

Integral features mentioned above (from Capital Allowances Act 2001 s.33A) include:

- electrical systems (including lighting systems);

- cold water systems (plumbing);

- space or water heating systems (heating and hot water);

- ventilation and air conditioning systems;

- lifts; and

- external solar shading

Please note that 'electrical system' does not include systems intended for other use i.e..phones, burglar alarm systems, fire alarms, etc

Other items not specifically mentioned include:

- Aerials.

- Automatic exit doors and gates.

- Bicycle holders or racks.

- Blinds and curtains.

- Burglar alarms.

- Cable TV provision and ducting.

- Cameras.

- Car park illumination and barrier equipment.

- Carpets and other loose floor coverings.

- Cleaning cradles (including tracks and anchorages).

- Closed circuit television (CCTV) equipment.

- Conduit for security alarm systems.

- Fans and heaters.

- Fire alarms.

- Fire protection systems and sprinklers.

- Fire safety equipment.

- Garden furniture.

- Intercom installations.

- Internal signs.

- Laundry equipment (in communal areas).

- Loose floor coverings and doormats.

- Loose furniture.

- Racking, cupboards and shelving (in communal or staff areas).

- Sanitary installations.

- Signage.

- Smoke detectors and heat detectors.

- Soft furnishings.

- Sprinkler systems.

- Telecommunications equipment.

- Wash basins and associated plumbing

Fixtures are anything physically attached to the property, and include:

- fitted kitchens;

- bathroom suites;

- fire alarm and CCTV systems.

In general, only the person who bought the item can claim. However if you buy a building from a previous business owner you can claim for integral features and fixtures that they have claimed for provided that the allowances have been 'pooled'. The way in which this works is that, if the seller has been claiming capital allowances, then the seller works out what proportion of the sale figure is attributable to the asset on which capital allowances have been claimed and this is carried through to the seller's capital allowance computation. However, the figures may vary if balancing allowances and charges are applied.

If an item is sold on which the seller originally claimed capital allowances, and the sale or value of the item is more than the balance in the pool, the seller must add the difference between the two amounts to their taxable profits (a 'balancing charge').

If the asset which is sold has had the AIA or first year allowance claimed, then the likelihood is that the 'pool' (see below) will have a zero balance; the amount you the asset is sold for (or its market value if it is given away or used privately) is the balancing charge.

This governs the buyer's figures for any capital allowance claim so you must agree the value of the fixtures with the seller as otherwise you can't claim for them. Agreeing the value also means the person selling the assets can account correctly for them. Since April 2014, the seller must have 'pooled' the expenditure on the plant and machinery in a chargeable period whilst owning the property. This means grouping items in accordance with the rates for which they qualify as follows:

- main pool with a rate of 18%

- special rate pool with a rate of 8%

- single asset pools (either 18% or 8% depending on the item).

The Enhanced Capital Allowances have enabled businesses to claim 100% accelerated tax relief in the year of purchase of equipment, plant and machinery that demonstrates a high standard of energy efficiency (listed on the Energy Technology List and the Water Technology List). This is also useful if you are considering buying an electric car.

This pooling acts alongside the requirement in s198 Capital Allowances act 2001 to fix the figure at which the plant and machinery is disposed of. The election under s198 must form part of or be attached to the contract.

The enquiries (CPSEs) raised by your solicitor should give you all the necessary information about allowances already claimed by the seller, so it's really important to share this information with your accountant at an early stage so that there are no nasty surprises about what you can claim.

You can't claim for:

- items you lease - you must own them;

- land and structures, e.g. bridges, roads, docks;

- items used only for business entertainment.

It used to be the case that you couldn't claim for the actual structure of the buildings, including doors, gates, shutters, mains water and gas. However, the Structures and Buildings Allowance introduced in 2018 has changed this.

This applies where you build, buy or lease a structure (leaseholds of at least 35 years) and you have paid some or all the costs towards the purchase, construction or renovation of the structure. You may be able to claim a 2% tax relief a year, on certain money you spend. This allowance may last up to 50 years.

All construction contracts must have been signed on or after 29 October 2018 and the structure must not have been used as residence when it was first used, nor during the period for which you are claiming.

You must be using the building for a qualifying activity, which includes:

- any trades, professions and vocations

- a UK or overseas property business (**except** for residential and serviced accommodation)

- managing the investments of a company

- mining, quarrying, fishing and other land-based trades such as running railways and toll roads

In addition, you must have an allowance statement which includes:

- information to identify the structure, such as address and description

- the date of the earliest written contract for construction

- the total qualifying costs

- the date that you started using the structure for a non-residential activity

If you buy a building that is already in use then you can only claim the allowance if you get a copy of the allowance statement from a previous owner. If you are the first user then you must create the allowance statement yourself.

If the building is sold or demolished, then claiming this allowance may affect the Capital Gains Tax or Corporation Tax position. It's important to consult your accountant first, to check that claiming the allowance will be beneficial.

#23. Trading and property allowances for individuals

From 6 April 2017, a small tax-free allowance of £1,000 per tax year is available for individuals earning property and/or trading income. If you have both types of income, you'll get a £1,000 allowance for each.

The allowances will not apply to partnership income from carrying on a trade, profession or property business in partnership and will not apply in addition to relief given under the Rent-a-Room Relief legislation.

The basic conditions allowing you to reduce the income you declare by £1,000 are as follows (but also refer to the individual sections below for trading and property allowances):

- If your annual gross property income is £1,000 or less, from one or more property businesses, you do not need to tell HMRC about this nor declare this income on a tax return.

- If your annual gross trading income is £1,000 or less, from one or more trades, you may not have to tell HMRC unless you are obliged to register for Self-Assessment and file a tax return (see below). You must keep records of this income. This is known as 'full relief'.

- If your annual gross trading or property income from one or more trades or businesses is more than £1,000 you can use the tax-free allowances, instead of deducting any expenses or other allowances. If you use the allowances you can deduct up to £1,000, but not more than the amount of your income. This is known as 'partial relief'.

Regarding the third point above, there is an optional alternative method for calculating profits where the relievable receipts of a property business are more than £1,000. This is an election that will apply to the calculation of the profits from property businesses for a particular tax year. The effect of the alternative method will be that the income receipts are brought into account only in calculating the profits for the tax year. Any expenses associated with the income receipts will not be brought into account. In calculating the profit a deduction is allowed for the £1,000 property allowance.

NB: If your expenses are more than your income it may be beneficial to claim expenses instead of the allowances. Even if your expenses are greater than £1,000 then it will work out better for you to claim the actual expenses as deductible, rather than using the allowance.

Property allowance

The property allowance is a tax-free allowance of up to £1,000 a year for individuals with income from land or property. Joint owners may each claim the £1,000.

If your annual gross property income is £1,000 or less, you won't need to tell HMRC unless you can't use the allowances (see *When you can't use the allowances* below). If it's higher, your property income must be declared.

This allowance is not available for income from letting a room in your own home under the Rent-a-Room Relief.

Trading allowance

The trading allowance is a tax-free allowance of up to £1,000 a year for individuals with trading income from:

- self-employment;

- casual services, for example, babysitting or gardening;

- hiring personal equipment, for example, power tools.

If your annual gross income from these is £1,000 or less, you don't need to tell HMRC, unless:

- you can't use the allowances (see When you can't use the allowances below);

- you are obliged to register for Self-Assessment and file a tax return.

If you have gross trading income of more than £1,000 or other income over £2,500 (not subject to PAYE) you must register for Self-Assessment. If your other income is between £1,000 and £2,500 you must notify HMRC who will inform you if you should file a tax return.

You cannot use the trading allowance for trading income from a partnership.

When can't you use the allowances?

The allowances cannot be used in any tax year where you have any trade or property income from:

- a company you or someone connected to you owns or controls;

- a partnership where you or someone connected to you are partners;

- your employer or the employer of your spouse or civil partner.

Also you can't use the *property* allowance if you:

- claim the tax reduction for non-deductible costs of a dwelling loan;

- deduct expenses from income from letting a room in your own home instead of using the Rent-a-Room Relief.

"What if I'm registered for Self-Assessment?"

If you're starting a new self-employed business and expect your annual gross income to be no more than £1,000, you may not have to register for Self-Assessment but you can do so if your gross income for the tax year will go above £1,000 and you want to be in Self-Assessment.

However, you do have to register for Self-Assessment and declare your income on a tax return when:

- you have made a loss and want to claim relief on a tax return;

- you want to pay voluntary Class 3 National Insurance contributions to help qualify for some benefits;

- you want to claim Tax Free Childcare for childcare costs based on your self -employment income;

- you want to claim Maternity Allowance, based on your self-employment.

In these cases you can still use the trading allowance but you'll need to complete a Self-Assessment return.

If your gross income for a tax year is more than £1,000, you must register for Self-Assessment by 5 October in the following tax year. If you're already registered for Self- Assessment, you can use the allowances by deducting them from your gross property or trading income on your tax return. NB: You can't deduct any other expenses or allowances if you claim the Trading or Property Allowances.

Keeping records

If you use the trading or property income allowances you must keep a record of your income, including:

- copies of your invoices (paper or electronic);

- a spreadsheet of your income receipts;

- emails confirming income received;

- statements from the company that paid you which show the amount you received;

- bank statements;

- bank deposit pay-in records;

- a diary or appointments book showing your income from each customer.

If your records are not accurate, complete and readable or if you don't retain them for the required period of time then HMRC may charge a penalty. One way in which you can make record-keeping easier (and also easier to provide to HMRC) is to use cloud-based accounting, via a system such as Xero or QuickBooks.

#24. Reliefs and schemes relating to CGT

What are reliefs and schemes?

I need to remind you of the section on Property Tax and the Law. There we established that your aim should be tax mitigation, the entirely legal and approved process of paying what you owe but no more.

So, what are these promising-sounding reliefs and schemes and how can they help with tax mitigation?

In essence they are tools that HMRC creates to give you some financial flexibility and business incentive but without them losing out on tax revenue in the bigger picture. They certainly offer opportunities to reduce your tax liability but only as a consequence of a decision made in relation to your business, not as a tax-reduction tool by itself. So the essential rule remains the same – what you gain in a tax reduction, you 'lose' in some form of additional 'cost' elsewhere.

This is also the case in other tax areas, and the point to consider will always be all taxation areas that apply and the overall impact of any action on your tax position. Whether the adjustment you make to be eligible for a relief or scheme justifies its use is ultimately your own decision made on the basis of where you're going with your business – but of course your accountant will always offer useful expert advice to help you.

Entrepreneurs' Relief (ER)

Entrepreneurs' relief applies when you dispose of shares in all or just part of your business, perhaps when you are restructuring it or changing your own level of involvement. ER reduces the CGT rate from a potential 28% to 10% of the value of the disposal. It is a very useful relief for smaller trading businesses and sole traders but it does only apply to trading businesses so a property investment business would not qualify (unless it is dealing in serviced accommodation). However, a property development business is likely to qualify and in section 3 above I've covered the distinction between a trading business and an investment business and how the classification works

To clarify, I'll cover the basic relief in detail first and then look specifically at how it impacts on a property business.

Material disposal: This is the basic definition upon which ER operates. A material disposal is

- the disposal of the whole or part of a business, where the business has been owned by the individual making the disposal throughout two years leading up to the date of the disposal

- the disposal of assets, or of interests in such assets, used for the purposes of a business that has now ceased, where:

    o the assets were in use for those purposes at the time of cessation, and

    o the business was owned by the individual making the disposal for a period of two years immediately prior to the cessation of the business, and

    o the disposal takes place within three years of that cessation -

- the disposal of shares in or securities of a company, or of an interest in such shares or securities, where either

    o throughout the period of two years ending with the date of disposal, the company was the shareholder's personal company, was a trading company or the holding company of a trading company and the shareholder was an officer or employee of the company or of one or more companies in the same group

or

o   the disposal takes place within three years of the company ceasing to meet the definition of a trading company (or holding company of a trading company) and the other conditions were satisfied during the two year period before the company ceased to meet the definition of trading (for this purpose).

An **associated** disposal is a material disposal which is associated with the individual's withdrawal from the business. I've given some examples further on.

Let's see how these definitions apply in connection with different business structures.

Sole trader: So, for example, if you are eligible for ER and you dispose of all or part of your sole trader business, instead of this being treated as a chargeable gain at the appropriate CGT rate you pay a flat rate of 10% (providing you meet the criteria for ER). Of course, disposing of the whole of your business will usually inevitably mean a cessation (see the landmark case of Rice in the *Appendix*). However if, say, you are a builder who also offers funeral services and you wish to dispose of the funeral business then you should also qualify for ER, as long as the assets disposed of constitute a distinct part which is ceasing.

Partnership: ER is also available where you dispose of a share in a partnership business, including a material disposal to the other partners. This could be for example where a partner reduces his or her share in the partnership but continues to be a partner, or on what amounts to a reduction in your partnership share where another individual joins the partnership.

If the partner also personally owned an asset used in the business (e.g. the business premises) or a share in that asset, and he or she was disposing of that at the same time (or within three years), the this would be an associated disposal, but only if the share of the partnership being disposed of if at least 5% (of the partnership), or, if the partner owns less than a 5% share, the whole of his share.

Unfortunately, you can no longer claim ER on the disposal of goodwill that takes place when you incorporate into a limited company (but see the section on incorporation relief, below, to see how this works).

Personal Limited Company: ER also applies where you dispose of some or all of your shares in a 'personal company' (defined as one in which you hold at least 5% of the shares and your shareholding gives you at least 5% of the voting rights). You must have held the shares for a minimum of 24 months (increased from 12 months in the Autumn 2018 Budget and the Finance Act 2019) and during that time the company must be either a trading company or the holding company of a trading company, and you must be an officer or employee of that company.

Alternatively, you can also qualify for ER on the disposal of shares in a personal company if the company ceased to be a trading company within the three years ending with the date of disposal and for a period of at least two years ending with that cessation the conditions set out above were satisfied. In this context 'cessation' does not necessarily mean that it ceased operation, but that it ceased to fulfil the qualifying conditions.

ER may also apply to shares acquired under an Enterprise Management Incentive Scheme and in this case the 'personal company' rules do not apply.

Alphabet shares: This is the name commonly applied where a company has different classes of shares. The rule is that ER only applies to material disposals of ordinary shares in the company. Measures brought in by the 2019 Finance Act indicate that ER will not apply to shares which do not rank 'pari passu' (i.e. on the same basis) with other shares in the company. However, as long as the alphabet shares are entitled to share in the distribution of assets on a winding up, or in the proceeds of a disposal, it does not matter that the directors may declare different rates of dividend on different classes of shares, nor that the alphabet shares may not have voting rights. As long as the individual shareholder has shares which entitle them to a 5% share of the assets on distribution or on the proceeds of a disposal, that shareholding will be eligible for ER if it meets the other conditions.

Limited companies and LLPs: Disposals of individual properties by limited companies do not qualify for ER (although a disposal of a material asset owned by a shareholder may qualify as an associated disposal). Where the company is an investment company, then ER is not available on either the disposal of the shares or on an associated disposal, because the company itself is not a trading company.

Although an LLP has its own 'legal persona' or separate identity, just like a limited company, the members of the LLP are treated just the same as ordinary partners in a non-LLP partnership for taxation purposes. Therefore each partner may claim ER on disposals. Also, in connection with the disposal of an interest in an LLP (whether or not to the other members) there is no requirement for the disposing member to have at least a 5% share (as there would be if the disposal were of shares in a personal limited company).

Trusts: ER is not available to the personal representatives dealing with the estate of a deceased person, although an ongoing trust set up by a will may, in due course, qualify under the general rules relating to trusts.

Disposals by trustees of trusts that are wholly discretionary in nature do not qualify for ER. However, a claim by the trustees of other settlements may qualify and the claim must be made jointly with the qualifying beneficiary for a trustees' disposal.

Material disposal of business assets

This is not only the disposal of a business, or part of a business, as set out above (including shares in a limited company), but also the disposal of any assets owned and used in that business. Sometimes certain assets of a business may be disposed of separately to the business itself - it depends what the deal is.

Suppose a sole trader disposes of his business but certain assets which have always appeared on his accounts as assets of the business are not purchased by the buyer. Provided these assets are sold within three years of cessation of the business (or disposal - if only a part of the business is sold) they still qualify for ER. See the Appendix for an illustration of this in the landmark Rice case that we handled. The same situation applies if the seller is a partnership.

However, with regard to the disposal of shares in a limited company, the situation is different. Anything the company itself sells, such as goodwill or a leasehold, will not qualify for ER. If the sale of the business proceeds by way of sale of shares (as opposed to company assets) then of course the company is still in existence - only the identity of the shareholders has changed. So, the disposal of business assets used by the company is irrelevant for any claim for ER by the individual shareholders. I've covered in the previous section the rules for claiming ER in respect of the shares themselves. However, if you have personal assets (such as a property) which you've allowed the limited company to use, then you can take advantage of the rules on an associated disposal, as long as you have not charged rent. If you have charged rent but at less than commercial rates, or for only a part of the occupancy, then you may be able to claim ER on a proportionate part of the gain.

Associated disposal: If you have allowed a personally held asset to be used as a material asset of your business, you can claim ER on the capital gain arising on the disposal (known as an associated disposal – see the example below) of that asset as long as you have allowed the business to use it for at least two years and the disposal takes place within 3 years of the cessation of the business or the disposal of your interest or shares.

This is known as an 'associated disposal', one that takes place in association with your *withdrawal* from a business carried on by either:

- a partnership of which you're a member;

- your 'personal' trading company in which you're an officer or employee.

So, in this case, in order to be eligible for ER there must either be a cessation of your sole trader business or, if you are a member of a partnership, a reduction of your interest in the assets of the partnership. If you hold shares in a personal limited company then you must dispose of at least some of these and cease to be an officer of the company. This is what is meant by 'withdrawal' in ER terms. Interestingly it is not necessary for you to actually reduce the amount of work which you do for the business.

Let's look at an example. You personally own a shop from which you trade in partnership with your brother. You have a 3/5 interest in the assets of the partnership and your brother 2/5. You and your brother decide to vary the partnership with the result that your interest in the business is reduced to 1/5 with 4/5 to your brother.

At the same time you also agree to sell the shop to your brother. Despite the alteration in the partnership shares, you go on working full-time in the shop.

What is the effect in terms of ER eligibility?

Your reduction of your partnership share is classified as a withdrawal from participation in the business, so you will be entitled to ER on any capital gain.

Since there was a withdrawal, the disposal of the shop also qualifies for ER as an associated disposal (subject to satisfying the qualifying conditions set out below), because it is associated with your withdrawal from the business. If you had sold the shop to your brother without at the same time reducing your partnership share, then the disposal of the shop would be unlikely to qualify as an associated disposal.

The associated asset must have been in use for the purpose of the business throughout the period of two years up to the date of your withdrawal or the cessation of the business. This was amended from one year by the Autumn 2018 Budget.

Restrictions

The amount of gain eligible for Entrepreneurs' Relief on a disposal of an associated asset may be restricted in cases where:

- the associated asset was in business use for only part of the time you owned it;

- only part of the associated asset was in business use during the period you owned it;

- you were involved in the carrying on of the business for only part of the period during which the associated asset was in business use;

- some of the period during which the associated asset was in use for the business falls after 5 April 2008 and for that period after 5 April 2008 you received any form of rent for letting the business use it.

Where one or more of these circumstances apply, only a just and reasonable proportion of the gain will qualify for relief. The periods involved and the level of any rent paid will be taken into account when working out this proportion.

Lifetime claim limit: There is a lifetime limit on the amount of ER which can be claimed and this is currently £10 million per individual.

Qualifying Conditions for Claiming ER

- The business must be a *trading* business

- The business, assets or shares must have been owned by you for a minimum of two years ending with the date of disposal (increased from one year in the Finance Act 2019 for disposals taking place on or after 6 April 2019).

- For an associated disposal the asset must have been used in the business for a period of at least two years ending with the date of cessation or withdrawal (increased from one year in the Autumn Finance Act 2019 for disposals taking place on or after 6 April 2019).

- In the case of shares in a personal company, the two-year minimum period of ownership usually applies. However, where the company ceases to be a trading company, or to be a member of a trading group, within the period of 3 years before the date of disposal, then the qualifying period ends on the date the company ceased to qualify as a trading company or a member of a trading group.

How ER benefits a property business

Here's an example – first the background: An individual running a property investment business will pay CGT on any gains resulting from the sale of a property. However, if this were established as a trading business then sales would be part of a trading activity and you'd pay Income Tax on the profit of the business as a whole, instead of CGT per property. With CGT at a possible 28% on residential property for a higher rate tax-payer, you'd need to do the maths to work out whether you're better off paying Income Tax year by year on the annual profits from a trade.

Now, what if you sell off the whole property portfolio as a business? Then you'd be entitled to ER on the gain providing you can establish it as a trading business rather than just private investment.

To secure ER, you have to cease trading - although the relief also applies to the disposal of your share in a partnership (even if the other partners continue), or a reduction in your share.

How about limited companies? ER is not available to companies themselves but it is still available to the individual company owners. So, if your property business is a limited company, then the disposal of all or part of your shares will attract ER on the capital gain irrespective of whether or not the business ceases or indeed whether you cease to work in the business. There are some conditions:

- You must be a trading company not an investment company;

- You must hold at least 5% of the shares and 5% of the voting rights, or be entitled to 5% of the assets available for distribution on a winding-up ;

- You must be an officer or employee of the company;

- You must have owned the shares for at least two years (or had the option for at least a year if they're EMI shares).

There is a lifetime cap for ER (currently £10 million).

NB: What happens when the company buys back shares? If a shareholder is retiring and selling his shares back to the company, this will be treated as a distribution by the company to the retiring shareholder unless the conditions of s.1033 Companies Act 2010 are met. This usually means meeting Condition A: that the transaction is made wholly or mainly for the purpose of benefitting a trade carried on by the company.

It's best to apply for HMRC advance clearance and framing the request for this can be quite complex. Please do contact us for help on this.

Winding up and ER

With a limited company, ER can also be claimed by the shareholders carrying out a members' voluntary winding up. The distribution of the assets is a chargeable gain which should qualify for ER. In these cases, the qualifying conditions must all be met throughout the year ending with either:

- the date on which the capital distribution is made; or

- if earlier, the date of cessation of the trading qualification and the capital distribution is made within 3 years of the cessation.

However, beware of *Phoenix companies*, so-called after the legendary phoenix bird that rises from the ashes of its death in flames. If one or more of the shareholders of the wound-up company form a new company to carry on all or part of the same trade, then the risk is that HMRC will regard the winding up as being for the purpose of gaining the tax advantage of converting income into capital and any distribution would be taxed as income and of course ER would not apply.

ER and Enterprise Investment Scheme (EIS)

EIS is discussed further below but I just want to mention it here. EIS is a scheme allowing employees to buy shares at advantageous prices. One feature of it is that the employees also benefit from the rules relating to ER but without having to hold a minimum of 5% shares.

Investors' Relief (IR)

You will see from the previous pages that ER is a valuable tool in mitigating the effect of CGT. Here we have a similar tax relief, brought in by the Finance Act 2016, but this time it helps reduce CGT for external investors of unlisted trading companies upon cessation. This is how Investors' Relief (IR) works.

- External investors in unlisted trading companies can claim ER for newly issued ordinary shares acquired for new consideration on or after 17 March 2016 (acquisitions of existing shares will not qualify);

- Investment must be held for at least three years from 6 April 2016;

- There is no requirement to hold 5% shareholding or voting rights;

- The share issue and subscription must be made for genuine commercial reasons at arm's length, and not form part of tax avoidance arrangements;

- Unlike the conditions for ER, neither the investor nor a connected person can be an officer or employee of the company, nor a connected company, at any time during ownership of the shares;

- £10 million lifetime IR cap will apply in addition to the £10 million lifetime ER allowance.

Who benefits from IR?

This relief is advantageous for investors in development projects. If the average development takes 18 months then you can look for potential investors. You might decide from the outset that you need two investment deals (which could be with the same person) and not then have to look for a second pot of funding. And on completion of the project, the investor pays only 10% on the eventual capital gain. A win/win situation that makes it much more attractive for potential investors (and hence an incentive for new development projects).

Incorporation Relief (S.162 Transfer of Capital Gains Act 1992)

This relates back to Section 3 (Investment business or trading business?), and represents one of the benefits when incorporating an investment business.

Incorporation Relief applies where:

"... a person who is not a company transfers to a company a business as a going concern, together with the whole assets of the business, or together with the whole of those assets other than cash, and the business is so transferred wholly or partly in exchange for shares issued by the company to the person transferring the business." TCGA 1992 s162(1)

The effect of s162 is that the capital gain arising on the disposal of the business to the company is 'rolled over' until the point at which the shares acquired are disposed of.

The transferor must be an individual or a partnership (general or LLP) and the transfer must be to a company in exchange for newly issued shares. If any other consideration is created (for example, creating a loan account for the owner) then CGT is chargeable on disposal by restricting the application of s162 relief. This is done by calculating the proportion of the consideration that is represented by the new shares and applying the relief to only that proportion of the capital gain.

Now, the eagle-eyed reader will have noticed in the definition above the requirement for there to be a 'business' – no mention of a 'trade'. This is significant as 'business' is not defined by statute. HMRC accepts that the meaning is wider than 'trade' and, in certain cases a property investment business can qualify.

The point has been considered in the Upper Tier Tribunal case of *Elisabeth Moyne Ramsay v HMRC* [2013] UKUT 0226. In this case, in 1987 the taxpayer inherited a one-third share in a single large property, divided into 10 flats, of which 5 were occupied at the relevant time. In 2003 she gifted one half of her one-third share to her husband and in 2004 purchased the remaining two-thirds interest in the property from her brothers. Then both she and her husband transferred all the interest in the property to a new company in return for shares, subsequently gifting all the shares to their son who became sole shareholder and director of the company.

It might appear that Mrs Ramsay had inherited a share in a property which she then ran as an investment business, but in fact she devoted some 20 hours a week to managing the block and had no other occupation during this period. The UTT held that the level of activity and taking the activities of the taxpayer "in the round", was sufficient to deem the business as being beyond the mere passive receipt of income and could satisfy the "business" test of s162.

So the point is that you need to examine the level of activity in the existing business to determine whether it is likely to be a business for s162 purposes. The turnover or profits of the business are not indicative of level of activity – a flat in Knightsbridge, London may bring in double the annual rent of 100 properties in a market town, but this doesn't mean that it will qualify for s162 relief. There's also some uncertainty whether a business is being carried on by an agent appointed by the taxpayer will qualify.

S 162 relief is applied automatically. However, if for any reason you don't want the relief to apply (in which case the capital gain arising on the disposal of the business to the limited company will not be rolled over) then you must make an election to HMRC by the second anniversary of the transfer. If however you dispose of the shares acquired on the transfer and do so within the same year of assessment as the transfer, then you must make the election by the first anniversary of 31st January next following the year of assessment in which the transfer took place.

Hold-over Relief

Assets: This relief for gifts and transfers at an undervalue disappeared years ago for most cases. So the general rule now is that a transfer for nil or reduced value is still a disposal - and if this is of chargeable assets you will have to pay CGT on any gain. But you may be able still to get the relief, if:

- you're giving away business assets and:

- you are a sole trader or business partner, or have at least 5% of voting rights in a company (known as your 'personal company');

- you use the assets in your business or personal company.

You can usually get partial relief if you used the assets only partly for your business.

Shares: If you're giving away shares, then the shares must be in a company that is either:

- not listed on any recognised stock exchange;

- your personal company.

The company's main activities must be in trading, for example providing goods or services, rather than non-trading activities like investment. However, it appears that the 'business' definition may apply (as in s.162 Incorporation Relief).

#25. Additional schemes relating to capital

The remaining items in this section may not relate specifically to CGT but as they concern the raising of capital I want to include them here. You will find some more relating specifically to developers in *Section 9. Property Construction and Development*. There is also Private Residence Relief which I discuss in *Section 10* (about inheritance tax).

Enterprise Management Incentive Scheme (EMI)

This scheme gives employees the option to buy shares at a pre-defined time in the future (based mostly on how quickly the directors expect the value of the shares to rise). When they are able to buy, the employees only pay the retrospective value of the shares when the EMI option was first given. So, if the real share value has risen in the interim, the employee is buying the shares at less than the current market rate.

Why offer an EMI Option?

Clearly this scheme is not the solution to a company's need for speedy additional capital, but it has other advantages. The general benefit is as an *incentive* in recruiting or retaining recruit key members of the team who can directly influence company performance and hence value. However, the common consensus is that any employee who has a direct interest in the company is more likely to 'go the extra mile', and so many companies offer EMI options to the whole, or a majority, of the workforce, not just to key employees.

Another use of the scheme is as part of the business planner's exit strategy. Using EIS to encourage growth makes it easier for the existing management to buy out the owner in a tax-efficient way.

Generally EMI Schemes offer a considerable degree of flexibility compared to other share schemes with favourable tax status. They allow companies to shape their staff incentives to fit their needs while giving them a direct interest in the equity value of the company. Meanwhile the owners retain all voting rights until options are exercised.

Taxation on EMI

The advantage to the employee is that the price at which the shares can be acquired is fixed at the time the option is granted. If the value of the shares has increased by the time the option is exercised, then the employee does not pay Income Tax nor suffer National Insurance (NI) on the purchase price nor on the increase is value.

However if at the time of offer, the employee was given a *discount* on the market value of the shares at the time of offer, then, should the employee exercise the option to buy, income tax and NI is payable on the difference between the offer price and the market value at the time of offer.

If the EMI shares are subsequently sold, Capital Gains Tax is payable (subject to the usual personal exemptions and reliefs) on any gain. However all EMI shares now qualify for Entrepreneurs' Relief (see above) and there is no requirement for the shares to amount to 5% of the company's issued shareholding).

To qualify for EMI:

- Company must not have assets in excess of £30 million;

- Company must not be under the control of another company and any subsidiaries must be 51% owned;

- Company must be employing fewer than 250 full time or FTE employees;

- Company must trade wholly or mainly in the UK;

- Companies that carry out 'excluded activities' cannot offer EMI schemes. This includes **property development** (but not other types of property businesses). However, if the excluded activity is only part of the company's business it may be possible to offer an EMI scheme;

- EMI options can only be offered to employees or directors who work a minimum of 25 hours per week for the company and spend 75% of their working time for the company;

- There is a limit on the values of share options which may be granted -£250,000 per employee over a three-year period (subject to a maximum holding of 30% of the total issued shareholding) - and an overall limit of £3 million for the total value of EMI shares offered.

And there are some more considerations:

- You will need to review and probably amend the company's Articles to include provisions to deal with leaving employee shareholders, pre-emption rights, rights of transfer and beneficial ownership and disputes between shareholders;

- Agreeing the value of the EMI shares with HMRC prior to offer is not mandatory but is strongly recommended;

- It is important that the scheme should specify that an employee's options lapse if they leave the company, and also to provide for the company's right to buy back the shares in these circumstances.

- The legislation requires the company to file documents with HMRC within 92 days of grant of the option. The company will obtain corporation tax relief based on the value of shares when the option is actually exercised.

Enterprise Investment Scheme (EIS)

EIS is designed to enable a company to raise up to £5 million per year (to a company lifetime maximum of £12 million) by offering tax reliefs to individual investors who buy new shares in the company. The limits mentioned above also include any venture capital investment. The EIS shares must be full risk ordinary shares and bought at their face value. The company issues a certificate on form EAS3 or EISS stating that the shares qualify. The investor then claims the tax relief on their personal self-assessment tax return.

The maximum amount an investing individual can claim relief on per tax year regarding any one company is £1 million, but as from 6 April 2018 relief can be claimed for an additional £1 million pounds invested in a knowledge-intensive company ('KIC') The EIS3/EAS5 will certify if a company meets this definition. The amount of EIS-qualifying investment that a company can receive in any 12-month period is limited to £5 million (£10 million for KICs).

The relief is at the rate of 30% on the aggregate amount of shares purchased (subject to the limits set out above). However if the investor's tax liability is not high enough to absorb the relief he or she has to forego any excess. You cannot claim a credit.

You can read more about EIS in *Section 9*.

SECTION 6: LEARN ABOUT YOUR TAX-DEDUCTIBLE EXPENSES

For some this may be the most appealing section in the book! Here we examine the wide range of potential expenses you can offset against your tax bill. You might very well think that this should be a simple topic as it follows a simple definition – *if you incur an expense in the course of your business, you can deduct it in computing your profit, providing that expense has been wholly and exclusively incurred for the purposes of your trade or profession.* However, of course it is very far from simple; and, as the choices you make when running your business may generate different types of expenses, there is good scope for some sensible tax planning. In addition, if you are seeking to claim an expense that you've incurred in your capacity as a director of a limited company (even if you are the only director), then you have to look at the rules for claiming expenses as an employee of the company. And these rules are not identical to the rules for an expense claimed by the business.

Later in this section we look at expenses issues that relate specifically to property businesses. First, however, let's take a broader look at this complex but rewarding topic; considering the general tax landscape for expenses will give you an overall view, before we narrow it down to property businesses.

#26. Tax vs profit and loss

When discussing business expenses in relation to tax – i.e. what you may or may not be able to deduct in order to reduce your tax bill – it is sometimes possible to confuse your tax scenario with your accounting for Profit and Loss. This is very easily done through no fault of the taxpayer.

Along with the Balance Sheet, the Profit and Loss calculation is one of the important measures of a business's performance and financial health. For Profit and Loss you deduct *all* expenses to arrive at your actual net profit and to show a comparison of income against expenditure (which includes direct costs of sales and also overheads). However, for your tax calculations you deduct only those that are permitted by the tax legislation. So for example, you may spend £1,000 on entertaining (in a form that truly benefits the business) – that would be a legitimate expense to insert into the Profit and Loss calculation. However, HMRC's interpretation of the rules might decree that only £400 of that is actually claimable against tax, and so for the tax computation you add the remaining £600 back in (£1,000 expended by company less the £400 which is tax-deductible). As I've said before, HMRC's interpretation is not law, so it is possible to challenge this, if you or your adviser feel that the legislation is capable of a different interpretation.

In the rest of this section, we are concerned with the expenses that can be offset against income to calculate the taxable figure on which your final tax bill is based.

#27. List of typical allowable expenses

It is important to understand that there are some variations in what is allowed depending on the nature of the business, i.e. sole trader/partnership vs limited company. It is also important not to confuse company director expenses with other expenses; a director is an employee of the company and therefore eligible to claim expenses like any other employee, but these must be incurred wholly, exclusively and **necessarily** in relation to doing the job itself. The word 'necessarily' is an important distinction because, for expenses to be tax-deductible in computing income from a sole trader or partnership business, the test is 'wholly and exclusively for the purposes of the business'.

If it can be shown that an expense claimed by an employee (including a company director) did not fulfill the criteria, then this will be classed as a benefit in kind in the employee's hands and the employee will suffer tax on the disallowed amount (and in some cases) the company as employer will be liable for Class 1A National Insurance. On the other hand, if the company chooses to pay or reimburse expenses that are not tax-deductible, then in certain cases these will legitimately decrease the company's profits so there will be that much less Corporation Tax to pay.

Let's look at a practical example:

A, a company director, uses a luxury car for both work and private use. It is considered by both A and his co-directors that this enhances the prestige of the company. A travels less than 10,000 a year on company business, and, for the purposes of this example, let's assume that all of those miles are travelled wholly, exclusively and necessarily on the company's business..

Now, as you will see below, if an employee is paid a mileage allowance of not more than 45p per mile (for annual business travel of less than 10,000 miles), HMRC have agreed that this rate does not amount to a benefit in kind. In other words, the payment at this rate is considered to be fair and reasonable reimbursement for the fuel and running costs for an employee using his own car for business.

However, A is paid business mileage at 65p per mile. What is the tax position on that additional 20p per mile?

As far as the company is concerned, provided that there is a contractual agreement for payment at this rate, (and I think it's fair to say that this is by no means an unreasonable rate of reimbursement for the running expenses of a car of this type), then this will be shown in the company's accounts as travel expenses and will be a legitimate expense of the business. So the profits will be less than if only 45p per mile were paid and consequently there is less Corporation Tax to pay. However the company, as employer, must pay Class 1A National Insurance (NI) on benefits-in-kind for directors and employees

In A's hands, the additional 20p per mile is classed as a benefit-in-kind and therefore is taxable but not subject to NI. Most benefits received by an employee from an employer do not result in NI being paid by the employee (unless they are in a form which could be sold on).

To give you a flavour of what we'll be examining, here is a list of the typical expenses you may be able to claim, providing that they are incurred wholly and exclusively for the purposes of the business and, in the case of directors and employees, also necessarily.. As a snapshot the list is not able to make all of the distinctions outlined above. Please note however that the rules are often complicated, so please read the relevant sections that then follow below, and always seek professional advice.

- **Salaries**

- **Executive pension contributions** (via an approved scheme).

- **Workplace pension contributions**

- **Employers' national insurance contributions** (NICs) payable on salaries paid to company employees.

- The cost of subsistence while away from your workplace (no claims after 24 months for **subsistence** at the same 'temporary workplace').

- **Accommodation** costs when away from normal place of business (although must not exceed 24 months at a 'temporary workplace').

- **Travel** and parking costs, mileage allowance if using own vehicle of 45p/mile for the first 10,000 miles, and 25p/mile thereafter. 20p/mile rate for bicycles. (If one employee allows another to travel in his car, then the passenger may claim 5p per mile)

- **Training** course fees as long as the content is relevant to the business and not it's not a new skill that is being acquired.

- **Stationery**, postage, and printing costs.

- **Business insurance**, such as professional indemnity insurance.

- **Telephone and broadband** packages (if the contract is in the company name).

- **Mobile and Smartphones** (if the contract is in the company name).

- The cost of **business calls** can be reclaimed on a residential phone bill.

- **Home office costs** For directors a flat £4/week without receipts is allowed by HMRC with a sliding scale flat rate, depending on hours worked, for sole traders/partners. Alternatively, you can work out a proportion of the household bills.

- **Computer equipment and software**.

- Costs of **advertising** and marketing your business.

- Business **gifts** up to £50 per individual are allowable before more complex rules apply. This does not apply to gifts of food, tobacco, and alcohol, nor to vouchers (as long as these bear the donor's logo).

- Incidental **overnight expenses** of £5/night (£10/night if overseas) can be claimed as a flat rate if you are working away from home.

- **Authorised bank charges**, e.g. standing charges each quarter.

- **Christmas party exemption** for directors and employees of £150 per person per year (you can include your partner or spouse).

- **Professional fees**, such as accountant or solicitor (depending on the nature of the legal services).

- A limited number of professional **subscriptions**, if allowed by HMRC.

- **Capital allowances** (depreciation of assets).

- Business magazines and **books**.

- An **eye test for employees** who use computer equipment.

- An **annual private health check** for employees.

- **Hire purchase agreements** (in the company name).

- **Company car expenses** If you're a director driving a car owned by the company, there is a benefit in kind charge for private use. If you're a sole trader or partner, effectively you can claim for the business use element.

- Company formation and ongoing costs (e.g. Annual Return fee), although the company formation fee is a 'capital cost', and cannot be set off against Corporation Tax.

The above list is not exhaustive by any means.

As *expenses* these are all items you can offset against your income before arriving at a tax-payable figure. This differs from a *tax relief* where you arrive at the tax-payable figure and then adjust it with the amount of relief for which you qualify (there is a good illustration of this later in this section, under Property rental operating expenses).

#28. Business operating expenses (against Income Tax)

Here we examine some common types of expenses and consider why they are (or are not) deductible.

SOLE TRADER AND PARTNER EXPENSES

Here is a list of the chief expense categories, along with some issues that we'll look at shortly:

- Motor expenses: *but there are two different ways of claiming your costs…*

- Travel: *the devil is in the detail; are those journeys really all for business, or are you just commuting between home and work?*

- Subsistence: *(should carry a government health warning!) Is your trade itinerant in nature, and what does that really mean these days?*

- Working from home: *yes, but how much, why and when?*

- Training costs and course fees: *what is being achieved when you train yourself to do something? This may colour what you can claim.*

- Repairs and maintenance: *newly acquired assets, dilapidations, renewal or capital improvement?*

- Employing the spouse and family: *but when are wages and benefits disallowed for tax?*

- Living expenses: *these are generally personal by nature so no claim is possible.*

- Entertaining and Gifts: *any chance of tax relief? Well…*

Now let's unpick some of these.

Sole traders and partnerships

Home office costs

We're talking here of the actual space in your house that you use to do some of your work, and the proportion of your household bills (heat and light, council tax, mortgage interest, etc) that you may be able to claim.

If you are self-employed (i.e. sole trader or partner) and you do some of your work at home irrespective of whether you also have an office, don't miss out on claiming tax relief. You have to bear in mind that HMRC may ask you to justify your claim. What is allowable depends on the particular facts, including the extent and nature of the trade activities undertaken in the home.

How does 'wholly and exclusively' apply to home office costs?

Put simply, it means that when a part of the home is being used for the trade, that is the sole use for it at that time. So if you work in one corner and your children simultaneously watch TV in another, you cannot claim for the room as office space. As always, this is a call that you as taxpayer have to make. If sometimes you use a room for work and at other times your children use it to watch TV (when you do not require it for work) then the room has duality of purpose and a suitable proportion could be claimed.

The obvious solution would be to use a space that cannot be used in any other way when you are using it for work. However, there is a trap for the unwary here! If you dedicate a portion of your home solely for business purposes (for example converting a bedroom into an office exclusively for your business work) then, if you dispose of your home you may not be eligible to claim Private Residence Relief for CGT on that proportion of the home (i.e. the former bedroom). *"Surely HMRC can't pick up on this?"* Oh yes it can. HMRC now uses powerful software that is able to review millions of returns and identify patterns and discrepancies. Another potential problem is that you may find that you are charged business rates on the part that you use solely for business.

So clearly, to avoid this risk, the rooms you use for business need to be available for use at other *times* for other domestic purposes as well. Some suggestions are: children's playroom, library/computer room, games room, guest bedroom, and certainly more than just for incidental storage.

As always, it's important to document this if you can. You can't make an agreement with yourself, but if the house is in the joint names of yourself and your partner, or if the 'business user' is a limited company, then you could for example have a short licence agreement stating that the business user is permitted to use the space on a non-exclusive basis. It's also a good idea to keep a log of dates and times of use. This may all sound like overkill, but it could save a lot of trouble if HMRC challenge the amount of home use.

If you use a separate building on your residential premises, you can claim back all the costs for maintaining that building or charge a proportion of the cost if the building has shared residential use. You'll still need to declare this on your personal Income Tax return alongside the expenses claimed. If the separate building is owned by the business, then more complex tax rules apply, as it will become a business asset rather than a personal one.

How do you allocate your home office costs?

In the case of Caillebotte v Quinn [1975] the judge stated '... *it is possible to apportion the use and cost of a room on a time basis, and to allow the expense of the room during the hours in which it is used exclusively for business purposes, in the same way as it is possible to calculate the business expenses of a car which is sometimes used for business purposes exclusively and sometimes used for pleasure.*'

Generally, if there is only minor trade use of the home then a reasonable estimate consistent with the underlying facts is usually acceptable. But if you use home space a lot, there can be more than one method of arriving at a reasonable apportionment and, even if the results may differ a little, they may be equally acceptable.

Some methods may be more appropriate for a particular type of expense. For instance, you could apportion by area based either on the number of rooms or on floor area. But if two different methods produce substantially different figures, then that is likely to be a sign that one may more closely reflect the underlying facts. Again, it's your responsibility as taxpayer to decide.

You can include mortgage interest (but not capital repayments) in calculating your use of home as office. Work out what a fair proportion would be to allocate to the time you spend working from home. From March 2017 new rules govern using mortgage (and other loan) interest, affecting higher-rate taxpayers (see Mortgage and loan interest relief, below).

Flat rate option

From April 2013, the new simplified expenses rules mean that unincorporated businesses (i.e. sole traders and partnerships) can choose to calculate the trade proportion of household expenses using flat rate allowances. This is a simpler alternative to allocating a proportion of household costs in your expenses.

Where a home is used partly for business purposes, the simplified expenses rules allow a flat rate deduction for household running costs. The deduction is based on the number of hours spent wholly and exclusively on core business activities in the home, and is only available if you work from home for *more than 25 hours per month*.

Core business activities comprise:

- Providing goods and/or services;
- Maintaining business records;
- Marketing and obtaining new business.

HMRC has approved the 'simplified expenses' method, which applies to business costs for vehicles, use of home, and living on business premises. I explain the application of this to vehicle costs under Business Travel (Method 1) below.

Use of the flat rate deduction for household running costs covers light and heat but you can still make a separate deduction for fixed costs such as council tax, insurance and mortgage interest, where an identifiable proportion can be attributed to business use. The flat rate calculation is not used for telephone and broadband/internet connection costs either, so you have to work out the proportion. If the private use is not significant the full cost of the telephone and broadband service can be claimed as a business expense.

The flat rates are as follows:

Number of hours worked	Flat rate per month
25 or more	£10
51 or more	£18
101 or more	£26

The deduction for a period is the sum of the flat rates for each month, or part of a month, falling within that period. If you have more than one home, then all the homes are treated as a single home for the purposes of calculating hours worked.

If you still prefer the 'proportionate method', there is no hard and fast rule about how this should be applied but you must base it on your actual business practice. HMRC may ask you to explain the system you've used and my suggestion is that you use a common sense approach that reflects your use of assets that are not used solely for business. This may mean using different methods for different assets used.

Partnerships

If two or more partners in the trade share a home only *one deduction* is available in calculating the partnership profits. Where the partners work different hours, the flat rate deduction is based on the aggregate hours worked and no hour is counted more than once. Where partners occupy different homes all partners' homes are to be treated in the same way.

Mobile phones (and landline unless exclusively a business line)

Phone bills can be claimed as a business expense, but if you use them for both business and private use you need to work out the proportion used for business.

The best way is to go through one or two sample months of bills each year and highlight your business/personal use to work out a basis for the percentage use to claim as a business expense. Alternatively, just work out a rule of thumb of 80/20, but remember that you might have to justify this to HMRC, so keep a note of our calculations.

Accountancy fees and other professional fees

Fees in relation to your self-employed business are a tax-deductible expense, but services relating to your personal affairs are not. Strictly speaking the fees for the preparation of your personal tax return are not allowable, but in practice as long as your tax return includes self-employed income any professional fees can be claimed.

Business travel

This one is a little more complicated.

Anyone self-employed can theoretically claim travel expenses such as fuel, parking, train or bus fares - but it all depends on the 'base of operations' where the self-employed person carries out their work. Travel between home and the base of operations is not an allowable expense. The exception is when you travel from home to a *temporary* base of operations, say a different office location for a week. Also, if your business is a 'travelling occupation' or 'itinerant in nature', for example if you are a travelling salesperson or regularly visit different clients, all business travel can be claimed.

Conversely, if your home *is* your base of operations then all business travel outwards from here will be allowable.

Here are some examples:

Let's say your business is run from an office unit some miles from your home. Travelling from your home to the office is not deductible. But what if you call to inspect a property on the way? In 2015 HMRC updated their guidance on business travel for employees and amongst the general principles you *cannot* turn a journey into business travel in this way just by fitting in a call en route. It has to be a **necessary** visit.

However, if you go to the office and then out to inspect the property, you can claim that journey. If you make a necessary all-day trip for business purposes and don't go to the office at all, then you can treat the whole as business travel.

And what actual costs can you claim for eligible journeys?

Public transport: You claim the full fare that you pay, as long as the journey is 100% for business (following the 'wholly and exclusively' rule).

Own vehicle: In addition to any parking costs, there are two methods for calculating the claimable expense:

Method 1 – Mileage rates (not for businesses above the VAT threshold)

You simply keep a mileage log of all allowable business journeys. Note the date of journey, start point, end point, purpose of journey and total number of miles. You then calculate how much you can claim on the basis (currently) of 45 pence per mile for the first 10,000 miles per year and 25 pence per mile thereafter.

You can only use the mileage rate method if at the point the car is first used for the business your business is below the VAT threshold rate. This is currently £85,000. If you are above this rate you would have to use Method 2 below.

Method 2 – Actual costs less private element deduction

This is more complicated but can be more tax-efficient, depending on your level of use. You keep a record of all motor expenses, including road tax, insurance, fuel, repairs and maintenance, breakdown cover and the interest costs if you lease. You can include warranty costs if you spread your claim over the life of the warranty.

You then work out the percentage of your vehicle costs that should be disallowed because of private use and claim the rest. In theory this means keeping a detailed mileage log of all work journeys plus a note of the mileage at the beginning and end of the financial year. Alternatively, you could keep a mileage log for a 'snapshot' of a typical period of, say, three months.

The purchase cost of the vehicle is a capital item so the expense can qualify as a capital allowance on a scale reflecting the vehicle's age and emissions rate. This means that when you sell the vehicle, if it is not entirely written down as a capital item, you could end up with a balancing amount that is taxable.

Subsistence

'Reasonable' costs of food and drink can be claimed as allowable expenses in conjunction with business travel. However, 'reasonable' is not defined by law, being a judgement made, when necessary, by the courts. Instead, use a simple rule of thumb relating to the business travel item above - if your journey itself is not claimable (for example, travelling from home to your usual office), then you can't claim any subsistence either.

So, you must be *either* in a trade or profession that is "itinerant" by nature or you only travel to the place occasionally and this travel is not part of a normal pattern of travel (or you have no normal pattern of travel).

Entertaining

This is a common expense which is easy to get wrong, so here are the guidelines.

Entertaining clients, customers or third parties

The cost of entertaining is not allowed as a deduction for tax purposes but should still be included as a business expense on your "Profit and Loss" account and added back for tax purposes (see Tax vs Profit and Loss, above).

However, if you hire a room for an event, as part of which you are entertaining clients, you may be able to claim tax relief on the cost of the room.

Entertaining yourself and your family

The cost is *not* deductible under the general principle of "wholly and exclusively". So, although family may play a vital role in, say, a networking event, tax law states that their element of the entertaining costs is not permitted as a deductible expense.

If family members are employees, however, the cost may be allowable providing that it is not excessive – see below.

Entertaining employees

Here at last is an entertainment expense you *can* claim, although it's actually because entertaining your staff is not treated as such but as staff welfare. NB: subcontractors and freelancers do not count as staff, so you cannot claim for their welfare.

Thinking of sending your employees on an all-expenses-paid weekend at a health spa and claiming against it? Think again. This would count as an employee's taxable benefit-in-kind (and both you and they would be liable for NI) *unless* it is an annual event, open to all employees at a total cost of no more than £150 per head for all such events in the tax year.

If you provide modest refreshments (for example, tea, coffee, soft drinks, biscuits) or indeed food (whether free or at a subsidized rate) then as long as this is available to all employees, the cost will be deductible as 'staff welfare' as explained above.

There is also a 'trivial benefits' exemption which enables employers to provide benefits for employees, as long as these meet all of the following criteria:

- it cost you £50 or less to provide

- it isn't cash or a cash voucher

- it isn't a reward for their work or performance

- it isn't a term of the employment contract

These are deductible and neither the employer nor the employee pays tax or National Insurance. There is no need to disclose these benefits to HMRC but of course, as always, you should keep records in case of challenge.

However, if trivial benefits are provided as part of a salary sacrifice arrangement, then they are not exempt and must be reported to HMRC using Form P11D. This will state the higher of:

- the salary given up

- the value of the trivial benefits

'Salary sacrifice' is an agreement to reduce an employee's entitlement to cash pay, usually in return for a non-cash benefit. The value of the non-cash benefit must be calculated for Income Tax and National Insurance purposes, but some benefits are exempt:

- payments into pension schemes

- employer provided pensions advice

- workplace nurseries

- childcare vouchers and directly contracted employer provided childcare that started on or before 4 October 2018

- bicycles and cycling safety equipment (including cycle to work)

Accommodation

What if you have to stay overnight when you are on a business trip?

You can deduct accommodation costs providing they are wholly and exclusively for the purposes of the trade or profession. If your accommodation is partly for business and partly for pleasure, you can claim an identifiable proportion as a business expense.

Claimable accommodation includes accommodation used as a workplace (for example, overnight in a hotel where you are holding client meetings), used as a stopover when travelling on business or used for any other business purpose.

Training

This is one that frustrates some people, and it's because you cannot claim the cost of a training or course fee for tax purposes if the object is to learn a new skill or qualification.

Why? Any new skill or knowledge obtained puts you in a place to better perform your duties and so it creates an intangible asset from the perspective of your business; i.e. it is something of enduring benefit that is totally personal to the individual.

However, on-going training and development *once a knowledge, skill or qualification is acquired* is claimable as a cost of up-dating or continuing professional development.

COMPANY DIRECTOR EXPENSES

We now come to that sticky issue of director expenses vs company expenses, mentioned earlier.

If a director incurs an expense in the course of his duties then we assume he is reimbursed for this by the company. The company will of course show this in its accounts as an expense in calculating its profit. If the expense was 'wholly, exclusively and necessarily' incurred in the course of the director's employment, then the company is not liable to pay Class 1A National Insurance on it as a benefit in kind. But even if the expense does not meet the criteria, then as a rule the company can still apply the test of 'wholly and exclusively incurred for the purposes of its business' and if so treat the whole of the expense plus any Class 1A NIC as an expense that can be included in the tax computation for Corporation Tax.(see comments above about this). There are one or two exceptions where a rule against this applies, notably in the case of entertainment expenses

With regard to a director's own Income Tax, then the position is the same as for any other employee. Generally speaking, an expense not 'wholly, exclusively and necessarily incurred in the course of the employee's *employment*' will be a taxable benefit in kind if reimbursed. If an employee incurs an expense which is not reimbursed by the employer, then he or she can only set it against personal income tax if the employee is obliged to purchase the items and the items are only used for work.

As you can see from the above, taxation on the director personally is based on his role as employee of the company. Corporation Tax however is based on the company's position as a separate legal persona running a business

Let's examine some director expenses in detail:

Home office costs

You might think that HMRC would use the same rules as for sole traders who work for themselves, but it doesn't. As you know, directors are technically the *employees* of the company, so they must follow the home-working rules relating specifically to employees.

So, what does this mean for a company director?

First of all you have to establish that you do indeed do some work from home – but this shouldn't be too difficult given that directors are directors 24/7 365 days of the year! However, there is more – and the key distinction is how *necessary* it is for you to work from home (a distinction that is not applied to self-employed people).

Before I go any further, let's look at what is meant (in taxation terms) by the word 'necessary'. You probably won't be surprised to learn that this is, or can be, a very grey area.

To start with, HMRC interpretation of what is 'necessary' for the purposes of an employment can vary dramatically between the different types of expenses. For example, an employee was denied relief for the cost of a projector used to improve the quality of presentations. Although HMRC accepted that this was used wholly and exclusively for business purposes, it was found that it did not meet the test of 'necessary', as it was possible to do presentations without it.

As you will know, it is common for senior executives to have first class rail travel when travelling for business. Since they could get around just as quickly using standard class it is difficult to see how the first-class element could be regarded as 'necessary'-but this point is rarely taken by HMRC in practice. If it were to be challenged then I imagine the justification would be along the lines of the need for comfort and privacy in order to combat the stressful nature of their employment and to facilitate working whilst travelling (including thinking and mental preparation for the forthcoming meetings).

There are two ways in which an expense may be classified as 'necessary' for the purpose of employment and these are 'practical' and 'contractual'.

'Practical' covers items that a director cannot do without, if he is to do his job properly. Examples include professional subscriptions, and 'tools of the trade'.

'Contractual' means items which are terms of the director's employment contract. If carefully worded (and appropriate to the director's employment duties) these are much less likely to be challenged by HMRC. However, do be careful about the wording - after all a literal interpretation of 'must provide own transport' could mean a bicycle.

Moving on, you must demonstrate that the expense has been incurred wholly, exclusively and *necessarily* (e.g. you can't claim home costs if it is perfectly reasonable and viable for you to work on company premises) in the performance of the duties of the employment (as these are the statutory conditions imposed by Section 336 Income Tax (Earnings and Pensions) Act 2003). And this means:

- The duties that the employee (director) performs at home are substantive duties of the employment. "Substantive duties" are duties that an employee has to carry out and that represent all or part of the central duties of the employment.

- Those duties cannot be performed without the use of appropriate facilities.

- No such appropriate facilities are available to the employee on the employer's premises – e.g. the premises are not available when the employee needs to work at weekends, or the nature of the job requires the employee to live so far from the employer's premises that it is unreasonable to expect him or her to travel to those premises on a daily basis)

- At no time either before or after the employment contract is drawn up is the employee able to choose between working at the employer's premises or elsewhere.

If one or more of those conditions is not met you are unlikely to satisfy the statutory tests in Section 336. Clearly these conditions are restrictive, so let's have a more pro-active look at how this might work for directors - who are after all a rather special class of employee!

Currently, HMRC allows a flat £4 per week fixed expense (excluding business telephone calls) for employees that can be claimed back from the company, without the need for any receipts. Of course this is a nominal amount, so what other options do you have?

One option is to rent a part of your home to the limited company (but remember the danger mentioned earlier about falling foul of CGT if you assign part of the home exclusively to business use).

As an alternative you could seek tax relief for a limited number of other expenses, The way in which you might do this is similar to the procedure for sole traders but you don't have the privilege of using the flat rate. You can, however, still claim a proportion of the household costs of running the building itself. Bear in mind however that, as a director, you can only claim the incremental cost of working from home. This means that any costs that are incurred anyway, by virtue of you being the householder, such as heat and light, insurance, cleaning services, cannot be included, unless you can show that a proportion of them were additionally incurred as a result of you working from home. You also need to beware of services which are already being provided for personal use or for dual purpose (such as a broadband line shared by the household as well as the business). If, for example, the broadband contract was already in place before you started working from home, then you may not be able to claim any part of the costs as an expense.

So in order to establish the proportion of household costs used by the business, you will need to work out the percentage of your property which is used for business purposes, what proportion of a utility bill that can be apportioned to business use (e.g. lighting or heating), and for how long each day the service is used for solely business reasons (for example, the business area only needs to have lighting for 50% of the day).

If you use a separate building on your residential premises, you can claim back all the costs for maintaining that building or charge a proportion of the cost if the building has shared residential use. You'll still need to declare this on your personal Income Tax return alongside the expenses claimed.

What about claiming back expenses from the company?

When we speak of claiming back expenses from the company, I'm referring to reimbursement to the director by the company for costs incurred (as opposed to the director claiming tax relief personally). Of course the company is at liberty to reimburse to whatever extent it thinks fit. The question is whether such reimbursement will first be allowed as legitimate company expenditure (this reducing the profits for Corporation Tax) and secondly whether the director will be able to claim such expenses as tax deductible personally.

As mentioned above, the tests are different. For the company the test is whether the expense was wholly and exclusively for the purposes of the business. So the company cannot usually pay (as a tax-deductible expense) directors' and employees' rent, mortgage interest, or council tax, these costs would have been paid personally anyway.

From the point of view of the director, the test also includes that word 'necessarily'. See the discussion above of how this works. Although sole directors are akin to sole traders, HMRC does not view them as such.

Directors' Expenses

For other expenses, the same criteria apply – your status as *employee* and the *necessity* of your personally-incurred expense; i.e.

- the expense must be 'necessary';
- the expense must be incurred for the purposes of your *employment*, rather than the business.

In reality, the majority of expenses (other than home office) incurred by a director will be either paid for or reimbursed by the company, so there is no need or opportunity to try claiming them against income tax.

Trivial Benefits

As set out above, an employer can award trivial benefits to an employee without any need to inform HMRC (i.e. no tax or NI to be paid). The company can therefore use this to award benefits to a director if it meets the set criteria:

In the case of a director of a close company (controlled by five or fewer directors, shareholders or participators), then there is an annual limit on the total value of the benefits of £300 per tax year.

COMPANY CARS AND VANS

Vehicles are costly but essential expenses for most businesses, but also an opportunity to make tax-beneficial choices.

Let's first look at some of pros and cons of vehicles for the business (and this broadly covers sole traders, partners and LLPs):

Pros and cons for the business

- If the business (limited company, partnership or sole trader) buys the vehicle for the owner/partner or employee to use it acquires a valuable asset (albeit a depreciating one) which it retains if the partner or employee leaves;

- If the car is leased (the favoured option for the majority of businesses) you're not laying out the cash but you should be able to get back 50% of the VAT on the lease costs (assuming that you use the car for both business and private purposes). You also don't incur heavy maintenance costs as the car ages, because typically the vehicle will be purchased new or nearly new. But if the car does more than the estimated mileage, you could be facing penalties;

- In some sectors (e.g. where company representatives traditionally incur regular heavy mileage) provision of a car may be essential, both for the business-owners and for employees;

- The burden of calculating the tax payable by the owner or employee on the use of the car falls on the business-owner/employer;

- As employer you have to pay Class 1A National Insurance on the value of the benefit to the employee of having the use of a company car;

- If you only use the car for business (and it is not available for private use) you can claim back all the VAT on the purchase or lease costs;

- If the car is used for both business and private use you can either reclaim all the VAT and pay the right fuel scale charge for your vehicle or reclaim only the VAT on fuel you use for business trips. However, in this case you must keep accurate records and you do need to do the maths. If you only do a low mileage, you may be better off not reclaiming the VAT at all, as the use of the fuel scale charge may leave you worse off.

- You can usually reclaim the VAT for all business-related running and maintenance costs, e.g. repairs or off-street parking, and any accessories you've fitted for business use even if you can't reclaim VAT on the vehicle itself;

- For sole traders, partnerships and LLP members there is no benefit in kind element to the private use of the car, but you do have to make the necessary private use adjustment (see below) so that the business is paying for (and claiming as business expenditure) *only* the business use.

- Capital Allowances also apply to vehicles and Enhanced Capital Allowances to electric vehicles. See the details in Section 5.

Private use adjustment

The easiest way to do this is to keep a mileage log so that you can differentiate between business and private mileage. This can then be used to allocate the proportion of running costs (excluding fuel) to be allocated to business use. For more details, see the section on business travel above.

Pros and cons for employees (including directors)

- The biggest benefit is that the employee does not usually have to bear the maintenance and repair costs of the car. On the other hand, if the employee leaves the employment, he is faced with the financial outlay of acquiring a vehicle;

- Unless the car is used exclusively for the company business (which means that it has to be left at the company's premises when not in use by the employee), the employee will pay tax on the private use as a Benefit in Kind (BIK) – see below.

Benefit in kind (BIK) tax on motor vehicles

- The tax paid by the employee depends on the value of the BIK and the employee's annual salary (excluding the BIK). If you're a 20% taxpayer you'll pay 20%, if you're a 40% taxpayer you'll pay 40% on the value over the 40% threshold. There is no cap.

- The value of the BIK is *not* the same as the cost of the car. Every car has a BIK band, based on fuel, type, CO_2 emissions, and a P11D value, which is the list price, including extras and VAT, but without the first year registration fee and vehicle tax. To calculate the BIK tax, multiply the P11D value by the BIK percentage banding and also adjust for the number of days in the year where the car was unavailable to the employee.

- Although BIKs are taxed, the employee does not have to pay NI on the value of the BIK

- If the employer pays for the fuel you use for personal journeys you pay tax (but not NI) on the value of this separately from the tax on the BIK

What happens if the employee contributes towards the cost of the car?

There are a few reasons why this might happen, e.g. to acquire a more expensive model, or to have certain extras added to the vehicle, or to reduce the BIK tax. In this case a lump sum (maximum £5,000) can be subtracted from the list price (or regular payments based on how long it is intended to keep the car) that is then knocked off the BIK calculations. This of course not only reduces the tax payable by the employee but also the Class 1A NI payable by the employer, because the value of the BIK is reduced.

One point that sometimes crops up is the situation where a car is provided for an employee (including private use) but a condition is that it bears the company logo, which may include advertising material. From the company's point of view, the cost of installing this would be a legitimate expense, but would not add to the BIK calculations.

However, what about the employee's position? It's tempting to say that a car plastered with company signage is not one which the employee would wish to use when not on business and therefore this ought to reduce the BIK figure. I'm not convinced that this is correct. The only exclusion is a vehicle which is not of a type commonly used as a private vehicle and not suitable as a private vehicle. Whatever your views, I can't see that the advertising makes the car a 'type' which is not suitable for private use.

Ultra-Low Emission Vehicles (ULEV)

These are vehicles that emit less than 75g of carbon dioxide (CO_2) for every kilometre travelled (typically electrically-powered cars and hybrid vehicles). They bring some tax advantages:

- No fuel duty, as electricity is not a fuel in this context;

- Reduced vehicle excise duty (zero emission vehicles valued less than £40,000 are now exempt);

- Electricity used to recharge vehicles at home is taxed at 5% VAT only;

- If you provide a ULEV for any employee (including directors) there's no car fuel benefit charge (as electricity is not a fuel);

- Income tax advantage for salary sacrifice in exchange for a ULEV as a benefit in kind;

- Lower taxation for company cars where the vehicle is a ULEV;

- Advisory Fuel Rates (the amount an employee may be paid for business mileage without it being classed as a benefit on kind) - if you have a hybrid you can still use the equivalent rates for petrol or diesel.

- Enhanced capital allowances - businesses that purchase ULEVs or ULEV recharging or refuelling infrastructure, are eligible for 100% first year allowance.

Vans

If you buy a van it will be eligible for the Annual Investment Allowance (AIA) so potentially the entire cost could be offset in the first year (assuming the van is used solely for business use and not, for example for travelling between home and work).

You can claim back VAT on the purchase and the running costs if the van is used solely for work.

#29. Property-related expenses and allowances

Let's start logically by looking at the situation for a new business.

Property rental start-up and pre-letting expenses

The basic principle involved in calculating tax-deductible expenses on property is covered by s.272 Income Tax (Trading and Other Income) Act 2005. This means that expenses are allowable in exactly the same way as for a trade – i.e. only if they are incurred 'wholly and exclusively' for the rental business. This principle cuts across the board whether you are a sole trader, partnership or LLP, and also interacts with specific reliefs such as Replacement of Domestic Items Relief and Mortgage Interest Relief. The rules for limited companies (that will be paying Corporation Tax) also follow the same principle.

Let's look at your start-up and pre-letting expenses in sequence.

When does the business start?

Generally, a property rental business will be deemed to start when the first property is marketed for letting (and not before). However, once the business has started, then all subsequent activities (whether related to the initial properties or to properties acquired later) will be treated as part of one and the same business as long as the properties are in the same ownership and located in the UK. Properties outside the UK would be treated as a separate business. There are also separate rules for serviced accommodation, which can usually be treated as a separate business.

For Income Tax purposes (or Corporation Tax if a limited company), the property owner is treated as receiving the profits of a business, but this will not count as a trade unless the rental business fulfills the HMRC definition of a trade (see the discussion in Section 3: Organisational Structure - What Does Your Business Look Like?) about the difference between trading and investment). So, since all the properties are assets of the one business, the allowable expenses relating to any one or more properties can be set against the income from the whole property rental business.

What about expenses incurred before the business starts?

Allowable expenditure incurred before the rental business begins (i.e. the date of the first property being marketed or advertised for letting) qualifies for relief under the general rules for pre-trading expenditure and can be deducted in the tax computation. In order to qualify the expenditure must:

- be incurred wholly and exclusively for the purposes of the rental business;

- not be capital expenditure;

- be incurred within a period of seven years before the date the rental business is started;

- not be otherwise allowable as a deduction for tax purposes (that is, it cannot be an expense that can be deducted under a different rule, irrespective of whether or not you personally have so deducted);

- have been allowed as a deduction if it had been incurred *after* the rental business started. For example, the reasonable costs of preparing a tenancy agreement or lease are deductible, so if you take the step of instructing your solicitor to prepare a draft document in readiness, before you start marketing, then the professional fees are still deductible.

Any pre-letting expenditure that meets these criteria is then treated as if incurred on the day on which the taxpayer first carries on their rental business, and so can be deducted from the first year's gross rents.

Capital or revenue expenditure?

Expenditure is only deductible from income for tax purposes if it is what is classed as 'in the nature of revenue'. Broadly speaking, this *excludes* any expenditure that results in a 'capital improvement'. The kind of expenses that will not be allowed for this reason include:

- the initial cost of the property;

- expenditure which adds to or improves the land or property, such as converting a disused barn to a home;

- the cost of refurbishing or repairing a property bought in a derelict or run-down state (unless this is classified as a trading activity, such as property-flipping or conversions of property with the intention of then selling);

- expenditure on demolishing a derelict building to clear space for a new building;

- expenditure on car parking or on an access road (where this is more than just repairs and maintenance);

- the cost of buying a new area of land for use with a property that is let.

However, it can sometimes be difficult to assess whether work is capital in nature or not. This tends to be a matter of fact and degree - an improvement might be so small that it may be counted as revenue expenditure in the absence of any other factors suggesting that it is capital improvement.

The nature of the work is important too, differentiating between repair and work that fundamentally changes the character of the property.

Here's a typical example. If you repair an older building using modern materials, e.g. replacing lead pipes with copper or plastic ones, then this will normally be classed as *revenue* expenditure. Similarly, replacements due to advancements in technology, such as replacing single-glazing with double-glazing, are generally treated as an allowable repair, where the functionality and character are broadly the same.

However, if your repair work is intended to upgrade the property, the *whole* of the cost is *capital* expenditure. This includes things like any redecoration after the main work has been done (even though redecoration would ordinarily be a revenue expense).

Whilst looking at the difference between revenue and capital expenditure, you need to bear in mind the rules on the replacement of domestic items, (which is set out below under Property Rental Operating Expenses). Although the replacement qualifies as a deductible expense (subject to the conditions), the cost of purchase doesn't qualify as capital expenditure.

All is not lost as, whilst you can't set the cost of capital improvements against income, you are of course entitled to relief in the form of enhancement expenditure against any capital gain ultimately made on sale or other disposal (as long as the improvement is still present on disposal). This is however likely to be a long way off so it makes sense to check, when your annual accounts are prepared, that all expenditure has been correctly classified, particularly where this qualifies as revenue expenditure.

Is the expenditure necessary?

There is a trap here! Just because expenditure is necessary, it doesn't make it automatically allowable as an immediate property business expense.

Where something needs to be fitted to a higher standard in order to be legal, specifically for letting, the implication is that it is an *improvement* on the original, and therefore a capital expense that cannot be claimed immediately. This often occurs where properties are to be used as HMOs.

For example, let's say you buy a flat where the kitchen and bathroom fittings are 'tired' and the whole flat needs redecorating. This expenditure will be allowable against the income because the property was clearly habitable before the work was done and the work would not significantly improve the underlying capital value of the property. Of course, the new kitchen and bathroom fittings are likely to be up-to-date and in that sense much better but as long as they are replacements of the existing fittings *when those previous fittings were new* then they will not count as 'capital improvements'. However, if you start adding additional fittings, such as extra units, then you are straying into the territory of capital expenditure. It's a fine line, and the best way to decide is to apply the 'like for like' test.

On the other hand, if you buy a large HMO and a recently imposed licencing regime requires it to meet various conditions before it can be let, then it is likely that some of the work will not be classed as revenue expenditure. For example:

- additional fire safety features (as opposed to simply replacing what is there);

- fire alarms and security measures to a higher standard;

- *additional* bathroom and kitchen fittings;

- electrical rewiring where this goes beyond simply replacing and upgrading to modern standards.

You can of course claim as deductible expenses any part of the work that is just replacing (even if this involves up-grading to the modern equivalent). But any work that is a capital improvement and any subsequent making good to the property as a result cannot be set against income. The trick is to judge where the dividing line is between upgrading and improving!

Wholly and exclusively

This term is misleading insofar as you are allowed to claim a part of an expense (a proportion of your phone bill, for example). The rule of thumb is that whatever you claim must be used wholly and exclusively for the business. There are some rules governing how you calculate an allowable proportion that we'll look at shortly.

There are a couple of interesting points in relation to this condition for claimable expenses.

1. If a property is let at *less* than the full commercial rent, any expenditure relating to that property will normally fail the 'wholly and exclusively' test. Strictly speaking no expenditure on such properties is admissible as an expense of the rental business, but expenses can be deducted up to the amount of rent derived from that property.

2. As mentioned earlier, where expenses are claimed by company directors, these must not only be 'wholly and exclusively' but also 'necessarily' incurred.

Records

Obviously it is important to keep all receipts and other records of expenditure as proof of your claim. And of course this is especially important for *capital* expenditure, as it may be some time before you need these for the purpose of calculating your capital gain on disposal.

Later in this section we look at property-specific issues such as 'Replacement of Domestic Items relief'. First let's move on to expenses incurred in the routine running of your business.

Property rental operating expenses

There are three main categories of claimable expense for rental property:

1. Replacement of Domestic Items Relief (this replaced the previous Wear & Tear Allowance);

2. Property Maintenance (allowable expenses);

3. Mortgage or loan interest relief on residential properties.

We'll examine each in turn.

1. Replacement of Domestic Items Relief

How it Works

Replacement of Domestic Items Relief, applicable since 5 April 2016, replaces the former Wear and Tear Allowance. It applies only to furnished lettings. There's no legal definition of 'furnished letting' so we are dependent upon common usage of the term in the lettings sector. It is generally taken to mean that the tenant can move in and live comfortably in the property without having to buy any furniture, carpets, curtains/blinds or white goods.

This is a valuable relief as the estimated cost for furnishing a 3-bedroom property could be c £15,000, depending on how generous the owner wants to be. So whilst no relief is due on initial setting up of a property, when it comes to replacing things, the money soon adds up.

However, unfortunately it's by no means as favourable as the former Wear and Tear Allowance that it has replaced - but we have to live with this change. As I mentioned above, you cannot claim it for the initial purchase of an item, only for a replacement.

There is a *like-for-like* requirement – so you can't replace an ordinary sofa with a sofa bed, for example. If you do, you must deduct the additional upgrade cost. And while the new washing machine you buy will probably be technically more advanced than the old one you can claim the full cost unless you have upgraded from a simple washing machine to a washer-dryer.

NB: The allowance is available for rental properties but not for *serviced accommodation*; these are dealt with through capital allowances.

So, what's included?

The relief is available for 'domestic items' which includes:

- Moveable furniture;
- Furnishings such as carpets, curtains and linen;
- Household appliances such as fridges and freezers;
- Kitchenware such as crockery and cutlery;
- Televisions.

But you can only claim if the items are provided solely for the use of the tenant within residential property.

How does the new relief compare with the old Wear and Tear Allowance?

The old allowance was simpler to use. Instead of keeping proof of cost of replacements, you could opt simply to claim up to 10% of the net rent each year (on furnished lettings) to cover ongoing wear and tear (instead of individual replacement costs as and when). There was also the option, as now, to claim instead in full against replacement items.

How do you get the most from this relief?

First, you keep detailed inventories as the professional letting agents do. This isn't just to review any damage when the tenancy comes to an end – it's really helpful if you want to be able to prove like-for-like replacements and claim the cost against rental income. You need to keep your receipts too.

Second, you can review the way you present your property. If you want to attract high quality tenants but not to pay out for high quality fixtures and contents, you could offer it unfurnished. There are some items any landlord must provide, and you can focus your spend on ones of high calibre. However, your top-quality tenant may be looking for furnished property so this may backfire. So if you furnish and stick with like-for-like, you know you will at least get full tax relief if and when you do need to replace that expensive sofa.

If you fear being worse off without the old 10% of net rent system, you can of course increase your rents to deliver the same net profit. However this may restrict your 'pool' of tenants who are prepared to pay a premium rent.

A more drastic alternative is to switch from tenancies to serviced accommodation; this way you can claim capital allowances instead (*see Section: 8 Buy-to-Let Businesses – What To Think About*)

2. Property Maintenance - Allowable Expenses

You can claim tax-deductible allowable expenses that you incur through maintaining your properties as long as these have been incurred wholly and exclusively for the purposes of renting out the property. And you *will* incur these. Common law and statutory obligations are implied in all residential tenancies, in addition to any repairing responsibilities expressly set out in the tenancy agreement. It's not just a legal requirement for landlords to keep their properties in a good state of repair and safety - it's also good practice!

Regular inspections are a good idea so that you keep matters under control, instead of having a knee-jerk reaction to a tenant's complaints. You also need to keep up-to-date with statutory requirements for regular inspections for gas and electrical installations and Health & Safety generally.

Expenses must be in the nature of revenue rather than capital expenditure (it is when you dispose of a property that you usually get tax relief for capital expenditure as a reduction in the level of taxable gain under Capital Gains Tax).

Here is a list of the typical expenses you may incur and claim against income:

- General maintenance and repairs to the property (but *not* material improvements such as replacing a laminate kitchen worktop with a granite worktop);

- Water rates, council tax, gas and electricity;

- Insurance, such as landlords' policies for buildings, contents and public liability;

- Costs of services, including the wages of gardeners and cleaners;

- Letting agent fees and management fees;

- Legal fees for lets of a year or less, or for renewing a lease for less than 50 years;

- Accountant's fees;

- Rents (if you're sub-letting), ground rents and service charges;

- Direct costs such as phone calls, stationery and advertising for new tenants;

- Vehicle running costs (only the proportion used for your rental business).

If you find that a particular expense is not incurred wholly and exclusively for the purposes of renting out the property, you may be able to make a partial deduction as long as you can identify a definite part of the expense that applies to the property or properties. Keep accurate records and receipts in all cases. Points to watch include:

- Use for a non-business purpose

- Dual purpose (i.e. part business/part private)

- Your motive or purpose in incurring the expense

- Whether or not the 'private' benefit is purely incidental

- The way in which you have apportioned the expense

3. Mortgage or Loan Interest Relief

New system for claiming loan interest

A key attraction in property rental as an *investment* has always been that you can claim interest paid on a mortgage or other loan used to acquire property as an expense against tax. This is in line with all other businesses who buy assets using loan finance and set the interest charges against the business income.

However, from April 2017, the tax relief on the finance costs on residential rental property (including buy-to-let) is being gradually reduced to the basic rate of tax. This is very unfair in my opinion, as it singles out property businesses. The transition follows a sliding scale between 2017 and 2021, ending up with a blanket credit (20%) for everybody on loan interest as their deductible claim.

Just to clarify, this is not a massive reduction from being able to claim 100% of the loan interest to only being able to claim 20%   The key point is that you can no longer simply treat loan interest as a deduction when working out your taxable income from property. Under the old rules, this meant that, if you were a higher rate taxpayer, you effectively received relief for Income Tax at your highest rate of tax. Under the new rules, no matter what Income Tax band you fall into (as an individual), your tax relief is limited to the 20% rate.

To clarify, under the old system the loan interest was *offset* as an expense against income to arrive at the pre-tax income figure that was *then* added to any other income and the whole taxed at the appropriate rate (20% or 40%). Under the new system, from 6 April 2017, instead of treating loan interest as an expense, you ignore it for the purpose of calculating your pre-tax income. However, you then look at the amount of interest and then apply the appropriate level of tax relief.

The restriction is the amount of loan interest that qualifies for relief and the rate at which the relief is applied. A 'sliding scale' is in operation which gradually increases the percentage of interest to which only relief at the basic rate (currently 20%) applies. If there is a change in the basic rate tax in the future, then the rate of relief should follow this (unless further changes are introduced).

The effect is that if your loan interest is, say, £50,000 and you are a higher rate taxpayer, then after 5 April 2020 you will only get tax relief at the rate of 20%. So you'll still be paying 20% tax (the difference between basic rate and higher rate) on that interest. You can carry forward unused relief to subsequent tax years, which is an advantage if your income from rental property is liable to fluctuate.

I've set out below a table of how the restriction is being phased in, and also a simple illustration of how it could affect the return.

The new system will hit higher-rate taxpayers but be aware that for *basic rate taxpayers* taxable income from just one rental property, when added to your other income, could take you into the higher rate tax bracket.

The new system in detail

The part of the loan interest to which the restriction to 20% basic rate tax applies (100% of loan interest from 6 April 2020) is not just a percentage of the loan interest but will be the *lower* of;

- The finance costs not already deducted from income in the tax year (25% for 2017-18, 50% for 2018-19, 75% for 2019-20 and 100% thereafter), *or*

- The profits of the property business in the tax year, or

- The total income (excluding savings and dividend income) that exceeds the personal allowance and blind person's allowance in the tax year.

However, those finance costs that fall under the new rules can include

- Mortgages

- Overdrafts

- Loans to buy furniture;

- Potentially any loans taken out to run a residential property letting business, whether the loan is for a business office, car or otherwise;

- Interest on a loan taken out to acquire an interest in a property letting partnership (but the rules differ slightly for these loans, especially regarding carry forward of unused interest relief).

- Incidental costs of obtaining the loans, premiums, discounts and returns under Sharia-compliant arrangements;

- Alternative finance returns.

If the relief is not fully utilised in the year it can be carried forward. If you are carrying forward significant losses it's always worth consulting your accountant on the impact of these and the reliefs available. You can only claim the relief while the loan is still in place and so you may wish to ensure your fully claim unused interest relief before repaying the debt altogether (if re-mortgaging then the relief will apply to the new loan).

There is no mechanism for utilising brought-forward interest that has not been relieved when a property rental business ceases and so careful planning may be needed before ceasing in the future, or incorporating your property business.

If you let both residential and commercial properties then only the loans or proportions of loans relating to the residential property business are caught by the restrictions on relief. You can claim the whole of the relief against the commercial property (which includes serviced accommodation).

Who do the new loan interest rules apply to? The new rules apply to individuals, partnerships, limited liability partnerships and trusts - but not to property-letting businesses run through limited companies (even non-resident companies), nor to serviced accommodation; nor does it affect property development businesses.

The new rules affect various types of property investors:

- Basic rate tax-payers – as mentioned earlier, those with income just below the higher rate tax threshold could easily find themselves entering it depending upon their full circumstances (and impacting on other things such as benefits being claimed);

- Higher and additional rate taxpayers who let out highly geared residential properties - who will in the future be restricted to interest relief at the basic rate only (so effectively the difference appears in the bottom line of profit) and will suffer tax at the higher rate;

- Individuals who live off a property portfolio with loans against their property and little other income. Their future income could be restricted even if they only have a small number of properties;

- Some individuals where interest relief could be carried forward indefinitely;

- Some individuals with property losses brought forward or losses arising;

- Trusts renting out property

Impact of the new rules on higher rate taxpayers:

The new rules will be phased in over a few years from 6 April 2017 and so by 6th April 2020 loan interest will be fully restricted. Here is the schedule of changes to the amounts of interest where relief is claimable, and relief rates:

Tax Year	Rate of relief
Pre-2017	100% of interest set against income so relief is @ taxpayer's income tax rate (40% or 20%)
2017-18	75% of interest @ taxpayer's income tax rate + 25% @ 20%
2018-19	50% of interest @ taxpayer's income tax rate + 50% @ 20%
2019-20	25% of I interest @ taxpayer's income tax rate + 75% @ 20%
2020-21	100% @ 20%

The new system can make a big difference – in the simple illustration below, a 93% increase in the tax liability:

Illustration

A higher rate (40%) taxpayer has rental income of £20,000 and pays loan interest of £13,000.

The position up to 5 April 2017:

Rental income	£20,000 (net of deductible expenses)
Less Loan interest	£13,000 (still deductible up to April 2017)
Pre-tax net	£ 7,000
Less tax @ 40%	£ 2,800
Remaining	**£ 4,200** in the hands of the property owner

With the new rules by 2020/21:

Rental income	£20,000 (net of deductible expenses)
Less loan interest	£13,000
Less tax	£8,000 (£20,000 @ 40%) (£1,000)
Plus tax relief	£2,600 (basic rate 20% on £13,000 loan interest)
Final net	**£ 1,600** in the hands of the property owner

So the amount of tax collected goes up from £2,800 to £5,400, an increase of 93%

Minimising the impact for higher rate tax-payers: There are various ways to minimise the impact of the new system:

- Spread property ownership between yourself and your spouse or partner, or other family members (depending on their tax position). This enables you to take advantage, as a family unit, of everyone's basic rate tax band. There may be Stamp Duty Land Tax to pay (see Section 7: All About Stamp Duty Land Tax) but there won't be any CGT on transfers between spouses;

- Look at converting suitable properties into serviced accommodation;

- Move into the commercial property market (*read more about this in Section 8. Buy-to-Let Businesses – What to Think About*)

- Look at incorporating your property portfolio in order to trade as a limited company. Just a word of warning here: do consult a property specialist accountant to ensure that this is done properly -it's easy to get wrong.

You could also reduce your debt burden by:

- Reviewing borrowings to see whether better interest rates could be achieved, although there could be a cost to re-mortgage the properties;

- Considering the sale of one or more rental properties or other assets to help repay some of the property loans and reduce the annual interest charge, but do keep an eye on possible Capital Gains Tax liability. I'm finding currently that quite a lot of investors are selling their entire portfolios.

You could also increase rent charged to tenants to offset the reduced tax reduction, but you need to be aware of potential pitfalls:

- Rent cannot normally be increased during a fixed term tenancy, unless there is a clause within the agreement that allows for it or the tenant agrees with the change.

- Plan carefully with specialist advice as there are required procedures for increasing rent.

- Tenants may be able to apply to a rent tribunal if the rent is significantly higher than other market rents in the area.

#30. Interest on personal loans to the business

When you need to raise money for your business, there are two basic routes – borrowing in the name of the business (business loan) or borrowing in your own name (personal loan) and lending the money to the business.

As discussed earlier, interest on a business loan is deductible when calculating your profit of loss, providing the loan is wholly and exclusively for a business purpose or a property letting if it is part of your business premises or a buy-to-let property. 'Wholly and exclusively' also applies to interest on overdrafts and credit cards. If you are a sole trader or part of a partnership and you also use the overdraft or credit cards for personal use, then you cannot claim **any** of the interest payments as a business expense.

However, what if you can't raise finance in the name of the business, or suppose the rates are more favourable if you take the loan in your own name? Is the interest on that loan a claimable expense against tax?

For accountancy purposes, if you personally raise money for the purposes of your limited company, LLP or ordinary partnership, it will be treated as a loan to the business in the business books and records.

You should be able to claim tax relief *personally* (via your Self-Assessment Income Tax return) against income tax for loan interest paid if the loan was a *qualifying loan*, as defined by HMRC.

Qualifying loans include those used for:

- Buying ordinary shares in, or lending money to, a close company in which you own more than 5% of the ordinary share capital on your own or with associates;

- Buying ordinary shares in, or lending money to, a close company in which you own any part of the share capital and work for the greater part of your time in the management and conduct of the company's business, or that of an associated company;

- Acquiring ordinary share capital in an employee-controlled company if you are a full-time employee – you will be regarded as a full-time employee if you work for the greater part of your time as a director or employee of the company or of a subsidiary in which the company has an interest of 51% or more;

- Acquiring a share or shares in, or to lend money to, a co-operative which is used wholly and exclusively for the purposes of its business;

- Acquiring an interest in a trading or professional partnership (including an LLP, other than an investment LLP);

- Providing a partnership, including an LLP, with funds by way of capital or premium or in advancing money, where the money contributed or advanced is used wholly for the partnership's business;

- Buying equipment or machinery for use in your work for your employer, or by a partnership (unless you have already deducted the interest as a business expense). Relief is only available if you, or the partnership, were entitled to claim capital allowances on the item(s) in question – if the equipment or machinery was used only partly for your employment, or only partly for the partnership business, only the business proportion of the loan interest or alternative finance payments qualifies for relief.

SECTION 7: ALL ABOUT STAMP DUTY LAND TAX (SDLT)

Anyone who has ever bought a house or some land is likely to have come up against this tax, either as the simple Stamp Duty of old or, since 2014, under the new guise of Stamp Duty Land Tax (SDLT). As with all tax legislation, changes aimed at either greater fairness or ease of calculation can lead to greater complexity in tax planning too. This current form, for example, has the flexibility of a sliding scale linked to the value of the purchase, which may influence purchasing decisions for investors. However, of equal interest is the question of claimable reliefs against SDLT – who is eligible and for how much. This section will provide the answers.

#31. Introducing Stamp Duty Land Tax

Stamp Duty Land Tax is a tax on the purchase of land or property, known as the purchase of a chargeable interest (which includes a lease of over 7 years). Much of this section looks at how this works when buying property, but we also touch on other forms of chargeable interest that are liable for SDLT.

The basic concept is simple:

"You must pay Stamp Duty Land Tax (SDLT) if you buy a property or land over a certain price in England and Northern Ireland." www.gov.uk

The names are different in Scotland (Land and Buildings Transaction Tax) and in Wales (Land Transaction Tax) but the basic concept is the same – once your purchase of property or land goes over a threshold, you pay a tax on the excess. An important difference to many taxes is that SDLT must be registered and paid quickly – within 14 days of completion of the transaction. So this is not a tax you can ponder at your leisure and plan for in arrears – all the more reason to learn about how it works.

SDLT liability is usually only generated through the purchase of property. It does not apply to gifts, for example if you are rearranging property ownership between spouses or other family members. Beware, however, if the property is mortgaged; if you make it condition of the gift that the donee takes over the mortgage obligations then SDLT will still be payable because a gift with conditions is not a gift for tax purposes.

'Purchase' of property, however, can include the transfer of property from an individual to a company, perhaps in return for shares. This then comes under Section 53 of Finance Act 2003, and will incur SDLT – see Limited companies: Chargeable considerations, below. It can also apply to another form of chargeable interest, the purchase of a share in a property investment partnership (see SDLT Reliefs: Partnerships, below).

Transactions not Documents: Please do remember that, unlike its predecessor, Stamp Duty, SDLT is essentially a tax on transactions, not on documents. So you cannot legally avoid SDLT by not committing a transaction to writing.

This is not as far-fetched as it sounds. Although transfer of legal title must always be in writing, I can certainly think of circumstances where a transaction can be inferred from a course of action. Suppose for example an individual A was the title-holder of a property, but consistently allowed the income to be paid to another individual B who also paid for all the expenditure on the property? A case could be made that, for example, the true owner of the property was B. The question would then be, was the transaction a gift (no SDLT) or was it on condition that B paid the mortgage (therefore not a gift and SDLT potentially payable).

#32. How SDLT works

SDLT is charged on the amount of the property cost above the tax-free threshold (£125,000 for standard SDLT), and on a sliding scale:

Purchase price £	SDLT rate	Enhanced rate for additional homes/ buy-to-lets where the cost (or deemed consideration) is over £40,000
0 – 125,000	0%	3%
125,001 – 250,000	2%	5%
250,001 – 925,000	5%	8%
925,001 – 1,500,000	10%	13%

Note that the tax is made up of increments – for example, if you buy a house as your only residence for £510,000, your SDLT bill is calculated as follows:

First £125,000 @ 0%	£0
£125,001 – 250,000 @ 2%	£2500
£250,000 – 510,000 @ 5%	£13,000
Total SDLT	£15,500

As you can also see from the table above, for additional properties the rate is 3% higher for each band.

However, there are a range of reliefs and special conditions attached to different types of purchases, examined below. The first category may not be of much interest to property investors, but it is always useful to understand the baseline of any taxation system when considering tax planning.

HOMEOWNERS
First time buyers

Definition of first time buyer: In order to count as a first time buyer in relation to SDLT, a purchaser must not, either alone or with others, have previously acquired a major interest in a dwelling or an equivalent interest in land situated anywhere in the world (but a lease or assignment of a lease with less than 21 years to run does not trigger the restriction). This includes previous acquisitions by inheritance or gift, or by a financial institution on behalf of a person under an alternative finance scheme.

First time buyer relief: Relief for first-time buyers was introduced in 2017 and applies to purchasers of *properties up to £500,000*, as long as the buyer intends to occupy as an only or main residence. The relief is applied as nil SDLT up to £300,000 and 5% of the balance above £300,000 up to £500,000.

The relief includes first time buyers purchasing through approved shared ownership schemes who do not elect to pay SDLT on the market value of the property but instead pay SDLT in stages. In the Autumn 2018 Budget this was extended further for shared ownership purchases with the same relief on the purchased share but no SDLT on the lease.

The relief only applies to individuals. If the property is purchased jointly, all the purchasers must meet the conditions in order to qualify for relief.

Overlap when replacing main residence

What happens if you own a single property – your main residence – and you are replacing it, but there is an overlap during which you technically own two properties?

Where you buy one property ahead of selling another, (with the intention of ending up with one main residence), the 3% additional property surcharge remains payable but this can be *reclaimed* if the old property is sold within three years of acquiring the new property.

The deadline for a successful reclaim is the later of:

- 12 months from selling the old home (extended from 3 months in the Finance Act 2019)

- a year from the filing date for the SDLT return for the new home.

As the three-year window for selling the old home still remains, the 2019 amendment simply means you now have a full 12 months after the sale to make your claim

Buying two houses to convert into the one main residence

What if you're buying two new main residences (as replacements) with a view to knocking them together into one residence?

It would be nice to think you can claim the refund of the additional 3% SDLT on each when you sell the old main residence within three years, but this is a grey area. On the one hand HMRC has stated that you can only claim the refund on one, i.e. one new residence for one old residence. *However* if both new dwellings are bought before you sell the old main residence then it appears there is no rule to prevent a refund

This scenario hasn't yet been tested by a tribunal, but it is clear that you can't 'double count' by selling the old main residence in the three years after buying a new one, claim the relief and then try to use it again on buying another main residence. Each main residence can only count once.

Buying an additional dwelling/residential property

The rules introduced from 1 April 2016 mean that anyone who already owns a *major interest* in a residential property pays additional SDLT on the purchase of a major interest in a further residential property or properties, irrespective of whether or not the further properties are let out.

The threshold is much lower (at £40,000) and the rates for each band are 3% higher than on the purchase of your main home (see table above). Also, if you exceed the £40,000 threshold, the 3% is payable on the whole purchase price, not just the excess over £40,000.

'Major interest' is used to exclude interests such as rights of way or of light. According to legal experts in this field there is uncertainty as to whether 'major interest' applies to an undivided share in land (that is, a tenancy in common) and if so then to what extent - so there may be scope for tax-planning there.

There was a loophole in the definition of the term 'major interest' in the context of SDLT. Case law indicated that the mere fact of owning a property jointly (an 'undivided share') did not of itself mean that each joint owner had a major interest. However the Finance Act 2019 provides that for transactions from 29 October 2018 onwards, undivided shares in land count for SDLT. In this context 'major interest' does not mean a majority interest but is used instead to exclude 'minor interests' such as rights of way and rights of light.

Mixed use property

See below under Commercial properties.

Where there is a residential element to a commercial property, then the transaction bears SDLT at the non-residential rates and therefore will not be liable for the Higher Residential Rate of 3%.

However, if a distinct part of the property is residential, then it is possible that part may bear SDLT at the residential rate and the remainder at the non-residential rate. I've included an example in the next section.

COMMERCIAL PROPERTY OWNERS
Limited companies and partnerships

There are two sets of circumstances affecting corporate bodies – buying a residential property and buying commercial property. However, there are exemptions that benefit property rental businesses and property developers.

Residential property

If buying a property that is a single dwelling over £500,000 (or which includes a dwelling), the limited company faces SDLT at 15% on the whole consideration that includes the dwelling. This also applies to partnerships and LLPs where one or more of the partners is a limited company. However, the company also pays the same additional 3% that is charged for second homes and buy-to-lets (regardless of whether the company owns additional residential properties) if it meets all of these conditions:

- The company is taking a majority interest in the dwelling; and

- The chargeable consideration for the transaction is £40,000 or more; and

- The new dwelling is not subject to a lease with an unexpired term of more than 21 years

Tax relief: The 15% rate will not apply where the property will be used for one of the following qualifying purposes:

- a property rental business (defined as one which acquires property in order to receive income by way of receipt of rents);

- property developers and traders;

- property made available to the public;

- financial institutions acquiring property in the course of lending;

- property occupied by employees;

- farmhouses.

Instead the standard rate SDLT will apply (including the additional 3% for purchases of dwelling by 'non-natural persons' i.e. companies, partnerships including a company and collective investment schemes).

There is a claw back if within three years the property ceases to be used for a qualifying purpose or is occupied by a 'non-qualifying individual' which means a director, director's spouse or a person related to either of them.

If you are buying more than one residential property through a limited company, then Multiple Dwellings Relief (see below) still applies and may reduce your SDLT bill further.

Commercial properties

Firstly, the definition of commercial properties includes a purchase of *at least six residential properties in a single transaction* (it also applies to property built for commercial use, to woodlands, agricultural property and to any land or property not used as a residence).

The additional 3% SDLT described above is *not* applicable to commercial property. Instead you pay on increasing portions of the property price for any purchase of £150,000 or more – 2% on the first £100,000 (i.e. £150,000 – 250,000) and 5% on the remainder.

Although the threshold is higher than for residential property the real advantage is that by buying commercial property (including six houses at a time) you avoid the additional 3% rate of SDLT. Furthermore, the purchaser can *choose* whether or not to treat the purchase of 6+ dwellings as a commercial transaction, and it is worth checking the figures to see which works our best, especially if Multiple Dwellings Relief applies (see below).

Mixed use properties

Where a property is used partly as a residence and partly for commercial, such as a shop with living accommodation upstairs, this will usually attract the commercial rate of SDLT. However, problems can arise where the sale is of a residence with a large amount of grounds and outbuildings – it cannot be assumed that these will count as residential. Previously, HMRC guidance (which was considered by the First Tier Tribunal in the 2019 case of P N Bewley Ltd v HMRC – see more below) was that only the land *necessary* for the enjoyment of the dwelling was classed as residential, but HMRC has now published guidance that *all* land that goes with a dwelling will be treated as residential (other than any part which has business use).

In another 2019 case, Hymans v HMRC, the taxpayers had purchased a house with 3.5 acres of grounds and argued that what was described as 'meadow' was neither garden nor grounds, as it was separated from the garden by a hedge and there was a public bridleway crossing the meadow. This argument, if successful, would result in the whole transaction being classified as 'mixed use' in which case the commercial rate of SDLT would have applied, not the residential rate.

In deciding in favour of HMRC, the judge took into account that 'meadow' was intended to be enjoyed with the house and to enhance its amenities, and was available for the house-owners' use. 'Grounds' was clearly a term which was more extensive than 'garden' (which also suggested a degree of cultivation). The judge ruled that it was not necessary for the grounds to be used for any particular purpose, nor was the separation by a fence, or the rights over the bridleway, conclusive.

It appears that use is a key factor and that only active use for agricultural or other non-residential purposes would allow for land to be classed as non-residential. However the judgement in this case did not specifically cover the situation where land ancillary to a dwelling is also used for a commercial purpose (for example, let out for shooting), so there may possibly still be room for argument there!

There is of course ample scope for nuances and interpretation of the HMRC stance, and no surprise therefore that cases go to tribunal. For example:

- Take a large house with former stabling used as an office and a former barn that you intend to convert to residential; the office will attract commercial rates, but the barn may not, depending upon the previous use of the barn and the planning status at the point of purchase. The crucial factor is not what the buyer intends to do with the barn but whether it has been used as part of the amenity of the house or as a separate facility that might be classed as commercial (see Properties under construction and derelict properties, below).

- It is also possible for agricultural land to be treated as being residential. For example, if a house has paddocks that are used for grazing, one would assume that use was not residential. However it could be held that the main benefit was the pleasant rural outlook afforded to the house - does this make it residential? The Hymans case suggests that this might well be so.

- Or, where a grazing licence (which clearly rendered the land agricultural) was terminated several days before completion and then reinstated on completion, isn't this just a ruse to dodge the commercial SDLT? Conveyancing law would not accept a 'scintilla' of time in the course of a transaction when, for example, a property is technically not subject to mortgage, as the seller's mortgage is redeemed and before the buyer's mortgage is actioned. Do similar considerations apply to SDLT law?

This distinction – and lack of clarity – is especially important when the purchaser is a company as the difference (for a property over £500,000) is between SDLT at the residential rate of 15% or the commercial rate of only 5% (and then only on the amount above £250,000 plus 2% on the £150-250k band).

The Bewley case, 2019, is still very recent at the time of writing, and we have yet to see its fuller impact on construction projects and derelict properties but you can read more about it in The Bewley Case, below.

Properties under construction and derelict properties

The rules relating to the purchase of properties under construction are complex, especially where these will be dwellings and so attract residential SDLT, and possibly at the higher rates.

The **HMRC definition of a dwelling** is unhelpful as it refers to a property that 'is a dwelling or is suitable for use as a dwelling'. So this means that if a property is capable of supporting habitation it will be classed as a dwelling. However, if the building is derelict yet someone is actually living in it, this will still be a dwelling even if the living conditions for the occupier are very uncomfortable. This is relevant in the light of the practice of installing a property guardian in an unoccupied property to prevent squatting. No matter what the state of the property the presence of the property guardian means that it's a dwelling.

This may seem clear, but the definition also has a second arm - that the term 'dwelling' also applies to a property that is in the course of being constructed or adapted as a dwelling. The question is: *At what point does this attract the residential rate of SDLT?*

At what stage does a building project become liable to residential SDLT?

Unfortunately this is currently rather a grey area. For example, with new build projects does the granting of planning permission for housing on some land for development bring the land within the residential regime for SDLT; what happens if the construction never goes ahead?

Attempts have been made to answer the fundamental question of when SDLT liability kicks in by using various tests, each offering a different stage in a project. For example:

- The 'golden brick' - a test commonly used in VAT, which basically means the development becomes residential when the first row of bricks is visible above ground;

- When the walls start to be built on the foundations;

- When the foundations are installed;

- When the excavation for the foundations starts.

Whatever the answer, it becomes even more complex if you are building a number of dwellings such as a block of flats, i.e. separate properties but all sharing the one foundation. As soon as the chosen test is met (e.g. the 'golden brick' test), *all* the dwellings will be treated as eligible for residential SDLT, even if the ground floor is intended for non-residential use (for example, where the building consists of a shop with flats above).

Land that is, or is to be, occupied or enjoyed with the dwelling, such as a garden or grounds (including any building or structure on such land), is taken to be part of the dwelling. This will usually be a question of fact depending on the individual circumstances of each case and please see my comments on Mixed use properties above and also the discussion of the Hymans case.

When does SDLT become payable?

Whatever rate of SDLT applied to the transaction, the rules regarding payment are the same. SDLT is payable within 14 days of the 'effective date'. So what does this mean?

In a transaction that consists of exchange of contracts followed by completion (even if this occurs on the same day) the effective date will be the completion date as the buyer will then be entitled to the property. Even if actual occupation is delayed, this will not alter the effective date.

However if you enter into a contract where the legal completion is deferred until the happening of a specific event, or until one party gives notice to the other, then the effective date may be different. The key to this is whether the contract has been 'substantially performed'. If so, then the date of substantial performance is the effective date and governs the liability to SDLT.

Generally, substantial performance is the point at which

- any payment of rent is made

- payment of most of the consideration other than rent is made

- the purchaser is entitled to possession

With regard to the last point, the purchaser does not have to have become entitled to possession under the terms of the contract. If, for example, the seller allows the purchaser to have possession on licence, then the purchaser has still become entitled to possession and SDLT will become payable.

The timing of the effective date will not usually affect the amount of SDLT payable as this will usually be set at the point of contract. However if, for example the sale is coupled with a construction contract which provides that the purchaser will carry out the work, then the consideration upon which the SDLT is calculated will be the value of the land plus any construction carried out on it at the date on which the land is transferred to the buyer.

The Bewley Case – SDLT on uninhabitable dwellings

That the term 'uninhabitable dwellings' appears to be a contradiction in terms is a good indication of the complexity of this issue. However, whether or not a property is classed as residential can make a big difference to the amount of SDLT payable, largely as a result of the imposition of the Higher Rate SDLT at 3% of the total consideration.

Fortunately, the First Tier Tribunal judgement on the January 2019 case of P N Bewley Ltd v HMRC should prove very helpful to any developer buying a property which is not suitable for habitation. There will no doubt be a number of new cases following this one, leading possibly to new legislation, so it is worth examining the case and its implications.

Before the case challenged the status quo, HMRC considered that if a building is not in use at the effective date (usually when you complete the purchase) but its last use was as a dwelling, it will be taken to be 'suitable for use as a dwelling' and treated as residential property, unless evidence is produced to the contrary.

However the Bewley case clearly established that the crucial words are 'suitable' for habitation, not 'capable ' of habitation. So, for example, if a property is in fact being lived in, but is not suitable for residence, this now appears to over-ride the HMRC definition of a dwelling (which includes a property that is 'used as a dwelling' as well as one that is 'suitable for use as a dwelling')

The Bewley case concerned the purchase of a dilapidated and uninhabited/ uninhabitable bungalow with the intention to demolish and build anew. The buyer's SDLT return was apparently made on the basis of the ordinary residential rate with the excess over £125,00 being charged at 2% = £1,500. However HMRC ruled that the Higher Rate of 3% also applied to the whole consideration which raised the SDLT to £7,500.

The taxpayer's case presented to the First Tier Tribunal was that whether or not the Higher Rate applied depended upon whether the property was habitable when purchased. The judgement established the principle that the crucial point is whether the property is habitable immediately on completion and, as I've mentioned, this means 'suitable'.

Of course whether or a property meets this criterion is a matter of fact in each case, but it is worth noting that the Housing Act 1957 states that a habitable property is one in which a functioning toilet, bathing and cooking facilities are available to the occupier.

The outcome of the Bewley case was that the Tribunal not only ruled that the Higher Rate did not apply but also went further and ruled that SDLT should have been charged at the commercial/non-residential rate, not the ordinary residential rate. The purchase price was £200,000 so this ruling meant that the rate of SDLT was still 2% but the threshold was £150,000 not £125,000. So the SDLT payable was reduced from £1,500 to £1,000 (the difference of 2% of £25,000).

So, how might this affect construction projects in the future?

It is still a very new case, but should be good news for anyone renovating derelict houses. Let's look at a couple of hypothetical examples:

1. A developer buys a dilapidated house for £79,500. This is below the residential threshold, but the Higher Rate of 3% applies, resulting in SDLT of £2,385.

   However, if it can be established that the house is not immediately habitable on completion, then non-residential SDLT will apply, so no Higher Rate, the price is below the threshold of £150,000 and no SDLT will be payable.

2. In another example, the house is purchased for £149,500 and the ordinary SDLT (2% on the band £125,001 to £250,000) is £490. However Higher Rate at 3% of the total price is a further £4,485. But if the house is not immediately habitable on completion, then the application of the non-residential rate means that, as the price is below the threshold of £150,000, no SDLT will be payable.

The only point to watch is the interaction of the Bewley decision with the part of the HMRC definition that catches property being constructed or adapted for use as a dwelling. This does not seem to have been a problem in the Bewley decision, although in that case the original bungalow was being demolished in order to rebuild, rather than being renovated. On the face of it, the Bewley decision means that any property uninhabitable at the completion date will be chargeable to SDLT as non-residential, irrespective of the buyer's future intentions.

Chargeable consideration for property transferred to a limited company

When property is transferred to a company, rather than being sold in a conventional way, it is still liable to SDLT, assessed on the basis of 'chargeable consideration'.

Section 53 of the Finance Act 2003 applies to all transactions between a company and a vendor (whether an individual or company), when the company is the purchaser. The chargeable consideration for such transactions will be not less than the market value at the effective date of the property transferred, irrespective of the consideration (or lack of it) actually passing.

It is important to understand that S53 also applies where vendor is connected (as an individual or a company) with the 'buying' company and receives shares in the company in consideration of the property transfer. The definition of 'connected companies' is in section 1122 Corporation Tax Act 2102 where sub-section (2) states:

A company is connected with another company if—

(a) the same person has control of both companies,

(b) a person ("A") has control of one company and persons connected with A have control of the other company,

(c) A has control of one company and A together with persons connected with A have control of the other company, or

(d) a group of two or more persons has control of both companies and the groups either consist of the same persons or could be so regarded if (in one or more cases) a member of either group were replaced by a person with whom the member is connected.

(And the Act also defines how specific individuals, rather than companies, may also be regarded as being 'connected'.)

In essence, a subsidiary company (or LLP) will always be connected to its parent because the parent controls the subsidiary and therefore whoever controls the parent also controls the subsidiary (see paragraph G for definition of group companies).

Transactions caught by section 53 will always be deemed to be at the market value (in this case, what you would expect to be paid for a long lease in an arms' length transaction), and the SDLT will be calculated on this basis.

What else can be included in a property transaction eligible for chargeable consideration?

As well as money, the consideration can include items such as:

- goods;

- works or services;

- release from a debt;

- transfer of (taking on) a debt.

The chargeable consideration includes any paid-for assets that form part of the land or property, including:

- buildings and structures that are part of the land;

- fixtures and fittings, including bathroom and kitchen fittings, but not carpets, curtains or free-standing furniture;

- intangible assets (for example, the value of goodwill attached to the land).

It also includes the estimated value of a commitment to do work or services (for example, a promise from the seller to repair the property).

Also, the SDLT return where you are buying commercial property (or mixed residential/commercial) asks whether this is part of the purchase of a business. Suppose for example you were buying a restaurant where the premises are valued at £250,000 and the goodwill at £100,000. HMRC rules say that SDLT is chargeable on any goodwill that forms part of the land on the sale of a business. According to HMRC guidance "What is described as the goodwill can actually form part of the land. This is often described as inherent goodwill because it is inherent in the land".

What does this mean? In this example, it would be difficult to separate the goodwill from the location of the premises, so the goodwill is inherent goodwill and accordingly SDLT should be assessed on the full £350,000 paid.

However, it's worth remembering that in a typical sale and purchase contract for a business, the purchase price will be apportioned between the various assets including any properties. The considerations for buyer and seller when agreeing these values are not aligned, so will be a matter of negotiation. I recommend always speaking to your accountant before agreeing these values to make sure you understand the taxation implications. Although you can alter the apportionments by making an election jointly with the seller (*see Section 5: Getting to Know Capital Taxes, Allowances, Reliefs and Schemes*) it's much safer to do it in the contract.

In the context of property and SDLT, if the value assigned to the property or lease is in fact an undervalue then on the face of it there isn't a problem. After all, if there is no SDLT on a gift, then an undervalue must mean it's partially a gift - right? Well, please refer to my comment above on the necessity for the chargeable consideration to reflect a fair market value or other fair and reasonable apportionment, and also on 'inherent goodwill'.

Just a reminder: where the transaction is between connected companies s.53 Finance Act 2003 provides that the deemed chargeable consideration will be not less than the market value at the effective date of the property transferred, irrespective of the consideration (or lack of it) actually passing. Also, as mentioned in Section 4. Understanding VAT, SDLT is calculated on the while consideration which includes the VAT incurred on the transaction.

One final point that you might need to consider is the situation where you as freeholder have leased a building to a tenant. You may have a buyer who wants to take free of the lease and you may be able to negotiate with the tenant for vacant possession. It is tempting to regard any payment made by way of compensation to the tenant to be a 'reverse premium' (which is exempt from SDLT). But beware; if the effect is that you 'enlarge your estate' (in other words the result is that you have the freehold with vacant possession, instead of subject to the lease) this is likely to be a chargeable event for SDLT. It's a complex area but the circumstances are not as unlikely as you might think, especially where the tenant is in fact a company connected to you.

#33. SDLT Reliefs
MULTIPLE DWELLINGS RELIEF (MDR)

The basic rule is that buying a second or subsequent residential property (unless it is to replace your main residence) will usually attract Higher Rate SDLT at an additional 3%. However, if you're buying more than one residential property (including a property with more than one dwelling in the same building), then MDR may help, provided that you are buying the properties in the same transaction or in a linked transaction (see below).

There is a minimum level of SDLT payable where MDR applies and this is 1% of the total consideration for the purchase. MDR does not apply to the transfer of a freehold reversion or head lease where a dwelling has a long lease of 21 years or more.

How MDR can help

MDR works by calculating the SDLT on each dwelling by reference to the average price of all the dwellings. So you may be able to save SDLT if you are buying where some properties are in the lower rates.

For example, *without* MDR: if you were buying three properties at the same time or in a linked transaction and the purchase prices were £500,000, £275,000 and £124,000 then the total purchase price would be £899,000. The SDLT (taken as a linked transaction) would be £34,950 plus Higher Rate of 3% of the whole consideration which is a further £26,970 making a total of £61,920 (unless one of the properties was for your main residence in which case the Higher Rate would not apply to this part of the transaction - or could be claimed back).

However, if MDR applies then the consideration per property for SDLT is the total price of the properties purchased divided by their number, so £899,000 divided by three is £299,670; and the actual tax calculation for each property looks like this:

SDLT (basic) on £299,670 = £4,983 with 3% Higher Rate = £8,990. Total SDLT £13,973.

You then multiply this figure by the number of properties in the transaction or linked transaction (in other words, averaging out the SDLT). And the result is that the SDLT on the whole transaction would be 3 x £13,973 = £41,919, a saving of £20,000!

A special case is the purchase of a house with a granny annexe (or similar). If the annexe is a 'dwelling' the on the face of it anyone buying the whole building would be purchasing two dwellings and therefore at least one of them would be liable for Higher Rate SDLT. HMRC defines dwelling as:

"a building or part of a building which is suitable for use as a single dwelling or is in the process of being constructed or adapted for such use."

However, an amendment to the rules at the time the Higher Rate SDLT was brought in indicates that a purchaser will not be treated as buying two separate dwellings for SDLT purposes (and therefore liable to Higher Rate SDLT) if:

1. An apportionment of the purchase price on a fair and reasonable basis results in at least two thirds being allocated to the main dwelling;

2. The 'subsidiary' dwelling is part of the same building or the same grounds.

So on a purchase of a house and annexe at a total of £500,000, as a main residence, the amount of SDLT would be £10,000 (0% on first £125,000, 2% on next £125,000 and 3% on the remainder) and there will be no Higher Rate SDLT as long as the qualifications set out above are met. If however, applying MDR, the apportionment were say £120,000 to the annex, then the average price would be £250,000 (£500,000 divided by 2) and the SDLT on this would be £2,500.

2 x £2,500 = £5,000 so again a large saving compared to the figure of £10,000 applied to the total cost of £500,000 as a single transaction.

Beware however if the transaction is liable for Higher Rate SDLT. Unless you are able to somehow separate the annexe from the main house (which is unlikely as HMRC will see it as a linked transaction), the whole transaction will bear a further 3% SDLT making a total of £17,500. Applying MDR will still mean that the average price is £250,000 but the SDLT on that will be £10,000 (£2,500 plus 3% of £250,000 - remember that for the Higher Rate the £125,000 nil rate does not apply).

2 x £10,000 = £20,000 so you would be worse off.

Claiming MDR

The good news is that MDR is not applied automatically – you can do the maths and decide which is the best option.

Bear in mind that, if you are buying 6 or more residential properties in the same transaction (or a linked transaction, see below) then you can elect to treat this as commercial and the commercial rates apply. This gives you a nil-rate threshold of £150,000 (for the total cost) but the real advantage is that the additional higher rate SDLT of 3% does not apply to commercial transactions. Also bear in mind that where you buy a property with mixed residential and commercial use (e.g. a shop with a flat above), you pay on the commercial scale and the higher rate doesn't apply.

The fact that the commercial threshold and SDLT rates apply does not appear to prevent you using MDR to average out the SDLT payable, but the benefit may be less. If you are buying between 2 and 5 residential properties, either in a single transaction or in a linked transaction, then although you are subject to the residential rate and the higher rate of SDLT, you can still use MDR to reduce the overall SDLT.

As MDR works by averaging out the price over the number of properties purchased, clearly it is only likely to be of benefit where at least one of the properties is worth substantially less than the other(s).

PARTNERSHIPS

Buying property: If a partnership already owns a residential property and buys another residential property for the partnership then the higher rate SDLT will apply. However, of you are a partner but are buying a property for yourself (and have no other properties in your own name), then the rules do not apply to the other partners unless they are your spouse.

Buying a share in a partnership: Although SDLT is a tax on land transactions, the sale of a share in a property investment partnership is treated as a sale of land.

Relief is available where one partner puts land into a partnership in which he is a partner, and is calculated on the basis of Market Value (MV) – the best price that might reasonably be obtained in a transaction between a willing buyer and a wiling seller 'at arms' length' on a given date. The principle behind the relief is that, as one of the purchasing partners, he already owns a share commensurate with his partnership shares. This is known as 'sum of lower proportions' (SLP) and works in relation to the definition of two key roles, *relevant owner and corresponding partner*. The process is quite complex (there is a simple illustration further below), but first let's define these two key roles.

A person is a *relevant owner* if:

1. immediately before the transaction, he was entitled to a proportion of the chargeable interest (the subject being purchased) and

2. immediately after the transaction, he is a partner or connected with a partner.

For each relevant owner, a person is a *corresponding partner* if, immediately after the transaction:

1. he is a partner, and

2. he is the relevant owner (or is an individual connected with the relevant owner).

If there is no relevant owner with a corresponding partner, the sum of the lower proportions is nil.

To calculate the relief:

For each relevant owner, find the proportion of the chargeable interest to which he was entitled immediately before the transaction, and apportion that proportion between any one or more of the relevant owner's corresponding partners. There is no set method of performing this apportionment and it can be carried out to give the most beneficial result.

Find the lower proportion for each person who is a corresponding partner in relation to one or more relevant owners.

The lower proportion is:

1. the proportion of the chargeable interest attributable to the partner (see below), or

2. if lower, the partner's partnership share immediately after the transaction.

The proportion of the chargeable interest attributable to the partner is:

1. (if he is a corresponding partner in relation to only one relevant owner) the proportion (if any) of the chargeable interest apportioned to him in respect of that owner;

2. (if he is a corresponding partner in relation to more than one relevant owner) the sum of the proportions (if any) of the chargeable interest apportioned to him in respect of each of those owners.

Add together the lower proportions of each person who is a corresponding partner in relation to one or more relevant owners.

The result is the sum of the lower proportions.

How are other parties treated?

Sometimes it is not simply a relevant owner and corresponding partner. Here are two other parties who might be involved in the process:

Joint tenants: People who are entitled to a chargeable interest as beneficial joint tenants are taken to be entitled to the chargeable interest as beneficial tenants in common.

Limited companies: A company is to be treated as an individual connected with the relevant owner in so far as it:

1. holds property as trustee, and

2. is connected with the relevant owner only because of section 1122(7) of the Taxes Act 1988.

Let's now look at a practical example.

Suppose a husband and wife are in partnership and the husband wishes to introduce land owned by him.

The formula for calculating SDLT liability is MV x (100 – (SLP))%

What this means is that if the land being put into the partnership is effectively retained by the transferor-partner (or persons connected with the transferor) after the transaction, you basically end up with:

MV x (100-100) = £0

If husband and wife owned the land 50% each, they could transfer the property to a company for 50% of the shares each and in theory there would be no SDLT charge.

NB: Going back to Section 2. Property and the law, you will realise that you need to satisfy HMRC that the any restructuring is for **Commercial Reasons**, otherwise it will be caught by anti-tax avoidance rules.

INTRA-GROUP RELIEF FOR TRANSFERS TO, BY OR BETWEEN COMPANIES

Transfers to, by or between companies are treated just the same as those for individuals. However, where the companies are in the same group (where one is the 75% subsidiary of the other or both are 75% subsidiaries of a third company – see What constitutes a company group, below), then *intra-group relief* may apply.

This relief allows groups to move property for commercial reasons without having to consider stamp duty land tax implications. You will notice the requirement for 'commercial reasons', so it's always a good idea to get advance clearance from the Stamp Duty Land Tax Office. If intra-group relief applies then it is claimed by ticking the appropriate box on the SDLT return made by the purchasing company and no SDLT will be payable.

There are, however, some restrictions:

- No relief is available where, at the effective date of the transaction, there are arrangements in existence which would mean that a person, or persons, could obtain control of the purchaser but not of the vendor (irrespective of whether or not this actually happens);

- Relief is not available where a non-group company or person is, directly or indirectly, to provide or receive all or part of the consideration for the transaction, and this is done in connection with, or in pursuance of, an arrangement;

- Group relief is not available where, in connection with, or in pursuance of, an arrangement or arrangements, the purchaser ceases (or could cease) to be in the same group as the vendor. There are clawback provisions, and an obligation to make a new SDLT return if the purchaser ceases to be a member of the same group as the vendor:

  o before the end of a period of three years beginning with the effective date of the relevant land transaction; or

  o in pursuance of, or in connection with, arrangements made before the end of a period of three years beginning with the effective date of the relevant land transaction

The Finance Act 2003 Schedule 7 introduced further restrictions, stating that group relief is not available where a transaction:

- is not effected for bona fide commercial reasons, or,

- forms part of arrangements of which the main purpose, or one of the main purposes, is the avoidance of tax

'Tax' in this context means income tax, CGT, corporation tax, SDLT or stamp duty - so quite wide-ranging!

The bona fide 'commercial reasons' test is crucial if any transaction in property has the capacity of triggering any of the restrictions. For example, suppose a property-owing company is acquired and then, after the acquisition, the property is transferred into another company in the group, Or suppose, after transferring the property out, the original property-owning company is wound up. Provided HMRC are satisfied that the transactions were not entered into with the objective of avoiding tax, then the relief will not be denied, and there is HMRC guidance setting out a list of transactions where, unless there is evidence of intent to avoid tax, group relief will not be denied. The list is not exclusive, and transactions of a similar nature would also qualify for relief.

Intra-group relief on granting of new leases

In a recent case, we were able to establish that intra-group relief for companies applies not only to transfers of freeholds and existing leaseholds but also to the grant of a new lease. Despite the first ruling from HMRC that the relief did not extend to new leases, we noticed that the relevant legislation (Schedule 7 Finance Act 2003) referred to 'transactions' not simply 'transfers' as stated in the HMRC SDLT Internal Manual. This experience shows that it's always a good idea to go back to the statutory authority, if there is one. We challenged HMRC on this basis and they agreed with our view!

We've also looked in detail at exactly how far the intra-group relief extends - with some interesting results. For example, as well as looking at leases entered into between companies on an ordinary commercial basis (e.g. a parent company leasing the business premises to a subsidiary trading company) we also looked at a company owning a freehold creating long leases (i.e. 99 years upwards) of flats to a subsidiary. These could then be sold on to residential purchasers be by way of an assignment (i.e. transfer) of the existing lease rather than the grant of a new lease. The assignment would of course be for a capital sum (the premium).

An attractive possibility is the creation of the new leases without any premium, but simply reserving the ground rent. In this case the SDLT would be assessed on the 'Net Present Value' ('NPV') that would be calculated on the ground rent payable during the first five years. For a 99-year lease with annual ground rent of £750 (plus VAT if an option to tax is in force), the NPV would be below the SDLT threshold.

The advantages would be that the management of the flats (including any short-term letting) would then be carried out by the subsidiary as a separate business. Also, should it be necessary to mortgage, most commercial lenders require there to be a leasehold structure in place for the whole building (a problem if only some of the flats have been sold on long leases).

What constitutes a company group?

For the purposes of group relief for SDLT, companies will be in the same group if one is the 75% subsidiary of the other or both are 75% subsidiaries of a third company. (Note: this requirement for 75% is higher than the general definition of group for company law or for other tax reliefs, which generally means over 50%)

So company B is the 75% subsidiary of company A if company A satisfies one or more of the following conditions:

- Is beneficial owner of not less than 75% of the ordinary share capital (either directly or through another company or companies as determined by sections 1155 to 1157 of Corporation Tax Act 2010) of company B;

- Is beneficially entitled to not less than 75% of the profits available for distribution to equity holders of company B;

- Would be beneficially entitled to not less than 75% of any assets of company B available for distribution to its equity holders on a winding-up

'Ordinary share capital' for this purpose means all the issued share capital of the company, by whatever name called, apart from share capital that only confers rights to a fixed dividend with no other rights to participate in the profits of the company.

Not just 'companies': Although all the HMRC guidance refers to 'companies' the legislation itself refers to 'a body corporate'. An LLP is in law a body corporate (although its members are taxed as individuals just as in the case of an ordinary partnership). HMRC initially took the view that group relief for SDLT did not apply to LLPs but this view changed in 2014. HMRC now accepts that for the purposes of SDLT group relief, a 'body corporate' does include an LLP. An LLP can therefore be the parent in a group structure. However, as an LLP doesn't itself have issued ordinary share capital it cannot be the subsidiary of other companies.

Also, an LLP cannot claim group relief itself because its chargeable interests in land are treated as held by or on behalf of the individual members, but it is possible that the members themselves (if limited companies) may be able to claim group relief if they themselves are in the same group.

To claim group relief, the group relationship must exist at the date of the lease or, if earlier, the agreement to grant the lease.

SALE AND LEASEBACK RELIEF

In one of the above examples I referred to the case of a parent company leasing business premises to a subsidiary. This will qualify for intra-group relief for SDLT (as it would in the less situation of the subsidiary leasing to the parent. However, care needs to be taken if the transaction involves the transfer of the freehold (or leasehold) between companies and the lease or sub-lease back.

Where this is two separate transactions (even if the linked transactions rules apply) then 100% intra-group relief should apply to both. However, in some circumstances intra-group relief will not apply but sale and leaseback relief may.

What is a sale and leaseback transaction?

A sale and leaseback transaction is one in which

- A transfers or grants to B a major interest in land, (the sale), and

- B grants a lease out of that interest to A (the leaseback).

This transaction is an exchange, so both parts of the transaction are, under the provisions of section 47 Finance Act 2003, chargeable on the greater of either the market value of the interests transferred, or the consideration given. However, where all the conditions of S57A (3) are met, the leaseback element will be exempt. These conditions are:

- the sale transaction must be entered into wholly or partly in consideration of the leaseback; and

- the interest leased back must be an interest out of the original interest; and

- the sale leg must be in wholly or partly in consideration of the leaseback, where partly the only other consideration is the payment of money or release from/assumption of a debt; and

- there is no transfer of rights under section 45 or 45A Finance Act 2003 involved in the transaction; and

- where A and B are both bodies corporate at the effective date they are **not** members of the same group for the purposes of group relief (paragraph 1 Schedule 7 Finance Act 2003).

The chargeable consideration for the sale leg will depend upon whether there was a written agreement, at the time of the sale, for the leaseback leg to be entered into. If there was, the chargeable consideration for the sale leg should take this encumbrance into account

Amendments inserted by the Finance Act 2004 extended the scope of the relief so that it now applies in circumstances where the sale is effected by the grant of a lease followed by an underlease back. The relief is also available in respect of sale and leaseback transactions in residential property. The leaseback element of an equity release or home reversion transaction may benefit from relief if all the qualifying conditions are met.

There is no particular requirement for a leaseback to be in consideration of only one sale, or for one sale to be in consideration of only one leaseback for the relief to apply. It is possible to have one sale with multiple leasebacks and also to have several sales with only one leaseback.

As you will see, there are two main points to be considered in looking at whether intra-group relief or sale and leaseback relief apply where the transactions are between companies. The first and most significant concerns the *contractual arrangement*, so it's really important to get this right. If the sale is arranged in such a way that part of the consideration is that the buyer will then grant a lease back to the buyer then, if there is a written agreement to that effect, s 47 Finance Act 2003 will apply. It's interesting to note that the effect of s.47, if it applies, is to govern the way in which SDLT on the sale and leaseback is charged. Unlike intra-group relief, it does not have to be specifically claimed and it's not a matter of choice. If it applies then the SDLT is paid on the sale but the leaseback is exempt

The second is that sale and leaseback SDLT applies to all purchasers, but the relief can only apply to transactions between companies if they are not in the same group   - whereas intra-group relief obviously can only be claimed if they are.

LINKED TRANSFERS

This is a 'trap' you can fall into if you decide to split up (artificially) a property transaction into several smaller transactions so that the total SDLT is reduced (for example, selling a house and the garden ground separately).

The problem is that where two or more property transactions involve the same buyer and seller, they count as 'linked' for SDLT. In this case SDLT is charged on the total value of all linked transactions. This may mean that you pay a higher rate of SDLT than if the transactions are counted individually. The 'same buyer and seller' includes 'connected' individual such as a relative, for example your brother, sister, parent, grandparent, husband, wife or civil partner - or one of their relatives. If the buyer or seller is a business, a connected person would be a business partner and their relatives. It also includes companies and groups of companies who are connected to the business, or companies connected to each other.

Transactions can also be linked if there's more than one transaction or the transactions are part of a single arrangement or scheme or part of a series of transactions. For example:

- if the transactions are part of the same single arrangement or scheme, whether you document them separately or not. If each transaction has a separate contract, and if the sales are part of the same deal, they count as linked for SDLT.

So in the example of splitting the house and the garden into two sales, one to a main buyer and the other to their relative, the two transactions are linked. They're connected people and they're buying things from the same seller as part of a single deal.

If a sale is followed by one or more related sales and there's something to link all the transactions together, they count as linked transactions for SDLT. There's no limit to the length of time between the transactions.

Examples include someone who is a property speculator buying a new house from a builder and later, you buy a second and finally a third house. Suppose the builder offers a special price for the second and third houses, then all three transactions will be linked. **How SDLT is charged in linked transactions**: Where transactions are linked, the amount of the SDLT due on the total chargeable consideration for all the transactions is calculated and then apportioned between the transactions in proportion to their share of the total chargeable consideration.

Whether or not any series of transactions is 'linked' is a matter of fact. For example, it is not beyond the bounds of possibility that a buyer could negotiate via the sellers' agent(s) for the purchase of two apparently unconnected properties, only to find that the seller of each property is the same. Subject to satisfying HMRC that this was merely a coincidence, this would not be a linked transaction.

There is no time limit beyond which a series of transactions will not be treated as linked - it is a matter of fact and, apart from the main criteria for connected persons or companies, the deciding factor will be whether the first transaction affects the subsequent transactions. So the length of time between transactions could be relevant - but the more closely the parties are connected, the more difficult it will be to show that the transactions are not linked.

Alternative options: Where you buy six or more residential properties in a single transaction, then you can apply the commercial threshold and rates of SDLT to the whole transaction. And you can still apply Multiple Dwellings Relief to a linked transaction, but you can't apply it if you've elected to treat 6+ dwellings as a commercial transaction - see which one works out best.

GENERAL EXEMPTIONS FROM SDLT

There are some general exemptions from SDLT and these include:

- transfers by way of gift (as long as there are no conditions attached to the gift, as discussed above)

- transfers of property out of the estate of a deceased person to the beneficiary entitled under the will or under the intestacy rules (whether they are entitled to the specific property or to a share of the estate)

- transfers on divorce or dissolution of a civil partnership

- purchase of a freehold property for less than £40,000

- purchase of a new or existing leasehold of 7 years or more, as long as the premium is less than £40,000 and the annual rent is less than £1,000

- grant of a new lease (or tenancy) for less than 7 years or the transfer of an existing lease with less than seven years to run as long as the chargeable consideration is less than the residential or non-residential SDLT threshold for leases

- transfers occurring as a result of using alternative property financial arrangements, for example to comply with Sharia law

Where a transaction is exempt, there is no need to file an SDLT return. However the computation of the SDLT thresholds for leases can be complex (relying on the concept of Net Present Value - which relates to the duration and the level of rent).

If a transaction is not exempt, but you are claiming one of the reliefs discussed earlier, then you still need to file an SDLT return, even if no SDLT is payable.

It's best to get professional advice on the liability to SDLT in all but the most straightforward of cases. Mistakes can be very costly.

STAMP DUTY ON SECURITIES TRANSACTIONS

As stated, this has been replaced by SDLT for property transactions. However it does still apply to transactions in securities.

Technically a transfer of 'certificated' shares will always require a stock transfer form (J30). You may feel that in this electronic age and with the use of computerised company secretarial systems, paper share certificates are a thing of the past. However, I notice that the current edition of the Model Articles (provided by Companies House) requires that a share certificate be issued (although I'm well aware that in many cases the record is kept electronically and paper shares are not issued). The transfer of certificated shares is therefore by a stock transfer form.

I understand that paper share certificates are likely to be a thing of the past by 2025. However as the moment, whatever company secretarial system you use, if you are transferring shares in your property company then you will almost certainly be transferring them by stock transfer form.

The significance of this is that this document may be liable to stamp duty. If the consideration for the transfer is less than £1,000, (and as long as it is not part of a larger transaction) then you can sign Certificate 1 on the back of the form and there is no Stamp Duty to pay. Alternatively, you can sign Certificate 2 if the transaction is exempt (for example by way of gift). Otherwise you must send the document to the Stamp Office with the ad valorem duty (currently at 0.5%). It is technically illegal for whoever keeps the statutory records to accept for registration a stock transfer form that is not stamped (unless it bears the appropriate certificate).

As a rule, there is no stamp duty to pay on the allotment (issue) of new shares to a shareholder, even if the shareholder is paying a premium over and above the face value of the share.

What if certificates cease to be required? Stamp Duty was originally paid on all kinds of documents, but this requirement has been eroded over the years until stamp duty on share transfers is virtually the only survivor. What will happen if certificated shares eventually die out? This is uncertain but I'm guessing it will be replaced with some other form of levy.

I notice a regrettable tendency, even amongst professionals, to refer to SDLT as 'stamp duty'. Now you know they are wrong.

SECTION 8: BUY-TO-LET BUSINESSES – WHAT TO THINK ABOUT

A buy-to-let business can be an attractive prospect. On the surface it would appear to offer two opportunities for financial gain – an income from the rent and an asset that is steadily increasing in value. Immediately, however, you can see that this attracts two distinct areas of taxation opportunity – on your income and on your investment. So, to make the most of this business choice you need to know exactly how HMRC will take an interest, and how you can plan for this intelligently. And there is another dimension to buy-to-let – it is not a passive hands-off investment option; so we start below by looking at the reality of running this kind of business on a routine basis.

#34. Setting up a buy-to-let business

Property of any kind is not the sort of investment that quietly looks after itself. A poorly managed property will very rapidly become a liability. Like a vintage car or a sailing yacht, a building requires maintenance to keep it working properly. And so does the business operation itself if you want to maximize your return from acquisitions (and sales) and of course manage an efficient letting process.

Right at the start there is the 'opportunity cost' - what it will actually cost you to get up and running. This comes down to simple arithmetic, weighing up any current debt, adding in costs for additional mortgages and any work required on the property. It also includes tax considerations (including restrictions and reliefs) relating to the type of business structure you use. This comes before calculating your income model based on predicted rental set against loans, insurance and maintenance.

Assuming these numbers stack up, you then examine your management strategy – just how hands-on do you want to be?

Styles of property management

Looking at property management generally, you have three basic models:

1.   Do-It-Yourself;

2.   Half and Half;

3.   Outsource to Professional.

Most of the property investors I work with choose this as an occupation, a way to run their own business and get out of the rat race. So it's a working way of life, not a passive investment – and hence they opt for one of the first two choices. What is interesting – and very relevant – is that, however proactive they are, they still routinely seek the help of expert professionals, from lawyers and surveyors to professional property managers and of course accountants. As with any business, you need the right team around you with the right expertise.

Even if you choose the third option, leaving it all to someone else to manage, you will still need to make your own decisions when facing tax mitigation choices, for example by ensuring you've qualified for and claimed all the available reliefs and allowances.

Now, assuming you want to run the business yourself to some extent, there are three roles to your job once you have acquired your property and some tenants:

1.   Managing the tenants;

2.   Managing property maintenance and inspections;

3.   Managing finances.

There are many good books on the first two; my focus here is to guide you through the third item where it relates to tax. But before we move on to that, let's just consider another decision you have to make - what sort of buy-to-let property to invest in; and we need to start from a financial angle.

Financial factors influencing the type of property

This is a business so it all ultimately comes down to money. Financial things to consider when you're choosing which sector of the buy-to-let market to enter include:

- Net cash flow: will the property generate sufficient rent on a month-by-month basis to cover the expenditure (including creating a fund to cover 'one-off' items and contingencies)?

- Value: not just the purchase price in isolation but within the wider market and within your own financial circumstances;

- Condition: will there be building or refurbishment costs, now or in the foreseeable future?

- Disposability: if and when you want to sell the property, how easy will this be?

- Maintenance and service costs: some buildings are inherently more expensive than others to keep in good order;

- Projected capital growth: how much and how fast can you expect the property to grow in value?

There is a further consideration that will determine the success of the business of renting out property *and* have financial impact:

- Tenants: consider the social and commercial demographic profile of the area. Make sure there is a market for your property.

Finally, there is the big question of whether your business will be regarded as a trading or an investment company. We discussed this in *Section 3. Organisational Structure*, and the tax implications crop up throughout this book, so it is definitely something to bear in mind. However, if you are set on enjoying the benefits of a trading business, you may need to consider Serviced Accommodation, discussed further below.

Tips for choosing the right properties

I have a few tips for anyone trying to make the right choices in the buy-to-let market. These are not definitive, as factors such as location, personal circumstances, goals and objectives, personal preference and economic climate all play their part. They may seem simplistic, but it's surprising how often they're ignored:

1. **Return on investment ('ROI')**: this should be an investor's first thought, whether it's property, a financial product, or time, effort and cost invested in a business. You need to be able to work out accurately what you'll get back, over a specified time, both in terms of income and cash flow and of capital appreciation; this should compensate you for your initial outlay and anything you spend to add value to the property, plus your ordinary expenditure over the whole period of ownership and the effort you'll be putting in.

2. **Going rate:** Review the 'going rate' in the area for rents for similar properties. Will this give you a good enough return (allowing for voids between tenants)?

3. **Renting or rebuilding?** This is rental, not property development, so you want a property that will 'wash its face' without a lot of initial further expense once you've purchased. So, avoid properties that require a lot of remedial work if your intention is to let it out (unless the work can add real tangible value);

4. **Avoid unnecessary expense and stress:** Don't buy a property that will be heavy on maintenance, as you'll just create a lot of needless work for yourself. The disappearance of the former 'wear and tear

allowance' means that you will have to itemise, and *justify,* every expense. And anyway, do you really want your tenants constantly demanding that work is carried out?

5. **Tenant vs property profile:** You may have in mind your ideal tenant, but you also need to consider the area and the type of available property. If you want a young couple with a family, is the property in a family-friendly area? If you prefer retired individuals, is it near to facilities or to public transport to access these? Is the property in an area that's relatively crime-free and generally desirable?

6. **Basic standards:** Put yourself in your tenant's shoes. The property doesn't have to offer superior luxury, but would *you* be happy to live in the rental property if you had to?

7. **Vet your tenants:** This means taking up proper references and taking a deposit. It's a good idea not to commit yourself to a long tenancy to start with but offer, say, a six-month contract. At the time of writing there is a statutory minimum of six months for shorthold tenancies. Following this period, you can review before deciding whether or not to extend. Conversely, if you get a good tenant, think about offering some form of incentive to keep them.

8. **Selective licensing:** Check whether or not the property is in an area where selective licensing is in force, because if so it will have to be licensed at additional expense.

9. **Engaging a property management company:** Think seriously about having the property professionally managed. Yes, it's an additional expense, but property management is far from easy and, unless you really enjoy working with property, you may find the expense you save is not worth the time and stress.

Now, with that in mind we need to ask another fundamental question – to invest in residential or in commercial property? As we'll see, there are some potentially very useful differences.

#35. Residential or commercial?

There are actually three broad categories of buy-to-let – residential property, commercial property/premises, and serviced accommodation. We cover the last of these later in this section, so here we look at the first two categories.

The basic operation is the same for both – you have to finance the purchase of property, bring it up to the required standard to go on the market, find tenants and then manage the tenancies on an ongoing basis. And you have to run the business, including all regulatory financial, accounting and tax compliance. But there are some interesting differences relating both to managing the properties and tenants and to the tax scenarios:

Commercial property

- Your tenants may stay for a longer term (but not always – bad businesses go bust and good ones can outgrow their premises);

- You can require the tenant to be fully responsible for the property (through either a full repairing and insuring lease or the reimbursement of costs);

- There are no regulatory requirements regarding the condition of property – it's just a matter of making the property attractive to the target tenant. However, under the terms of the lease you may still have health and safety responsibilities and you will usually be responsible for the safety of any fixtures and fittings you install, including gas and electricity installations and fitting. The tenant is responsible for anything installed by the tenant;

- You may need to carry out an asbestos survey as you will be responsible for the management of any asbestos in the building;

- You will need to provide an Energy Performance Certificate because under s 49 Energy Act 2011 it's unlawful to let a non-domestic property that "falls below such level of energy efficiency (as demonstrated by the energy performance certificate) as is provided for by the regulations. For new lets (or renewals) after 1 April 2018 this means not below 'E' rating and from 1 April 2023 this will apply to all lettings";

- Deposits are not regulated as they are for residential property, although in practice this is governed by market forces, with a norm of three or six months' deposit. There is frequently a condition, either in the lease or in a separate rent deposit deed, that if the tenant is in breach of his obligations (for example, to keep the property in repair), then the landlord can dip into the rent deposit and require the tenant to top up the deposit to restore the original total;

- You can exclude tenant's right to a further lease if you wish (Landlord & Tenant Act 1954);

- You can obtain possession quickly in the event of tenant's breach;

- There is no restriction on mortgage interest relief.

- The rate of CGT is lower on commercial properties (10% to 20% as opposed to 18% to 28% on residential).

Now let's compare this with residential properties.

Residential property

- The length of tenancies may be shorter (although there are proposals for tenancies to be for a minimum term)

- As landlord you are responsible for the structure of the building;

- You are also responsible for sanitary fittings, pipes and drains, heating and hot water, gas appliances and electric wiring. You cannot require your tenant to contribute to any repairs or replacements;

- You must comply with regulations concerning deposits by paying them into one of the statutory deposit-holding schemes. Also, as from 1 June 2019 the Tenants Fees Act 2019 makes it illegal to charge residential tenants an agent's fee for taking up references or drawing up the tenancy agreement, and there is a cap on deposits of no more than 5 weeks of rent (or 6 weeks if the annual rent is £50,000 or more). You are also limited to one week's rent as a 'holding deposit' (with a timescale for repayment), and the Act also limits the fees and payments that can be demanded from the tenant if in default;

- Where applicable you must comply with regulations concerning HMOs and selective licensing;

- With an asssured shorthold tenancy you can terminate at the end of the fixed term (or after the fixed term has expired by giving 2 months' notice in the statutory form. However;

- You cannot seek to evict a tenant without a court order (but there is an accelerated court procedure for assured shorthold tenancies);

- There is a limit on mortgage interest relief.

The landlord also has a statutory responsibility to:

- Make sure gas and electricity installations are safe and maintained;

- Fit and test smoke alarms and carbon monoxide detectors;

- Follow fire regulations if the property is a purpose-built block of flats or a house converted into flats;

- Take action on any Health & Safety enforcement notices issued by local authority;

- Have an Energy Performance Certificate;

- Check that the tenants and anyone else living in property over 18 has the right to remain in UK and rent a property;

- Issue a 'How to Rent' checklist.

From this brief comparison it might appear that commercial is the easier and more flexible option. On the other hand, some investors may only feel happy dealing with residential if it feels more familiar to them. However, I would always recommend seeking expert professional advice when making your decision as there may be other unique issues to consider.

#36. Serviced Accommodation

This is an attractive option for some, a more hands-on operation with an added hospitality flavour, while also investing in a business that can be easy to sell on. It also offers some interesting tax reliefs and schemes.

Serviced accommodation

The good news is that, unlike other property ownership businesses, although this is not classed as a trade, HMRC allows the same reliefs, for certain tax purposes, as those enjoyed by a trading business, as long as the criteria for serviced accommodation are met. This means you can benefit from the following:

- You can claim a range of Capital Gains Tax reliefs for traders (Business Asset Rollover Relief, Entrepreneurs' Relief, relief for gifts of business assets and relief for loans to traders);

- You are entitled to plant and machinery capital allowances for items such as furniture, equipment and fixtures;

- The profits count as earnings for pension purposes.

NB: If you have serviced accommodation as well as *other* types of property rental income, you'll need to keep separate records for the serviced accommodation in order to make the appropriate claims on your tax return.

To retain the status and benefits of being Serviced Accommodation, you will need to meet some criteria during each financial year:

- The property must be in the UK or (unless Brexit changes things) in the European Economic Area (EEA) ;

- You must provide sufficient furniture for normal occupation and your visitors must be entitled to use the furniture;

- The property must be commercially let - that is, you must intend to make a profit. N.B. if you let the property out of season to cover costs but did not manage to make a profit, the letting will still be treated as commercial;

- Your property must be available for letting as furnished holiday accommodation letting for at least 210 days in the year, and of these days you must actually let the property commercially as furnished holiday accommodation to the public for at least 105 days in the year. So you can't count any days when you are staying in the property yourself, and when calculating the 105 days you can't count any days when you let to family and friends at a zero or substantially reduced rent;

- If you let to one party for a continuous period of more than 31 days then you can't count this towards the 105 commercial days unless the 31 days is extended owing to unforeseen circumstances, such as the occupier falling ill or their travel arrangements being cancelled.

There's another point about longer lettings: if the total of all lettings that exceed 31 continuous days is more than 155 days during the year, this condition is not met so your property will not be an FHL for that year.

Now, you might be growing uneasy with the challenge of meeting minimum letting targets – what will happen if you don't?

Well there are ways to mitigate this in the forms of an 'averaging election' (if you have more than one property) and a 'period of grace election'.

Averaging election

If you let more than one property as a FHL, and one or more of these properties does not meet the letting condition of 105 days, you can elect to apply the letting condition to the average rate of occupancy for all the properties you let as FHLs. You make an averaging election up to one year after 31 January following the end of the tax year. Note that you can't mix UK and EEA FHLs for this purpose.

Period of grace election

This is leeway that you can use if you suffer a bad year. You must be able to show that you had a genuine intention to let the property in the year. Evidence of successfully meeting the letting conditions in previous years will be helpful, or evidence of bookings cancelled due so unforeseen circumstances, including extreme adverse weather.

You can make an election where the property met the letting condition in the year before the first year you wish to make a period of grace election (either on its own or because of an averaging election). If your property again doesn't meet the letting condition in the following year, you can make a second period of grace election (as long as you made an election in the previous year).

If, however, your property doesn't reach the threshold by the fourth year, after 2 consecutive periods of grace elections, it will no longer qualify as a FHL.

And how do these threshold periods work for new lets or when you cease to let?

For an ongoing let, you apply the test to the tax year, i.e. from 6 April one year to 5 April the next. For new or ceased lets, the following rules apply:

- For a new let, apply the tests to the first 12 months from when the letting began;

- For a ceased let, apply the tests to the 12 months up to when the letting finished.

If your property is only used as serviced accommodation and is closed for part of the year because there are no customers, you can deduct all the expenses, such as insurance and loan interest, for the whole year, provided you do not live in the property.

Partial letting: If you let part of the property as serviced accommodation, or you use the property privately for part of the year, you need to apportion your receipts and expenses on a reasonable basis.

What to do if you cease to qualify as Serviced Accommodation: If your property ceases to qualify as serviced accommodation, the special tax treatment will no longer apply. You will need to work out any balancing allowance or balancing charge for capital allowances and any Capital Gains Tax reliefs will be affected.

Are there any disadvantages to Serviced Accommodation? Not really, provided you observe the rules and conditions. From a VAT point of view, the provision of holiday accommodation is a taxable supply so you will be required to register on reaching the VAT threshold.

Rent a Room Relief

People have had lodgers for as long as they've had homes. But the rise of innovative internet-based services like airBnB has also encouraged people to offer spare accommodation in their home as a holiday let. Strictly speaking, of course, this does not equate to property investment (unless it enables you to finance a larger property, thereby increasing your capital investment). However, it does offer a tax relief and is worth including here.

In essence, you can earn up to £7,500 from renting out living space in your home before incurring any tax liability on this income. You can use the scheme if:

- you let a furnished room in your main home;
- your letting activity amounts to a trade, for example, if you run a guest house or bed and breakfast business, or provide services, such as meals and cleaning.

However you cannot use the scheme if the accommodation is:

- not part of your main home when you let it (e.g. a separate granny annexe);

- not furnished;

- used as an office or for any business (but you can use the scheme if your lodger works in your home in the evening or at weekends or is a student who is provided with study facilities);

- in your UK home and is let while you live abroad.

If you own the property jointly with your partner, then the relief is divided, half each. However, if one of you does not pay tax you cannot transfer your 50% of the relief – it is simply lost.

Claiming rent-a-room relief

The relief applies to your gross receipts, that is, rent received plus any sums for meals or services. If this is below the relief threshold you get it automatically. If it's above then you have a choice of how you claim tax relief.

Method A

You pay tax on your actual profit - your total receipts less any expenses and capital allowances.

Method B

You pay tax on your gross receipts over the Rent-a-Room limit - that is, your gross receipts minus £7,500 (or £3,750 per joint owner). You cannot deduct any expenses or capital allowances if you choose this method.

HMRC will automatically use your actual profit (Method A) to work out your tax, so if you want to pay tax using Method B, you need to advise HMRC within the time limit (31 January following the end of the tax year in which the income was received). You may revert to Method A at any time by advising HMRC (again within the time limit).

If you pay tax using Method B, this automatically stops if your rental income drops below the £7,500 (or £3,750) limit.

So, you need to do the sums to work out whether you are better off using Method A or Method B.

#37. Buy-to-lets - company or individual?

As with any type of property investment, the question arises of how to structure a buy-to-let business – and whether to hold the property in your own name or in a company name.

This raises many of the topics that fill this book – but I include a simple comparison here for anyone who is starting out on a buy-to-let venture. For more information you can refer to the relevant sections of the book.

Issues and comparators, personally owned vs company owned

Held personally	Held through company
Income Tax	**Corporation Tax**
• Taxed on profits at marginal tax rate (up to 45%), regardless of when the money is withdrawn from the business. • Difficulty in classifying as a trade unless these are Furnished Holiday Lets • Full relief for mortgage interest is withdrawn from April 2017 Corporation Tax	• Letting is a business for corporation tax purposes. • Profits and gains on disposal are taxed at Corporation Tax rates • Accommodation - PAYE considerations if there is private use by company owners.
Tax on disposal of the property	**Tax on disposal of the property**
• Residential subject to capital gains tax (CGT) after deducting any available annual exemption. • No indexation allowance for CGT • The lower rates of CGT introduced from April 2016 do not apply to the disposal of residential property. • CGT payable 31 January in year after tax year of disposal	• An indexation allowance is frozen at 31 December 2017. • Payment date is subject to ordinary corporation tax payment deadlines.

Extraction of funds	**Extraction of funds**
Income	Income tax
• In general profits are available for the individual as fully taxed either as rental income or CGT on disposal.	• Tax charge when profits extracted as dividends by higher rate taxpayer, or by basic rate taxpayer from April 2016, subject to annual allowance. £2,000 for tax year 2019/20
Capital	
• A disposal of a property at a profit will trigger a capital gain.	• Tax above the allowance is on three dividend tax bands: 7.5%, 32.5% and 38.1%
• A disposal is treated in most cases at market value.	• Tax credit abolished
Incorporation	• Dividends received by pensions and ISAs are unaffected
• Incorporation will trigger a capital disposal.	Capital gains tax
	• Profits may be extracted as a capital distribution on striking off or winding up.
	• Subject to new anti-avoidance rules from 6 April 2016.
Ownership	**Ownership**
• The maximum number of legal owners of land and property is restricted to four.	• A company may have multiple shareholders.
• Owners need to decide whether to hold property as joint tenants, or tenants in common.	
Losses	**Losses**
• Losses may be offset against other property income or carried forward.	• Locked into the company and cannot be offset against the owner's other income.
	• Losses can be offset against total company profits of the current or future years, as long as the rental business continues.

Annual Tax on Enveloped Dwellings (ATED)	Annual Tax on Enveloped Dwellings (ATED)
• No ATED charge.	• The ATED regime applies to high value residential properties held by non-natural persons (e.g. a company) subject to exemption when the property is let on a commercial basis. • The ATED charge is payable if the letting business ceases
Stamp Duty Land Tax (SDLT) • Charged on purchase. • From April 2016 a 3% premium applies on the purchase of an additional residential property.	**Stamp Duty Land Tax (SDLT)** • Charged on purchase from or gift by an individual to their connected company. • From April 2016 a 3% premium applies on the purchase of residential property by companies. Stamp Duty • Applies at a rate of 0.5% on share acquisitions of £1,000 or higher. • See Stamp Duty Land Tax rates and reliefs
Inheritance Tax (IHT) • IHT Business Relief will not apply in respect of let property as it is an investment asset. Beneficiaries of the estate on death will receive the property at market value so there would be no capital gains tax for them to pay on an immediate sale. • IHT only applies to UK situated assets for a non-UK domiciled individual. • From April 2017, IHT extends to non UK domiciled individuals (or their trusts) where UK residential property is held indirectly through a foreign company or partnership.	**Inheritance Tax (IHT)** • IHT Business Relief will not apply to shares unless the company has significant other non-investment activities. • On death a shareholder's shares will benefit from an uplift to market value in the hands of the beneficiaries for CGT purposes. Property held in a company receive no similar uplift. • From April 2017 IHT extends to non-UK domiciled individuals (or their trusts) where UK residential property is held indirectly through a foreign company or partnership.

De-enveloping	De-enveloping
N/A	• The transfer of a residential property from a company back to its shareholders will only attract SDLT if there is a debt to a third party which the shareholders take on.
VAT	**VAT**
• Residential lets are always exempt, however commercial letting can be standard rated if the owner has opted to tax. • If the property qualifies as a furnished holiday let, then the income generated is standard rated and the owner will have to charge VAT if they are registered.	• Income from property letting is exempt from VAT with the exception of commercial letting which is standard rated if the company has opted to tax the building. • The letting of furnished holiday lets is a standard rated activity.

#38. Non-UK resident landlords

Some buy-to-let owners who are happy to have a hands-off approach choose this business model so that they can enjoy the fruits of living abroad. However, being classed as a landlord not resident in the UK has tax implications. You will be classed as a non-resident landlord if you live outside the UK for six months or more per year. N.B. this is still the case even if you're classed as UK-resident for other tax purposes.

Individual-owned residential property

You can receive your rent gross provided HMRC has agreed to this and issued a certificate (which won't happen unless your tax affairs are up to date!). Otherwise your agent must deduct basic rate tax from the rent (after deducting their expenses). If you don't have an agent and the tenant pays more than £100 a week then they must deduct the basic rate tax.

If you dispose of residential property in the UK you must notify HMRC within 30 days (or you will suffer a penalty) and pay any CGT attributable to the gain. This also applies if you are a close company (5 or fewer controllers or participators) but in this case you can apply Indexation Allowance to the acquisition costs (up to 31 December 2017) to compute the capital gain.

Some property does not count as residential for this purpose e.g.

- Care or nursing homes and hospices;

- Student accommodation provided it is purpose-built for at least 15 students and is occupied by students for at least 165 days in the year;

- Building land provided no residential building has started (but not acquisitions 'off-plan').

Company-owned residential property

A company is a 'non-resident landlord' if it receives income from renting UK property and either:

- It is main office or business premises is outside the UK, or

- It is incorporated outside the UK.

The arrangements regarding remittance of rent and disposal of residential property are the same as for individuals.

From 6 April 2019, the disposal of shares in property-rich companies by non-resident shareholders with 25% or more (with connected parties) interest will be subject to CGT.

Gains from property that is subject to the Annual Tax on Enveloped Dwellings regime (see Section 5. Getting to know your capital taxes, reliefs and schemes) will be subject to ATED capital gains tax.

Currently non-UK companies with UK residential property pay on the same basis as individuals for Income Tax and CGT. The rate for income tax for companies is 205. However there has been an HMRC consultation to bring such companies within the Corporation Tax regime.

On disposal of residential property in the UK, if you are a close company (5 or fewer controllers or participators) the rules are the same as for individually-owned property: you must notify HMRC within 30 days (or you will suffer a penalty) and pay any CGT attributable to the gain. You can however apply Indexation Allowance to the acquisition costs (up to 31 December 2017) to compute the capital gain.

Proposed non-resident SDLT surcharge

At the time of writing there is a proposal (consultation ended on 6 May 2019) that purchases of residential property by non-UK residents should bear an additional 1% SDLT. For these purposes non-UK residents will be individuals with fewer than 183 days in UK in the preceding 12 months. However a refund claim can be made if they then spend at least 183 days in the UK in the following 12 months. There are separate tests proposed for companies and trusts.

It appears that the surcharge will not apply where a non-UK resident buys off-plan and then flips to a UK resident because relief from SDLT is available.

Commercial property

For non-UK-resident investors in commercial property the income tax provisions are relatively straight forward compared to residential property.

The ATED regime does not apply to commercial property.

Disposals of commercial property by non-UK companies are exempt from CGT

NB: The above points refer to property-owning by non-UK residents as an investment. Should the activity be classed as trading then different rules apply. This could be the case if the non-UK resident or company is dealing in development land.

#39. How to deal with property losses

Even the simplest business operation can make a loss. Fortunately, the tax legislation does provide ways in which a buy-to-let loss can be alleviated.

If you make a loss but are continuing with your property business, the loss can be carried forward against future profits. However losses made in one rental business can't be carried across to any other rental business you may carry on at the same time in a different legal capacity. This relief applies only to commercial losses made from genuine commercial activity – i.e. you cannot offset losses incurred by letting a property at a nominal rent to a relative. In these cases, expenses can only be deducted up to the amount of the rent or other receipts actually generated by the nominal agreement.

If this isn't appropriate to you, then there are limited circumstances in which losses can be set against general income. Until the 2010/11 tax year, relief against general income could be claimed to the extent the loss was due to furnished holiday lettings, but this is no longer the case. You can claim certain capital allowances against general income but you must claim the full amount. The amount of net capital allowances is the amount of capital allowances that can be claimed less any charges due and you must make the claim on or before the first anniversary of 31 January following the end of the year of assessment.

Post-cessation relief

Given the fluctuating nature of some rental businesses, it might seem hard to determine whether such a business is still in operation or has ceased. But for tax purposes it is very clear. It will be treated as having ceased if, after a given date, the activities are:

- only concerned with winding up the activity, or

- a continuation of the business for the purpose of realising assets; e.g. you continue carrying on the business, perhaps in the hope of selling a going concern for a higher price.

However, in these circumstances you can claim some tax relief against the remaining business activity.

For tax on post-cessation receipts, you can deduct any allowable business losses that were left unrelieved when the business ceased and also other expenses that would have been allowable had the business continued. For example, if you recover a bad debt after cessation, you can deduct the costs incurred in collecting that debt. Or you could deduct the cost of background heating for empty premises to keep down condensation and so maintain the value of the property for later sale.

You can of course set post-cessation expenses against post-cessation receipts but if there are no receipts then you may be able to set the expenses against other taxable income and capital gains of the year in which the debts proved to be bad or the payments were made.

SECTION 9: PROPERTY CONSTRUCTION AND DEVELOPMENT

So far, we have barely mentioned an important part of the property investment sector, property development. The past decade or so has seen a rise in the number of entrepreneurial 'flippers', people who buy up property, renovate or improve it and then sell it on, and those who buy commercial properties in order to convert to residential use. Also, of course, there are other entrepreneurs who buy up undeveloped land and build from scratch, as well as larger building companies. While the long-term investment potential of property is absent here, there are still plenty of property-specific tax issues to consider ranging from employment to Capital Gains Tax, and including a number of useful schemes and reliefs.

#40. Construction Industry Scheme (CIS)

Purpose: to prevent subcontractors from avoiding tax and NI

If you're in the property development or renovation sector, you're almost certainly going to need to use the Construction Industry Scheme ('CIS'). In essence, if you are deemed to be a contractor, under CIS you must deduct money from payments made to your subcontractors and send this to HMRC. The deduction is an advance payment towards the subcontractor's tax and NI.

The big question that arises is who is or is not a contractor or a subcontractor – more on this in a moment.

CIS doesn't just apply to large companies building new homes – anyone involved in renovation needs to be aware of CIS too. After all, even a single residence renovation project is likely to need skills and disciplines beyond the self-renovator's scope – you'll be using subcontractors at some point. To comply with CIS you will need to make the same decision as any other employer about whether or not a subcontractor is truly self-employed or effectively your own employee.

Deductions under CIS are from payment made for labour, travel expenses and subsistence; they are not made in respect of materials or VAT.

Contractor, subcontractor or employee?

To add a layer of complexity, a sub-contractor may in turn hire help (becoming a contractor). Hence a sub-contractor may also need to apply CIS! To clarify:

A contractor is a business or other concern that pays subcontractors for construction work. Contractors may be construction companies and building firms, but may also be government departments, local authorities and many other businesses that are normally known in the industry as 'clients'.

Some businesses or other concerns are counted as contractors if their average annual expenditure on construction operations over a period of 3 years is £1 million or more. Originally this expenditure threshold also applied to buy-to-let investors (as you would expect) but in 2012 HMRC changed their stance to indicate that where a property investor business undertakes   activities attributed to those of 'property development', it will be considered a mainstream contractor during the period of that development and will be required to observe CIS.

A subcontractor is a business that carries out construction work for a contractor. A subcontractor may in turn hire workers in which case the rules for contractors also apply.

Employees: As explained in Section 3, there is no grey area regarding employee status; it's a matter of whether the working relationship meets the HMRC criteria. So if you're satisfied that an individual is correctly classed as an employee, and you're paying them as an employee, then CIS does not apply (but PAYE and NIC do!)

Who must register for CIS?

The scheme covers all types of businesses and other concerns that work in the construction industry, including:

* Companies;

* Partnerships'

* Self-employed individuals.

There is very little flexibility over registration:

* All contractors must register with HMRC for the CIS;

* Subcontractors do not have to register, but if they don't then deductions will be taken from their payments at a *higher* rate;

* Before a contractor can make a payment to a subcontractor for construction work, they must verify with HMRC that the subcontractor is registered. HMRC will then advise the rate of deduction that must apply to the payment, or whether the payment can be made without any deductions.

The general rule is that it is illegal to carry out construction work within the UK without being registered. However, there are some important exceptions, the main ones being:

* Ordinary householders that are having work done on their own premises, such as new house building, decoration, repairs or an extension;

* Businesses which don't include construction operations whose average annual expenditure on construction work over the last 3 years has been less than £1 million;

- Businesses and other concerns that are otherwise mainstream or deemed contractors may not need to apply the scheme for certain types of work (e.g. work on property used in own business or for another company in group). There are a number of these exceptions;

- LEA maintained schools;

- Work for charities;

- Small contracts (less than £1,000) if authorised by HMRC.

- Work up to £1,000 on land owned by sub-contractor if authorised by HMRC.

What type of work is covered by CIS?

- CIS covers all of the following if carried out in the UK (including territorial waters up to the 12-mile limit):

- Site preparation

- Alterations

- Dismantling

- Construction

- Repairs

- Decorating

- Demolition

There are some exceptions such as architecture, surveying, carpet fitting and so on – if in doubt, seek advice. The scheme doesn't apply to construction work carried on outside the UK. However, a business based outside the UK but carrying out construction work within the UK must register for CIS.

CIS Returns and Payments

For CIS, contractors have to calculate and deduct the correct amount from the subcontractor's pay. They must record all details of the deduction and supply a statement of deduction along with the net payment to the subcontractor.

Then, each month, the contractors send HMRC a complete return of all the payments they have made within the scheme (including a report of no payments if appropriate), including:

- Details of the subcontractors;

- Details of the payments made, and any deductions withheld;

- A declaration that the employment status of all subcontractors has been considered;

- A declaration that all subcontractors that need to be verified have been verified.

The contractors must send the deductions to HMRC each month (or in some cases quarterly by special agreement).

Applying to be paid without deductions

Subcontractors can apply to be paid gross if they meet all of certain qualifying conditions, including:

- A history of paying tax and National Insurance on time in the past;

- Business does construction work (or provides labour for it) in the UK;

- Business is run through a bank account and has an annual turnover of at least £30,000 (sole trader) or £30,000 for each partner or director with total turnover of at least £100,000.

#41. Enterprise Investment Scheme (EIS) for construction companies

Purpose: to incentivise investment in companies trying to grow

The Enterprise Investment Scheme (EIS) is designed to help you raise money to help grow your business. It does this by offering tax reliefs to individual investors who buy new shares in the company.

Under EIS, you can raise up to £5 million each year, and a maximum of £12 million in your company's lifetime. This also includes amounts received from other venture capital schemes. Your company must usually receive investment under a venture capital scheme within seven years of its first commercial sale (in the case of a group of companies, this means the earliest sale in the group) and the money must be used for a 'qualifying business' (see below).

However you can receive the investment after the seven-year period provided that you can show that:

- the money is required to enter a completely new product market or a new geographic market; and

- the investment you're seeking is at least 50% of your company's average annual turnover for the last 5 years.

This requirement also applies if you are receiving an investment for an activity which is different to the activity for which you have received previous investment under EIS.

You must follow the scheme rules so that your investors can claim and keep EIS tax reliefs relating to their shares. Tax reliefs will be withheld or withdrawn from your investors if you do not follow the rules for at least 3 years after the investment is made.

Qualifying for EIS

Your company (or group of companies if you're a parent company) may qualify if at the time of investment it:

- Has a permanent establishment in the UK

- Is unquoted – although AIM and PLUS Quoted companies do qualify

- Does not control another company other than qualifying subsidiaries*

- Is not controlled by or has more than 50% of its shares owned by another company

- Has no more than £15 million in gross assets before new shares are issued and not more than £16 million after;

- Has fewer than 250 employees;

- Does not expect to close after completing a project or series of projects

- Been more than 7 years since its first commercial sale.

> * Qualifying subsidiaries - your company must own more than 50% of the shares and only your company or another qualifying subsidiary controls the company. There must be no arrangement which could lead to control by anyone else.

However, the share ownership requirement goes up to 90% if business activity to be funded by the investment is to be carried out by the subsidiary, or if the subsidiary's business is mainly property or land management.

Unlike the parent company, the qualifying subsidiary can close after completing a project or series of projects, as long as the projects support the growth and development of the main company.

The money raised by the new share issue must be used for a qualifying business activity, which is either:

- A qualifying trade;

- Preparing to carry out a qualifying trade (which must start within 2 years of the investment);

- Research and development that's expected to lead to a qualifying trade.

The money raised by the new share issue must:

- Be spent within 2 years of the investment, or if later, the date you started trading;

- Not be used to buy all or part of another business;

- Pose a risk of loss to capital for the investor;

- Be used to grow or develop your business.

Most trades will qualify, including for any research and development that will lead to a qualifying trade. However it may not qualify if more than 20% of the trade is property development, leasing activities, or running a nursing home or hotel.

Knowledge intensive companies

This relates to companies that innovate new technologies, and although not immediately relevant to property investors, it is possible for some construction work to come within this category and enjoy enhanced investment conditions. See also R&D Tax Relief, below.

These companies can apply outside the 7-year period and the time limit is within 10 years of **either** the first commercial sale **or** the annual turnover exceeding £200,000.

To qualify, the company and any qualifying subsidiaries must have fewer than 500 full-time equivalent employees when the shares are issued and:

- **either** be carrying out work to create intellectual property and expect the majority of their business to come from this within 10 years

- **or** have 20% of employees carrying out research for at least 3 years from the date of investment - these employees must be in a role that requires a relevant Master's or higher degree

The company must apply a percentage of its overall operating costs on research, development or innovation. This must be:

- **Either** 10% a year for 3 years

- **Or** 15% in one of 3 years

The company must have met this requirement in each of the 3 years before the investment or, if the company is less than 3 years old, it must do so in the 3 years following the investment.

A knowledge-intensive company can raise

- £10 million of investment per year;

- £20 million of investment in the lifetime of the company and any subsidiaries.

How can you make EIS work for developers?

Being the developer yourself may mean that your company does not qualify for EIS. However, a developer could be looking for someone who can provide a turnkey solution for the development of their land. This person/ company may be EIS-eligible. For example, the EIS company will manage the building of high-quality units, turning over a high volume of properties. By subcontracting the construction, the EIS company can manage several projects at once and thus fulfil the definition of trading, without falling foul of the exclusion of being itself a property developer.

It's a somewhat complex strategy, but worth considering if you have or can acquire the necessary in-house expertise.

#42. Research and Development (R&D) Tax Relief

Purpose: to incentivise meaningful research and development of new practice

Research and Development Tax Relief is a valuable scheme (available to limited companies only), but it can be tricky to apply it to developers and construction businesses.

We'll try to address that in a moment. First of all, let's just have a brief look at how R&D Relief works in general as it's often mistakenly thought that it only applies to 'white coat' research or to high technology. But as you read through the conditions and exclusions you will begin to see why it can be difficult (but not impossible) to justify it for property construction work.

WHAT IS REGARDED AS R&D?

R&D covers work on a specific project intended to make an advance in science or technology. This can include, for example, devising and developing systems and working practices, inventing/devising new products and making improvements to existing products or systems. There are some provisions:

- It cannot include artistic fields, social sciences like economics or a theoretical field like pure mathematics;

- The project must relate to your company's existing trade, or a trade that it is intended to start up based on the results of the R&D;

- You can claim relief for projects which were ultimately unsuccessful provided they meet the other conditions;

- You can claim for work carried out as a sub-contractor.

What do you need to show for a successful claim?

- The work must be an advance in knowledge *in the field generally*, not just for your business. So, simply using an existing technology or a commercially innovative process for the first time is not sufficient unless you have incorporated specific advances which meet this criterion;

- There must have been uncertainties to be overcome. If you and your staff were puzzling over finding a solution this suggests that the work may qualify for R & D Relief;

- You must show the work you carried out to overcome the uncertainty;

- You must be able to explain why a 'competent professional' could not easily provide you with a solution. This does not prevent you using consultants to work on the project.

Deadline for claim: You must file your claim within 2 years of the company year-end in which the work took place. Where the project lasted for more than one company year you must make a claim for each year.

So, back to the original question:

CAN R&D TAX RELIEF APPLY TO PROPERTY CONSTRUCTION?

Before I try to answer this, let me just give you an example of a recent R & D claim that my firm is putting through. For reasons of confidentiality, I can't give too many details as, unless this ultimately goes to Tribunal, it isn't in the public domain.

The taxpayer is a family business working in an ecologically-sound business which involves recycling. It's a very hands-on environment and, to be frank, the business premises resemble a cross between a scrapyard and a timber-yard. In saying that, please do bear in mind that these people are involved in recycling waste products.

Our first idea was that the clients had mentioned various modifications made from time to time to their processing equipment and we felt that these might qualify for R & D Tax Relief. However, the client indicated that the expenditure on these was relatively slight. We made a site visit to check this out and by chance it was mentioned that a large amount of expenditure had been incurred when one of the client's biggest customers had changed the specification. Apparently satisfying the customer requirements had involved the investment of a large amount of time in modifying the processing equipment, testing it and also disposing of the reject material used in the testing. Expenditure in a single year was nearing £1 million.

A solution was not simply a matter of buying in new equipment or getting an industry specialist to advise. The clients had to find the solution through a trial and error process. This is exactly what R & D is all about.

The claim is still with HMRC and, although certain elements were included that are borderline, I'm expecting that at least some of the expenditure will qualify. You could say that we ourselves are to some extent pushing open the envelope here, as this industry sector was far from the typical source of an R & D Tax Relief claim.

Now for R & D claims in the property sector:

It's not the most obvious application, but I feel there's a lot of scope here. The criteria are the same as for any other business. If you, your staff or external consultants are spending an appreciable amount of time on devising products, systems and practices or working methodology that is different to what anyone else is doing, then it's worth looking to see if the criteria apply.

As you can see from the example above, I'm always keen to spot an angle which can mitigate my clients' overall taxation.

HOW R&D TAX RELIEF WORKS

Which companies will qualify?

The company must be an SME, which for R&D purposes means:

- A staff headcount of less than 500;

- Turnover of not more than 100m Euros or balance sheet of not more than 86m Euros.

If the company owns more than 50% shareholding voting rights in another company then it is a 'linked company' and the other company's data must be included.

If the company owns more than 25% of another company, or is more than 25% owned by another company then it is a 'partner company' and a proportion of the other partner company's and that proportion of the other partner company's data must be added in (although certain types of investors are excluded).

What relief is available?

If you are an SME, you can *either*

- Deduct an additional 130% of qualifying costs from annual profit, resulting in a tax reduction or refund equivalent to 24.7% (19% Corporation Tax on 130% of costs); or

- If the company is loss making in year of claim, tax credits worth up to 14.5% of the surrenderable loss.

Large companies can claim R&D Expenditure Credit (RDEC) as a tax credit of 12% of qualifying expenditure. Both SMEs and large companies who have been sub-contracted to large companies to do this work can also claim RDEC.

Please note: if you have received notifiable State-aided grant this may restrict your claim to tax credits, especially if the grant was non-project-specific.

How to assess if you have a possible R&D claim

Ask yourself the following:

- What were the commercial goals for the R&D?

- What were the technical objectives of the R&D?

- What were the technical uncertainties that you needed to overcome?

- Why could you not obtain a solution from a competent professional in the field?

- Regarding any staff/sub-contractors/consultants who worked on the project - how were they qualified e.g. professional qualifications, industry experience?

If you carried out R&D for other entities:

- What percentage of your total R&D was for other companies?

- What was the split between SMEs and large companies?

#43. Land Remediation Relief (LRR)

Purpose: to incentivise proper treatment of contaminated land

LRR is a relief available to a developer that is remedying contaminated land. This includes the removal of asbestos from buildings, breaking out buried structures and treating harmful organisms and natural contaminants such as the invasive plant, Japanese Knotweed.

LRR is available to property investors and developers alike, but is a relief solely against Corporation Tax so only available to limited companies. Developments, regeneration projects and refurbishments or fit-outs are all eligible if they meet the qualifying conditions.

There are three types of relief:

- Owner occupier / investor rate - 150%

- Developer rate - 50%

- Tax credit for loss making companies – 24%

LRR Qualifying conditions

- Work carried out must qualify for relief (see above);

- Where property is held as an asset (e.g. a rental portfolio), the full 150% must be claimed in the year in which expenditure is incurred;

- Where property is traded by developers **all** the expenditure on construction will have been shown as expenditure in the profit and loss account in the usual way, so effectively providing 100% relief against Corporation Tax. Then the qualifying expenditure incurred by companies in cleaning up land acquired from a third party in a contaminated state attracts the additional relief of 50%. As this only applies where land is *traded*, it follows that the additional 505 relief is only claimed on the disposal of the property;

- LRR is available for both capital and revenue expenditure but the company must elect, within two years of the end of the accounting period in which the expenditure is incurred, to treat qualifying capital expenditure as a deduction in computing taxable profits;

- HMRC will deal with any late claims under their general procedure for time limits for Corporation Tax Self-assessment, but in general the time limit for retrospective claims for LRR is three years from the end of the accounting period to which the claim relates

There are some restrictions where LRR cannot be claimed:

- The claiming company caused the contamination in the first place;

- The claimant company does not have a 'major interest' (freehold or a minimum lease of 7 years);

- The expenditure has been subsidised, for example by grant funding;

- The acquisition cost of the land was specifically discounted in order to account for the cost of remediation works and stated as such in the purchase agreement.

Why would you claim LRR?

Claiming LRR can provide cash savings, in particular where the 150% owner occupier / investor rate (for UK companies only) is claimed. However you do have to claim the relief – it does not happen automatically.

Calculating the anticipated LRR is useful tool at an early stage. The likely savings can be factored in if you are working out what to bid for the property, or putting together a case for borrowing or investment. However don't forget that the claim has to be made, and you need to build the timing into your cashflow.

Land Remediation/Derelict Land Tax Credit

If a UK company qualifies for LRR but makes a loss for an accounting period in which it incurs LRR-related expenditure, it may elect to receive a payable credit from HMRC. The amount of tax credit that can be claimed is 16% of the qualifying LRR for the accounting period the claim relates to. For both investors and developers, the cash return is equivalent to 24% of the expenditure incurred (16% x 150%).

Derelict Land Relief and Vacant Building Credit

This is not the same as LLR but is worth mentioning here.

Derelict Land Relief was introduced by Finance Act 2009 to encourage abandoned sites to be brought back into productive use. To qualify, a site must be listed on the English National Land Use Database as being derelict since 1998, or have been derelict for 10 years. For qualifying sites, generous relief is available on demolishing and preparing the site for redevelopment.

Vacant Building Credit is somewhat similar. Introduced in November 2014, it was then the subject of challenge in the High Court. It applies to any building that has not been abandoned that is brought back into any lawful use, or is demolished to be replaced by a new building. The developer is offered a financial 'credit' equivalent to the existing gross floor space of relevant vacant buildings when the local planning authority calculates affordable housing contributions.

Following the High Court clarification in May 2015, vacant building credit has now made its way into the national Planning Practice Guidance.

#44. Some Capital Gains Tax and VAT issues for developers

There are two areas of interest that raise specific questions about CGT and VAT – converting property into flats and buying and developing land.

CONVERSION TO FLATS

This is a popular type of development project that needs consideration. For taxation purposes there are two areas of potential interest – CGT and VAT. Let's examine three different scenarios.

1. Acquiring, converting and selling

To take a simple one first, a property developer may see the potential of acquiring a large property such as a disused public house or office block and converting it into flats. From the tax point of view, it's likely that the developer will already be classed as trading, so it will be a commercial rather than investment activity with the benefit that the costs and profits will be taxed on the basis of a trade. As the developer is trading, CGT is not an issue and there will be no chargeable gain.

I must however point out the case of Terrace Hill (Berkeley) Ltd v. HMRC (2015), where the company had acquired and refurbished a property that was then disposed of but only *after* it has been let as offices to various tenants. The challenge was that this had all the hallmarks of a trading activity, but the verdict was that this was an investment activity. The directors were able to establish that the original intention had been to retain the property as an investment and the plan had only changed when the returns from letting proved disappointing and they received a good offer from a purchaser.

In this case, this was exactly the outcome the directors had hoped for, but beware that the Tribunal could come to the same logical conclusion in a case where you definitely did not want to be judged an investment business!

2. Landlord converting rental house into rental flats

In another scenario, maybe a landlord decides to convert his rental property into flats to maximise both rental income in the short term and profit on sale in the longer term. He goes ahead with the conversion of a large house that has previously been let out, lets the flats for a few more years and then sells them.

The landlord will be subject to CGT on any gain made from the sale of the flats. However, he will be able to deduct the costs of the conversion when computing the gain. If, however, the landlord develops the property into flats and sells the flats upon completion then CGT and Income Tax will be payable. CGT for the period it was an investment property and Income Tax during the period it became a development business.

3. Homeowner converting house into flats

Another similar scenario is the person who wants to convert a former family home into flats to realise the maximum possible gain on disposal. The principles are the same as the last case but there may be other factors to take into account when computing the CGT. For example, the owner may have resided in the family home as his or her main residence, in which case Private Residence Relief may apply (although the timescale will only allow for a very tight window). Another factor is that the family home may have passed though the parents' estate and as such been acquired by the present owners at the market value at the date of death (a tax-free uplift for CGT purposes).

So in this example, the person converting the family home may well be in a more advantageous position for CGT than the investment landlord was. But he will have to pay Income Tax on the development element of the profit.

What about VAT?

Whether or not your ownership is classed as a trade, if you are letting property you have the option of electing that VAT should apply to the property. I've discussed earlier how this works (Section 4. Understanding VAT) and in particular the process of dis-applying the election on Form 1614D.

Let's just look at how VAT works on supplies for conversion. If you are converting a non-residential building into flats this will usually qualify for the 5% VAT rate. The 5% rate also applies to conversions that change the number of dwellings, for example, converting flats into one house, or a single property into multiple apartments. Furthermore, if a residential building has been empty for two or more years, the 5% is also available for most renovation and alteration works. So this means that you can dramatically reduce your construction budget where the supplier of the building/construction services is VAT-registered.

If you simply buy in materials then you'll pay 20% VAT on this supply. However if you contract out both materials and labour then you'll only pay 5% VAT.

This is quite a complex topic but well worth looking at.

DEALING IN DEVELOPMENT LAND

Whether the acquisition and development of land is a trade or an investment depends upon the activities and intentions of the taxpayer. In turn these determine liability for CGT.

If it is a trade then the developer will pay Income Tax on the profits or, if a limited company, Corporation Tax. The sale of the land will be sale of trading stock and will not be a chargeable capital gain. If it is classed as an investment, the Capital Gains Tax will be charged on the gain realised on sale (and Corporation Tax charged on the capital gain if the developer is a limited company).

CGT and Income Tax on disposal of investment land by non-UK residents

Historically, disposals of UK land held as an investment by non-UK residents were not subject to UK CGT, unless the property was residential. If a non-UK resident was classified as trading, the profits were only taxed where either:

- The profits and gains were attributable to a UK permanent establishment; or

- The company had a residual liability to UK income tax in respect of its UK source trading profits (unless this was relieved by a double tax treaty); or

- The diverted profits tax legislation applied.

However the Finance Act 2016 changed this so that the profits of a trade carried on by a company are subject to UK Corporation Tax where the company is:

- dealing in UK land; or

- developing UK land with a view to disposing of the UK land.

This applies regardless of the residence of the seller, and whether or not it has a UK permanent establishment, and also applies where the company's main purpose (or one of its main purposes) is broadly to realise a profit or gain from disposing of or developing UK land.

Similar legislation applies to income tax.

#45. New Structural and Buildings Allowance (SBA)

This was proposed in the Autumn 2018 Budget and introduced by s. 30 Finance Act 2019 and is available from 29 October 2018 on qualifying construction costs for new non-residential structures and buildings. Relief will be given at an annual rate of 2% on a straight-line basis.

Unfortunately s.30 immediately refers to the regulations that 'may' be introduced and at the date of publication this had not yet happened. Below is the framework that has been proposed (and note under 'Dwellings' that whilst the scheme is intended solely for non-residential construction, there is scope for some relief in association with residential construction).

SBA will relieve the costs of physically constructing new structures and buildings and encourage investment in the construction of new structures and buildings that are intended for commercial use, the necessary works to bring them into existence and the improvement of existing structures and buildings, including the cost of converting existing premises for use in a qualifying activity. Although these assets may already be depreciated in your accounts, actual tax relief has not previously been available.

The principal proposed features are:

- Structures and buildings must be intended for commercial activity. Neither land nor dwellings will be eligible for relief.

- Where there is mixed use relief will be reduced by apportionment. No relief will be provided for workspaces within domestic settings, such as home-offices.

- Relief will be limited to the original cost of construction or renovation, relieved across a fixed 50-year period, regardless of ownership changes.

- SBA will be allowed as a deduction from profits at an annual rate of two percent. The relief will be available to businesses that chargeable to income tax and companies chargeable to corporation tax.

- The two percent writing down allowance will be at a flat rate, calculated on the amount of original construction expenditure. There will not be a system of balancing charges or balancing allowances on a subsequent disposal of the asset. Instead, a purchaser will continue to claim the annual allowance of two percent of the original cost.

- Relief will not be available for structures or buildings where a contract for the physical construction works is entered into before 29 October 2018, nor where the construction activity began before 29 October 2018.

- Relief is available for UK and overseas structures and buildings, where the business is within the charge to UK tax.

- Relief will be limited to the costs of physically constructing the structure or building, including costs of demolition or land alterations necessary for construction, and direct costs required to bring the asset into existence.

- Claims can only be made from when a structure or building first comes into use.

- Land costs or rights over land will not be eligible for relief, nor will the costs of obtaining planning permission.

- The claimant must have an interest in the land on which the structure or building is constructed.

- The sale of the asset will not result in a balancing adjustment - instead, the purchaser takes over the remainder of the allowances written down over the remaining part of the 50-year period.

- Expenditure on integral features and fittings of a structure or building that are currently allowable as expenditure on plant and machinery, will continue to qualify for writing down allowances for plant and machinery including the Annual Investment Allowance (AIA) up to its annual limit.

- SBA expenditure will not qualify for the AIA

- Where a structure or building is renovated or converted so that it becomes a qualifying asset, the expenditure will qualify for a separate two percent relief over the next 50 years.

Qualifying expenditure for SBA

SBA will be available for capital expenditure on structures and buildings brought into use for the following qualifying activities:

a) a trade, including a ring-fence trade in the oil and gas sector;

b) a profession or vocation;

c) a UK or overseas property business that is an "ordinary" business for the purposes of the Capital Allowances Act 2001;

d) a concern listed in section 12(4) of the Income Tax (Trading and Other Income) Act 2005 or section 39(4) of the Corporation Tax Act 2009 (mines, transport undertakings etc.);

e) managing the investments of a company with investment business, to the extent that any profits or gains from the activity are chargeable to tax.

'Structures and buildings' include offices, retail and wholesale premises, walls, bridges, tunnels, factories and warehouses. Capital expenditure on renovations or conversions of existing commercial structures or buildings will also qualify. The costs of construction will include only the net direct costs related to physically constructing the asset, after any discounts, refunds or other adjustments. Capital expenditure does not include costs that can be allowed as a deduction in calculating the profits of the business.

'Dwellings'. Expenditure on residential property and other buildings that function as dwellings will not qualify for the SBA. Dwellings are buildings primarily intended or used for long-term residence. This would include university or school accommodation, military accommodation and prisons, but premises used as hotels and care homes will qualify for the SBA.

Where the business itself develops the structure or building, rather than acquires it, the cost of any land preparation necessary for construction will qualify for relief.

Where a structure or building is acquired from a developer, then an apportionment of the purchase cost from the developer will be required to separate the amount of the cost that is attributable to the land. The eligible costs will be the overall acquisition cost less the value of the land acquired.

Integral features and fixtures that are functional assets within a structure or building, such as its lighting or heating system, will continue to qualify for relief as plant or machinery, as they do now, including the AIA within the annual limit, and will not be taken into account for the SBA.

Allowances can be claimed once the structure or building comes into qualifying use. As with any capital allowance, qualifying expenditure can only be claimed once where separate provisions of the Capital Allowances Act 2001 might apply to the same expenditure. Therefore, where parts of a structure or building qualify for allowances as plant and machinery such expenditure will not also be allowed under the SBA. Capital allowances are not due on any costs deductible in calculating profits chargeable to tax, such as land remediation relief.

SECTION 10: MANAGING YOUR PROPERTY FOR INHERITANCE (PART 1) – INHERITANCE TAX

This topic touches a great many people with an interest in property, from the owner of a portfolio proprietor to a family homeowner. The topic is also large and complex, so I have split it into two sections: this section covering Inheritance Tax, and Section 11 covering Trusts. There is also an interesting in-depth case study in Section 12.

Looking to the future and deciding how to pass on property (or whether instead to sell it) is a weighty responsibility, driven sometimes by logical business consideration and sometimes by powerful emotional instinct. Across this spectrum there are important decisions to make regarding tax. Some will affect you while others will affect those who inherit from you; some give useful opportunities to restructure your property holding using trusts while others help you to decide the optimum time and method for transferring ownership to your spouse or children. At stake for all is the risk of losing value in the inheritance through tax that need not have been incurred.

#46. Setting the scene

Anyone building a property-letting business may be looking to pass on the asset to the next generation. The same of course goes for homeowners for whom the home may be the chief source of inheritable wealth for their surviving family.

Key to understanding IHT is that it relates both to assets passed on death and to asset ownership that is transferred while still alive. So, there are two basic ways of enabling a third party to benefit from your property:

1. transferring over full legal title and beneficial possession, either on death or at an earlier stage through some form of gifting: or

2. creating and gifting a formal interest in the property and/or its revenue.

Within these there are some further options. You can gift property into a trust; this is especially useful if the recipients are underage or if you want to benefit a class of recipients. You can hold the properties in one or more limited companies and then gift the shares instead of the properties themselves. This gives maximum flexibility out of a single property or a group of properties and moreover will enable you to keep some control (if you are the director) over the management. You can also create different classes of shares, usually referred to as 'alphabet shares' (discussed in Section 3. Organisational Structure).

Whichever route you choose, there are four main taxes to watch out for!

THE FOUR MAIN TAXES

This is just a brief summary (and we will examine the first two in more detail shortly).

The first pair of taxes – inheritance tax and capital gains tax - are the ones that most readily spring to mind when considering inheritance planning.

Inheritance Tax (IHT)

A gift of either property or shares (or indeed any asset including cash), whether made during your lifetime or on your death will be a chargeable transfer that is liable for IHT, at the value of the asset as at the date of transfer, unless it falls within one of the exemptions (which I'll be discussing later). However the transfer may still not suffer tax if it falls within your nil rate band for IHT.

'Gift' also includes a transfer at an undervalue. The difference between the true value and the amount paid for which it is transferred will still be subject to the IHT rules.

The passage of time is very important in relation to IHT liability, rendering some transfers as potentially tax-exempt. So, a transfer made while you are still alive may be a 'potentially exempt transfer' (PET) that will actually drop out of the tax computation providing you survive for a further seven years. The main exception to this is a gift into what is known as a discretionary trust (about which more later!). But be aware that if you attach conditions to the gift for your own benefit (for example gifting a property which you then continue to live in rent-free), this will usually result in it being a 'gift with a reservation'. This means that, although it is still a gift, for the purposes of IHT the seven-year period for which you need to survive commences only when the reservation ceases, and the gift is treated as being made at the value on that date. If you die whilst the reservation is still in force, then the asset is treated as being part of your estate. I will be discussing later on how PETs and gifts with reservations interact with IHT on death.

Capital Gains Tax (CGT)

The key term to look out for here is 'disposal'. If there is a disposal (sale, gift, or transfer with conditions) of the property (or a share in it) or of shares, and there has been an increase in value since the date you acquired the asset, then there is likely to be a chargeable gain which is subject to CGT at up to 28% (tax year 2019/20). There is an annual exemption for each individual (£12,000 for tax year 2019/20) which is set against the earliest disposals in each tax year, together with certain other exemptions, the most useful of which is that transfers between spouses or civil partners are completely exempt.

Unlike IHT, CGT does not apply to gifts of cash.

The other two taxes below may appear more relevant to the acquisition and running of property, but they can impact on inheritance planning too.

Income Tax

There can be many reasons why you might gift an asset to a son or daughter whose age makes them legally a minor. However, the general rule is that, for as long as the child remains a minor, any income arising from the asset (to which the child is entitled) is taxed as if it were income of the parent and at their current tax rate.

If, however, the gift is of shares, then, by creating a separate class of shares, the dividend income can be restricted during the child's minority, leaving the main advantage for this period to be capital growth rather than income.

The good news is that gifts to grandchildren or other relatives are not affected by this provision.

Stamp Duty Land Tax (SDLT)

Is the giving of property or land treated the same as a sale, and therefore liable to SDLT? Where the transaction is a pure gift the answer is 'no'. But, if there is any condition attached to the gift, such as taking on the mortgage, then this isn't a straight gift and SDLT may be payable on the then value of the transfer, taking into account any 'consideration' involved (for example the amount of the mortgage debt). This can have some surprising consequences and, in some cases, (such as a transfer to a company with which you are connected) may mean that SDLT is levied on the market value of the property itself.

Similar considerations apply to the transfer of shares (where stamp duty is potentially payable unless the transfer is genuinely for 'nil consideration', or falls within one of the other exemptions, such as being 'in consideration of natural love and affection' or on divorce).

> * Now, inheritance planning isn't just for the next generation; sometimes it is to benefit a surviving spouse. So before going deeper into the topic, it's useful to clarify the legal definition of 'spouse' and see how this might impact on your tax planning.

DEFINITION OF 'SPOUSE'

There are some exemptions and reliefs for both IHT and CGT that only apply to married partners. However, we live in a multi-cultural society with a wide range of social customs, so it is important to understand how current law interprets married partner or spouse.

The term is not defined in tax legislation and we therefore have to rely upon general law. No matter how binding the parties may consider a relationship to be (for example because they have undergone a religious ceremony), it is only a lawful marriage under English law if one of the following applies:

- It is a marriage entered into after the reading of banns under the law of the Church of England (no other Christian denomination has this privilege, although I believe there may be special rules for Quaker or Jewish marriages);

- It is by registrar's certificate and conducted in a building registered for marriages;

- It is by common licence or special licence (the latter is issued by the Archbishop of Canterbury);

- It is entered into outside the UK, valid according to the law of place where it is conducted and not repugnant to English public policy. Each of the parties must be free to marry according to the law of the place where he or she is domiciled.

A civil partnership entered into under the Civil Partnerships Act 2004 now also qualifies for the spouse exemptions. At the time of writing, the Act applies only to same sex couples, but it has been announced that, following a landmark Supreme Court ruling in June 2018, the right to enter into a civil partnership will be extended to heterosexual couples.

Living together does not make you a spouse for capital tax purposes, no matter how long the relationship has lasted and there is no such thing in modern English law as a 'common-law-marriage'.

Of course a bigamous or polygamous marriage is never valid (unless the fourth alternative above applies) and a forced marriage (or a sham marriage) will be 'voidable'. This means that you can apply to have it annulled, but until annulment takes place it remains legally a marriage.

As regards succession in the estate of a deceased person, not being married means that automatic rights to inherit under the intestacy laws do not apply. The survivor of an unmarried couple (or civil partners) is likely to be able to make a claim for fair and reasonable financial provision under the Inheritance (Provision for Family & Dependents) Act 1975 - but only if she/he can show a degree of financial dependence on the deceased person.

Income-splitting to a spouse – legal or not?

Before going on to look at specific tax liabilities and reliefs, there is a particular tax issue that can arise when income-splitting - transferring income to a spouse (or to a child under the age of 18).

There are various instances where it might seem advantageous to transfer some income over to a spouse. However, if done for example as an attempt by a higher rate taxpayer to deliberately avoid some tax by passing income to a lower-rate taxpayer, HMRC will simply treat the income in question as being that of the original taxpayer and levy Income Tax on this basis. It may also be classed as tax evasion and the legal position on this is clear, with legislation deliberately designed to prevent schemes that make use the annual allowances and lower rates of tax of other family members for what is really the income of one member of the family only.

The exception, however, is that the rule does not apply to an outright gift from one spouse or civil partner to another, as long as all the income produced by the gifted property goes with it to the spouse, and provided that the property given is not "wholly or substantially a right to income". This was tested in a leading case on the issue of income from dividends split between husband and wife:

The Arctic Systems Case: a cautionary tale

In November 2005, the Court of Appeal heard a tax appeal that was of vital importance to family businesses in the UK. HMRC had argued that Mr and Mrs Jones, proprietors of Arctic Systems Ltd, had attempted to reduce their tax liability by ignoring the 'settlement' rules on income from dividends. The court, however, found *against* HMRC and in favour of Mr and Mrs Jones. Here's the outline argument that led to that decision.

Mr & Mrs Jones were the proprietors and shareholders (the company had been formed with two shares, of which they each held one) of Arctic Systems Ltd. The 'key person' and driver of the business was Mr Jones, as a computer consultant, with Mrs Jones providing back-office support. Although the company paid salaries to both Mr & Mrs Jones, the bulk of their income was received as dividends. At that time, the advantages of receiving income via dividends and of dividing that income evenly between them were considerable.

HMRC's case: HMRC had argued that a business carried on by a husband who then allowed his wife to take a substantial percentage of the profits through dividends would constitute a "settlement" for the purposes of section 660A Income and Corporation Taxes Act 1988 (latterly section 619 onwards of the Income Tax (Trading and Other Income) Act 2005). The case went all the way through the Special Commissioners, the High Court and the Court of Appeal before reaching the House of Lords in June 2007.

The legal opinion: The House of Lords judgement concluded that there had been a settlement but that it fell within the spousal gift exemption (as set out above), thereby rejecting the final appeal from HMRC.

This was good news for Mr & Mrs Jones and, as a leading case, has considerable authority in similar situations. Had it gone against Mr & Mrs Jones, the amount they would have been obliged to pay in arrears of tax, interest and possibly penalties would have been very considerable.

The value of professional advice and good records: I must point out that HMRC has subsequently won other cases involving husband and wife businesses with income splitting arrangements where the situations were not identical to the Arctic systems case. This is all the more reason to take specialist professional advice before embarking on this type of arrangement. It is also a useful reminder that important distinctions are made by the courts in such cases, including:

1. between inaccurate returns that are made from innocent error and those that are made negligently or deliberately: and

2. between disclosures made voluntarily and those made only on prompting from HMRC or indeed discovered by HMRC without any disclosure by the tax-payer.

This all goes into the consideration of what an appropriate penalty may be. As I have urged elsewhere in the book, keeping good records and evidence of professional advice prudently taken can help alleviate the level of penalty should HMRC's argument win the day.

Let's now get to the heart of the matter and examine IHT in depth.

#47. Inheritance Tax (IHT) in essence

HOW IHT WORKS

"Inheritance Tax is a tax on the estate (the property, money and possessions) of someone who's died. The standard Inheritance Tax rate is 40%, charged on that part of the estate that is above the threshold." www.gov.uk.

And that threshold? Currently the standard arrangement is that you can leave an estate up to the value of £325,000 without incurring IHT (called the nil rate band, discussed below).

However IHT also applies to lifetime transfers, subject to the concept of the Potentially Exempt Transfer (PET) which I'll be discussing later. Any lifetime transfer which is not within the PET rules will eat into the £325,000.

But there are other breaks too, outlined below.

IHT RELIEFS AND EXEMPTIONS

The following giftings are exempt from IHT

- Gift to spouse or civil partner;

- Gifts on marriage (up to £5,000 for child, £2,500 for grandchild or great grandchild, anyone else £1,000);

- Annual gifts of not more than £3,000 in total per year (1 year carry-forward);

- Individual gifts of not more than £250 each (as long as not combined with another exemption);

- Gifts to charities or political parties.

In addition:

- The rate of IHT on death is reduced to 36% (on most assets) if you leave at least 10% of your estate to charity;

- Normal expenditure out of income is free of tax; this means that IHT is not going to apply every time you give an expensive birthday present! If your level of income and assets is such that you can easily afford to make lavish gifts and this is a normal thing for you to do (or the occasion on which you make the gift fits into your general way of living or family life) then these are not chargeable transfers (nor PETs) for IHT. It is of course possible that you will be required to demonstrate to HMRC that this is normal expenditure for you.

- S11 IHTA 1984 provides that expenditure incurred for the maintenance of a dependent are normally not subject to IHT e.g. provision of education for child or grandchild

- Chargeable lifetime transfers into trusts generate IHT at 20% (if over nil-rate band) but drop out of the overall computation if you survive seven years. Otherwise on death the rate of tax increases to 40%.

Any IHT charged is based on the value at the time of the gifting (except in the case of a 'reservation of benefit', discussed earlier).

BUSINESS ASSETS RELIEF AND AGRICULTURAL ASSETS RELIEF

Business and agricultural assets have their own system of Business Relief for IHT, which applies to both lifetime transfers and on death.

Business Relief

This applies where the transfer is of a business belonging to the transferor or an interest in that business and works by reducing the value of the asset for IHT purposes.

The relief is 100% for a business or interest in a business owned by you or for shares in an unlisted company

50% relief applies for shares controlling more than 50% of the voting rights in a listed company, or for land, buildings and machinery owned by you personally and used in a business in which you were a partner or which you control (or used by a business but held in a trust from which it had the right to benefit).

In each case you must have held the asset for at least two years before the date of transfer. You cannot claim Business Relief on an asset to which Agricultural Relief applies (see below).

Relief is not available for a business that is wholly or mainly making profits from investments. There are, however, some grey areas for this including property management and the development of properties where there is a large element of letting, management and buying and selling of properties, and also holiday letting businesses.

Agricultural Relief

This applies to agricultural land or pasture used for growing crops or intensively rearing livestock. It also includes farmhouses farm cottages and farm buildings. Some other assets also qualify such as growing crops, stud farms and milk quotas.

Farm equipment and machinery, harvested crops, livestock and derelict buildings do not qualify (but may qualify for Business Relief).

The property must be part of a working farm and have been owned for agricultural purposes for 2 years immediately prior to transfer, if occupied by you or your spouse or civil partner or a company controlled by you. If it is occupied by anyone else then the period is 7 years.

The relief applies by reducing the value of the asset for IHT. Relief is 100% of the property if you farm the property yourself, it is used by someone else on a short-term grazing licence, or it is let on a tenancy that began on or after 1 September 1995. (It may also qualify in some circumstances if it was owned prior to 10 March 1981 and you had no right to vacant possession between that date and the date of transfer). In all other cases the relief is 50%.

If Business Relief or Agricultural Relief is not available, the properties pass to the beneficiaries at the market value and this may give rise to an IHT charge. If this is a lifetime gift then you'll need to look at the possible CGT implications (and it is possible that Entrepreneurs' Relief will apply). If however the transfer occurs on death then there is an immediate tax-free uplift in value (without charge to CGT) to the value agreed for probate.

N.B. Agricultural Relief is quite a complex relief (as is the law relating to agricultural property) so I recommend you take advice from a professional specialising in this.

NIL RATE BANDS

This tends to be the linchpin of tax-planning for IHT, being the part of your estate that suffers tax at a nil-rate:

- The standard nil rate band is currently £325,000 per individual and this is a 'rolling' figure for lifetime transfers (with PETs – discussed below-dropping out of the calculation after 7 years). The nil rate band is not likely to go up before 2021.

- Where an individual dies without making full use of the nil rate band (for example because the estate has passed to a spouse and is therefore exempt from IHT), then the spouse/civil partner can take over the unused proportion.

Enhanced nil rate band

- This applies only to transfers on death where an interest in a property that the deceased occupied some time in their life is transferred to a lineal descendant (including foster/stepchildren). It applies an additional £150,000 for the tax year 2019/20, increasing the nil rate band to £475,000 provided the estate does not exceed £2 million.

- The enhanced nil rate band will increase by £25,000 per year until 2020/21 and then be set in line with Consumer Prices Index.

- The unused enhanced band is also transferable to surviving spouse/ civil partner.

Read more under Using Enhanced ('Residential') IHT Nil Rate band for the family home below.

#48. Some IHT planning options
ALPHABET SHARES

I discuss these in *Section 3. Organisational Structure*, but mention them again here as a useful option when you want to transfer shares to your minority-aged child but want to restrict the income until they reach a certain age. For more information please refer to Section 3.

POTENTIALLY EXEMPT TRANSFERS (PETS) AND LIFETIME GIFTS

A gift made while still alive is potentially exempt for IHT and so can be a useful way to transfer assets. It is completely exempt if the donor survives seven years after making the gift. But if the donor dies before this, the gifted asset is taxed as if a part of the deceased's estate (valued as at the date of gifting). However:

- There is tapered relief via a sliding scale tax rate for PETs where the donor dies more than 3 years after the gift (from 32% down to 8%);

- Quick succession relief is also available where both donor and donee die within seven years of gift.

Legal definition of a PET

What is and is not a PET?

A PET is a lifetime transfer of value that, first of all, satisfies three conditions:

1. The transfer is by an individual on or after 18 March 1986;

2. It would be a chargeable transfer if it were not for s. 3A of Inheritance Tax Act 1984 (or, if only partly chargeable, is a PET to the extent that it would be chargeable); and

3. It is a gift to another individual or a transfer into some types of trust (but NOT if this is a gift into a discretionary trust, where the trustees have complete discretion to decide how the trust assets are dealt with).

Transfer of Value: It is worth just pointing out that value is assessed on the basis is the loss to the transferor. A simple example would be where a shareholder with a 51% holding transfers 2% to a third party. By so doing the transferor gives up a controlling interest in the company (because someone with 51% can govern ordinary shareholders' resolutions which require a simple majority). So that 2% is worth a lot more to the transferor than it is to the transferee and it is the 'diminution in the value of the transferor's estate' that is the measure of value for IHT.

Exempt transfer: A transfer of value that is wholly covered by an exemption is an *exempt transfer* and *not* a PET, whether or not the three conditions above are satisfied. An example would be a transfer between spouses. This is completely exempt from the start and therefore not a PET (nor a chargeable transfer) – see IHT exemptions and reliefs, above.

If it is not an exempt transfer or a PET, then it will be a chargeable transfer attracting IHT. However, whether or not IHT is actually payable will depend upon whether and by how much the value of the transfer exceeds your unused nil rate band at the time of the transfer.

Finally, remember that IHT is all about gifts. If an individual makes a transfer at open market value and receives payment (whether in terms of cash or otherwise) then IHT does not apply. If however the transfer is at an undervalue, then IHT will apply to the amount by which the consideration is at an undervalue.

When is a transfer not a PET?

The two main gifts that are not classed as PETs are:

- Transfers into a relevant property trust (which includes what is generally known as a discretionary trust) because the gift is not to an individual (unless the trust is set up under s89 Inheritance Tax Act 1984 for the benefit of a disabled beneficiary);

- Transfers to a company.

In addition, the following will not be PETs:

- Transfers by a close company (i.e. one that has five or fewer participators). N.B. Although IHT does not apply to limited companies, HMRC will 'look through' the company structure and treat it as a transfer by the individual participators;

- The deemed disposition on the alteration in the capital or share rights of close companies;

- The release of a life interest between 18 March 1986 and 16 March 1987;

- The transfer of woodlands (IHTM04062) subject to an outstanding Estate Duty charge, which only qualifies for partial PET treatment.

As time goes on it becomes less likely that either of the last two categories will apply.

Who pays the IHT on a failed PET?

Where a gift ultimately fails to qualify as a PET (for example, if the donor dies within seven years), the primary tax burden is on the recipient, not on the donor's estate.

So in a net estate of say £700,000 on top of which the deceased had made a PET of £100,000 in the three years before death, IHT would be 40% of the full £800,000 = £320,000. In this case, IHT is payable by the recipient on the failed PET of £100,000 (1/8 = £40,000) and the remainder is payable from the estate. If death occurred after three years (but before seven years) the 40% rate on the PET would be reduced on the sliding scale.

So, if you make a PET, consider whether, in the event of your premature death, the beneficiary of the PET should pay the outstanding IHT. If you don't want this to happen, ensure that your will is drafted to avoid an unexpected tax burden.

Transfers to a company or by a close company

The picture can get murky when value is transferred to a company for the benefit of an individual – does this meet the rules regarding PETs?

Let's say A owns X Ltd and owns all of the issued share capital. Then A's mother gifts A by giving the company £200,000.

Although this is a transfer of value, it does not satisfy the condition of being a gift to an individual and so is not a PET.

The gift is a transfer of value by an individual, so it will be chargeable to IHT unless it is either exempt or a PET. But because it does not satisfy the condition of being a gift to an individual, it is not a PET. It is not an exempt transfer (and would not be exempt even if the transfer had been made directly to A as an individual) so it is a chargeable transfer.

However, the annual exemption of £3,000 will still apply (as will the previous year's exemption which can be carried forward for one year) as long as A's mother has not already used this up on other transfers. The balance of £194,000 will be the amount of the chargeable transfer and will be taxed at a nil rate (assuming that this has not already been used up by earlier PETs of chargeable transfers).

When a close company **makes** a transfer of value, HMRC will look through the company and charge tax as if each individual participator has made a transfer of the amount apportioned to them by reference to their rights and interests in the company immediately before the transfer. So, it's deemed to be a transfer of value by the participators as individuals. An example is where a company transfers a house to a director for no consideration, or a consideration at less than market value.

Just to clarify, a 'deemed transfer of value' is one where there is no actual transfer by the individual but the operation of tax law results in the situation being treated as if a transfer had taken place. You also find this terminology where there is a transaction (other than a straightforward gift) but actually there is no 'consideration' (e.g. money paid) or the consideration is below open market value, but nevertheless the transaction is treated as being a transfer of value (usually at open market value).

What if the transfer is by a company that is not a close company?

If it's a transfer for no consideration or at an undervalue, then, depending on the circumstances, the taxation consequences could be significant but IHT will not apply as it's not a transfer by an individual nor is it deemed to be a transfer by individual(s). It could be classed as a benefit in kind, or it could be an arrangement under an Employee Incentive Scheme.

PETs and Discretionary Trusts

We examine trusts in detail in Section 11, but I want to mention them here when used in conjunction with PETs.

One way to make use of the nil rate bands and the tapered rates if you die within seven years of gifting is to work with both PETs and discretionary trusts (where no beneficiary has an actual right to a benefit but it is left instead to the discretion of trustees to distribute trust assets to one or more of a stated pool of beneficiaries). Effectively you gift directly to individual beneficiaries via a PET and you also put some money in to a trust. This can significantly change the total IHT but it can also change who must pay it - your estate or your recipient?

A transfer to a discretionary trust is not a PET but a chargeable transfer, and as such, if the gift takes you over your nil rate band, IHT will be payable by you on the portion of the gift that exceeds the nil rate band. If the chargeable transfer does not take you beyond the nil rate band and you survive seven years, it drops out of any IHT computation. And as already explained, if you die within seven years of making a PET it is treated as a chargeable transfer but the IHT is reduced on a tapered scale if four years elapsed since the date of the transfer (but with the IHT payable by the donee, not by your estate).

A word of warning however -if you are making both PETs and chargeable lifetime transfers, you do need to be careful in what order you make them, as if you then die within 7 years of the last transfer, there can be some surprising IHT consequences.

Taxation of discretionary trusts

- IHT is charged when trustees vest property to a beneficiary (referred to as 'exit charge') to a maximum of 5.85%

- 10-yearly IHT charge (maximum 6% of value of assets in the trust where these exceed nil-rate band)

- Nil-rate band trusts (i.e. transfer within the settlor's individual nil rate for IHT) are very tax-efficient;

- Income tax is charged on trustees (38.1% to 45% and note lower trustees' annual allowance) unless the property has been 'appointed'. The term 'appointed' means that the trustees have decided to pass the assets to one or of the beneficiaries. This could be either a direct transfer or the trustees could themselves set up another trust vehicle. This could be the type of trust where the beneficiary is entitled to the income but not the capital (an 'interest in possession trust') and in this case the income tax would be charged on the person receiving the income (at their personal rate of income tax.

- As with most trust, CGT is chargeable to the trustees on disposal of assets to a third party (and subject to trustee's annual CGT exemption) and is payable out of trust assets.

So how can you benefit from this dual option?

If you are considering making both PETs and gifts into discretionary trusts, it's generally best to make the chargeable transfers first - at least from the donor's point of view for IHT. This is because the order of gifting may deliver different tax outcomes. But you do need to do the maths! Let's look at an example, comparing outcomes depending on the order of gifting:

X makes a gift of £400,000 to Y in March 2014; this qualifies as a PET.

X then makes a gift of £250,000 in May 2016 into a discretionary trust; this becomes a chargeable lifetime transfer ('CLT').

As no other gifts have been made, X's estate will be able to use the annual IHT exemption of £3,000 (annual gift limit) with regard to both gifts for the tax year of transfer and the preceding year. The exemptions for 2012/13 and 2013/14 reduce the amount potentially liable to IHT from £400,000 to £394,000 and those for 2015/16 and 2016/17 reduce the amount from £250,000 to £244,000.

At this stage, the CLT generates no IHT liability because the PET does not come into account and the £244,000 is within the nil rate band.

X then dies in November 2018, within less than seven years of making the first gift. The resulting IHT adjustments and calculation are as follows:

The PET becomes a CLT of £394,000 which exceeds the nil rate band of £325,000 by £69,000. IHT of 40% would therefore be payable on the £69,000 (£27,600) but because 4 years and 8 months have elapsed between the gift the rate of IHT is reduced by taper relief to 24% (£16,560). This tax is payable by the **donee** of the gift.

However, the fact that the first lifetime gift used up the nil rate band means that the second lifetime gift into the discretionary trust (which was not a PET) now falls to be taxed at 40% instead of being taxed at the nil rate. No taper relief is available, so IHT is due at 40% of the gift which (allowing for the annual exemptions available at the time the gift was made was valued at £244,000. The tax is payable by the donor (or rather, as he is now deceased, out of his estate) at 40% of £244,000

(£97,600). Whatever else remains of the deceased's estate is also taxed at 40%.

Now let's see what happens if the gifts took place the other way around.

The first gift (in March 2014) of £250,000 into the trust is a CLT, not a PET and the annual exemptions available reduce the value to £244,000. However this comfortably comes within the nil rate band and so will not be subject to IHT.

The second gift (May 2016) of £400,000 (reduced to £394,000 by the annual exemptions available) would be a PET, so with no IHT liability when the gift is made.

On the death, the PET becomes a chargeable transfer but the unused nil rate band (£325,000 less £244,000 = £81,000) reduces the chargeable transfer value to £313,000. As in this scenario less than three years have elapsed between the date of the gift (May 2016) and the date of death (November 2018) taper relief is not available and so the rate of IHT remains at 40% (125,200).

So the total IHT in the first scenario is £114,160 and in the second £125,200. On this occasion the total IHT is greater on the second occasion. However, from the point of view of the donor's ultimate personal tax bill, (paid out of his estate as a liability incurred as a result of lifetime transactions) the second scenario is much better.

This is because there is of course a difference in who pays the IHT. In the first case the donor's estate pays most of it, with the donee of the PET being liable for only £16,560 (as a result of the taper relief) and in the second case all the IHT is on the failed PET and therefore is paid by the donee. The donor's estate pays nothing. It can easily be an unintended consequence that the donee of the PET ends up paying any IHT and therefore if you are making a PET you may want to consider whether or not you should make provision in your will the estate to pay any IHT resulting from you dying within the 7 year period.

There is also a trap for the unwary if you have made both PETs and chargeable transfers in the seven years before your death. The calculation for IHT on death generally takes into account only the transfers made in the seven years before death. However if you die within seven years of gifting into a discretionary trust, not only do the gifted assets (a chargeable transfer) affect the calculation of your nil rate band, but other gifts that were made in the previous seven years before the establishment of the trust, also form part of the calculation. So you could end up looking back 14 years instead of just 7

The above illustration is just a simple example, and more extreme consequences can occur. So, before you make lifetime gifts, especially if these include gifts into trusts, do look at the IHT consequences if you were to die prematurely.

PETs and GWR rules

One final caution about PETS - beware of making gifts with a reservation of benefit ('GWRs').

To be a PET the gift must transfer its full benefits to the recipient – you cannot 'reserve' part of the benefit for yourself, even if you do not make use of it. An example of this would be if you gift your residence to your children but continue to live in it yourself. This would be a valid gift but not a PET, and only gains PET status when you cease to reserve any rights to benefits.

The aim of the GWR rules is to prevent you from reducing the IHT charge by making gifts while not actually making any change to your basic situation. Whether or not it is a GWR depends upon the facts and the nature of the benefit reserved.

PRE-OWNED ASSETS TAX (POA TAX)

Although this is not an Inheritance Tax issue as such, it links into the whole regime of lifetime gifting for IHT purposes out of what would be an individual's estate.

The rules were introduced by Schedule 15 of the Finance Act 2004 to tackle instances of people managing to get around the Gifts With Reservation (GWR) rules explained above. They impose an annual income *tax* charge where the individual is still able to benefit from the asset (referring primarily to land and buildings but also apply to chattels and certain interests in trusts). So not only does the gift (if a PET) run the risk of no longer qualifying as a PET for the 7-year rule until the donor ceases to reserve the benefit (because of the GRW), but also he/she is taxed as if they get income from this.

Here is an illustration:

A wants to gift his home to B as an outright gift – but A still wants to live in the house. Following the GWR rules, this would mean that the house continues to be counted as part of A's estate for IHT.

If however A had used a home loan scheme in making the gift, POA rules would apply, charging A income tax on the loan and removing the asset from A's estate. This would be the case even if A only lived in the home part of the time.

If A sold his home to B for full market value neither the POA nor the GWR rules would apply.

The rules also catch situations where an individual has contributed towards someone else's purchase of property from which the individual later benefits, unless the period between the original gift and the occupation of the property by the individual exceeds seven years.

So if A made a cash gift to B and B then used the cash to buy a property which A moved into, the POA rules would apply unless more than seven years had elapsed since the gift. This would still be the case even if B had used the cash to buy an asset that he later sold to buy the property.

There are a number of exclusions from the rules, one of the most important being that transactions will not be caught where a property is transferred to a spouse or former spouse under a court order.

Despite the fact that the regime is only effective from 6 April 2005, it can apply to arrangements that may have been put in place at any time since March 1986.

How is POA tax calculated?

The charge is based on a notional market rent for the property. Here is an example:

Assuming a rental yield of, say, 5%, the income tax charge for a higher rate taxpayer on a £1 million property will be £20,000 each year. The rental yield or value is established assuming a tenant's repairing lease.

Properties need to be valued once every five years. In situations where events happened prior to 6 April 2005, the first year of charge was 2005/06 and the first valuation date was 6 April 2005. In these cases, a new valuation should have been made on 6 April 2010 and 6 April 2015.

If the occupier pays a rent, the charge is reduced accordingly, and there is no charge where a full market rent is paid.

The charge will not apply where the deemed income in relation to all property affected by the rules is less than £5,000.

The rules are more complex where part interests in properties are involved.

Avoiding POA tax

1. You can avoid the charge by electing to treat the property as part of the IHT estate – this election cannot be revoked once the first filing date for a POA charge has passed. The effect of the election using the example above is that the annual £20,000 income tax charge will be avoided but instead the £1 million property is effectively treated as part of the IHT estate and could one day give rise to an IHT liability of £400,000 for the donee. The election must be made by 31 January in the year following that in which the charge would first apply. In other words, if it would apply for 2015/16 the election should have been made by 31 January 2017

2. Where a share of your family home is given to a family member (say an adult child) who lives with you, both IHT and the POA charge can be avoided. The expenses of the property should be shared. This course of action is only suitable where the sharing is likely to be long term and there are not other family members who would be compromised by the making of the gift.

3. Equity release schemes whereby you sell all or part of your home to a commercial company or bank are not caught by the POA rules. If the sale is to a family member, a sale of the whole property is outside the POA rules but the sale of only a part is caught if the sale was on or after 7 March 2005. The cash you receive can then be given away using other IHT exemptions.

USING ENHANCED ('RESIDENTIAL') IHT NIL RATE BAND FOR THE FAMILY HOME

First, a reminder of the conditions of enhancement rates that are added to the ordinary nil rate band:

Enhancement rules

The enhancement rate is only available to property left on death by someone who at some point used it as a residence and who leaves it to a linear descendant. The additional element is as follows (relating to the year of death):

- £100,000 in 2017/18

- £125,000 in 2018/19

- £150,000 in 2019/20

- £175,000 in 2020/21

- Then indexed by reference to the Consumer Price Index rounded to nearest £1,000.

The rules can be clarified further:

- One additional rate band per individual only;

- Can be used for any residential property that has at some point been a residence for the deceased (not necessarily the most recent). Does not have to be the principal residence;

- Linear descendants include children (both legitimate and illegitimate), grandchildren and remoter issue, step-children, adopted children, foster children and where the donor has been appointed by the court a guardian;

- Also available where deceased leaves interest in home to the spouse of a lineal descendent;

- Can apply where the deceased has an interest in the property which is less than a full interest in the freehold or long leasehold e.g. a life interest;

- Can also apply where the deceased has sold the property and either replaced it with another property or retained assets in the estate of an equivalent value ('downsizing relief' available for disposals after 8 July 2015).

Enhanced nil rate band and trusts

Enhanced nil rate band is generally not available where a home is passed into a trust but there are a few exceptions, including:

- Homes placed in trust for surviving spouse will benefit on spouse's death;

- Discretionary trust where asset is 'appointed out' within 2 years of death;

- Some trusts where beneficiary is a minor or under 25 or treated as if they own the property themselves.

Unused enhanced nil rate band

Unused enhanced nil rate band is transferable to a spouse or civil partner in the same was as unused ordinary nil rate band. To work out the transferable amount, you calculate the proportion of unused band on first death, then apply that proportion to the available band for the survivor. Now, since the government might choose to revise bands to keep them in line with economic factors, this proportional basis is important as it can in turn change the financial value of the unused band that is passed on to surviving spouses/civil partners.

Here's an illustration – and keep an eye on those percentages of bands that are unused and passed on:

Husband (H) dies in May 2017. At the time of death, as a result of lifetime transfers, H has only used 75k of the available nil rate band (325k). This means that 76.93% of his nil rate band is unused.

He also leaves an interest worth £75,000 in a qualifying residential property to a lineal descendent, and so eligible for the *enhanced* nil rate band (100k for 2017/18). This means that he uses up 75%, leaving 25% of unused enhanced nil rate band.

The rest of the estate passes to his wife.

Wife (W) then dies in June 2018 leaving all her estate to the children of the marriage. Let's now examine her position at the time of death – and this is where we see the proportional calculations taking effect if nil rate bands have changed in the intervening time between deaths.

The available ordinary nil rate band has not changed – it still sits at 325k. So, her own ordinary nil rate band is £325K, and the unused 76.93% of H's nil rate band that she took on remains the same at 250k.

However, by the time of her death, the *enhanced* nil rate band has been increased, from 100k to 125k. And assuming W has a qualifying residential property, she has her own enhanced nil rate band. But H's unused band that passed to her is now worth 25 % of 125k, not 100k, which equals £31,500 instead of £25,000.

Suppose in the above example, H owned the family residence (worth £500K) as equal tenants-in-common with W and had left this interest in trust to her for her life and then on to the children of his first marriage.

The gift of the life interest would be exempt from IHT. The gift of the interest in another qualifying property would still use up 75% of the enhanced NRB.

On W's death, as life tenant she would be treated as the donor of the H's 50% share, but this would be to her step-children so these are still treated as her lineal descendants. The gift of her own 50% also qualifies for the enhanced NRB.

She can still take over H's unused NRB and enhanced NRB so the amount of available relief remains the same but how is the relief applied?

Bear in mind that an individual can apply the enhanced NRB in respect of one residential property only.

The point is that it depends on how the will is drafted!

The reliefs apply to W so her personal representatives ('PRs') may choose which assets bear the tax (subject to the operation of law and the wording of the will).

The PRs could therefore (in the absence of directions by H or by W in their wills) nominate the whole of the enhanced NRB to W's 50% of the property. As regards the ordinary NRB this is usually allocated to the residuary estate as it is the residue that effectively bears the IHT (again in the absence of directions to the contrary).

Tapered enhanced nil rate relief on estate exceeding £2m

Estates over £2.2m will have no enhanced nil rate band. However, if the value of the deceased's estate (including the capital supporting a life interest) exceeds £2m but not £2.2m, the enhanced nil rate band is reduced – the reduction is calculated as the excess over £2m divided by two.

Additional points on enhanced nil rate bands

- The carry forward of the enhanced nil rate band must be claimed within 2 years of second death;

- Varying the disposition in an estate by means of a Deed of Variation (see Deeds of Variation in Section 12) will still allow for qualification for the enhanced nil rate band.

Also, make a will and be sure that the wording is precise and correct; and don't leave the planning until the death of the surviving spouse – things in life can change!

IHT AND CAPITAL GAINS TAX ON DEATH

There are not many opportunities to talk about a tax-free uplift, but here's one.

As you can see, the IHT situation on death is pretty clear. You add up the value of your whole estate, plus any gifts in the preceding seven years (less any debts). Then you take away:

- surviving spouse exemption (if any)

- unused nil rate band

- enhanced (residential) nil rate band (if applicable)

- unused nil rate band and enhanced nil rate band from spouse/partner who pre-deceased you.

Whatever is left will bear IHT at 40% (subject to any of the reliefs discussed earlier) - end of story.

However, Capital Gains Tax is unlikely to be a concern. Why?

Usually, if you dispose of a capital asset to which CGT applies, even if you gift it, there is a chargeable gain calculated by reference to the value at the date of disposal, less the acquisition value, less the costs of acquisition/disposal and less the costs of capital enhancement.

However, the law states that when you die there is a notional disposal by you of all your assets at the moment of your death and a notional reacquisition at the then current value by your personal representatives *but without any charge* to CGT.

Unless your PRs hang on to the assets (e.g. in a trust set up by will) or the assets themselves fluctuate wildly in value, CGT will be irrelevant.

So the trick is to balance the CGT you may suffer in disposing of assets during your lifetime (allowing for the annual exemption for CGT and your personal tax position) against the 40% IHT your estate would suffer if you still own them at your death.

PROPERTY-HOLDING – JOINTLY-OWNED PROPERTIES

There can be advantages to have joint ownership of a property, either as a joint tenancy or a tenancy-in-common:

- **Joint tenancy:** If one owner dies, his or her share goes automatically (without any formal transfer document) to the other co-owner(s).

   While all the co-owners are alive they are deemed to have equal shares.

- **Tenancy-in common:** Legal title (i.e. the persons named as trustees) is a joint tenancy (and can't be anything else) but the beneficial interest can be in any shares, equal or unequal.

   Each co-owner can give away his or her share by will or deed. Other benefits include:

   o   Safeguarding individual co-owners' shares where contributions are not equal;

   o   Safeguarding the succession of a co-owner's heirs to his or her share of the property;

   o   For tax-planning purposes.

Income from jointly owned properties

It may be that you want income to be apportioned unequally between joint owners. However, the usual rule is that the income of jointly-held properties (whether joint tenancies or tenancies-in-common) will be deemed to belong equally to the owners. But s.836 Income Tax Act 2007 provides an important *exception* by allowing individuals to make a declaration to HMRC of their unequal beneficial interests on Income Tax Form 17.

The rules are as follows:

- This option only applies to couples (husband and wife or civil partners) who are living together;

- You must be *tenants-in-common*. A form 17 election cannot be made (i.e. the property income cannot be split other than in equal shares) if the couple own the property as 'joint tenants';

- HMRC requires evidence that the couple's beneficial interests are unequal, such as a written declaration or deed. If the property is jointly held in equal shares, it is not possible to make a declaration for income to be divided in unequal shares;

- The declaration on form 17 must be made by both co-owners jointly. For example, it cannot be made by one co-owner if the other disagrees;

- The declaration on form 17 must reach HMRC within 60 days from the date of signature of the last co-owner to sign; otherwise, it is invalid. HMRC generally enforces this time limit strictly;

- The form 17 rule only applies to income arising from the date of the declaration (s 837(4)). Thus, a declaration made very late in the tax year may have little or no effect on the couple's overall tax position for that year;

- HMRC treats a valid declaration on form 17 as continuing to apply in later tax years, until one co-owner dies, or the couple separate permanently or divorce, or the beneficial interest of a co-owner in the property or income changes.

Please note, this is an instance where property law and tax rules can diverge! If property is owned as tenants-in-common, as a matter of law the income belongs to the owners in the same ratio as the capital. But for income tax purposes the assumption is that it is owned in equal shares unless a valid Form 17 declaration is in force.

Valuations of undivided shares in property

It's useful to insert a note here about valuing shared property. When a property is in a single name, valuation is simple - you just need to arrive at the current market value. However, if you're looking at the value of a share in a property then as a rule it's not just a simple arithmetical calculation using the value of the property and the ratio of the shares.

HMRC is likely to adopt the following guidelines:

- A 'broad brush' approach;
- Co-owner remains in residence: discount of 15%;
- Co-owner has right to reside but chooses not to: 10% - 15% (original purpose);
- Some current benefit, but not residence: 10%;
- Majority interest: 10%;
- Minority interest (little control): 20%.

DEEDS OF VARIATION FOR POST-MORTEM TAX PLANNING

We have now looked in some detail at the process of leaving an estate, and of receiving from a deceased person's estate. But what do you do if you prefer what you inherit to go to someone else?

As a rule, when you inherit something there is no legal reason why you cannot give it away to another person in whole or in part. As a straightforward gift, this might be in the form of a PET or, if you create a discretionary trust, a Chargeable Lifetime Transfer, with related tax implications. However, under s.142 of the Inheritance Tax Act 1984, if you can identify how you would have preferred the will to work, you can, at the point of inheriting, change the terms of the will in a tax-efficient way. You can also do this if the deceased didn't leave a will.

The tool is the Deed of Variation – so called as it varies the provisions of someone's will of the devolution of their estate.

To understand its value, let's look at what normally happens first.

Let's say you inherit a substantial asset that you have no use for and want to pass it on to someone who could really make use of it. Being a completely separate action from your inheriting the asset, this makes it a gift by you with consequent IHT or CGT implications. However, if you make the gift more or less straightaway, there is unlikely to be any significant increase in value since you received it (although of course there could be!) so there is unlikely to be any chargeable CGT gain.

The problem occurs when, for IHT purposes, this is a potentially exempt transfer or even, if you use a discretionary trust, a chargeable lifetime transfer and you will have to survive at least 7 years in order for it to drop out of your IHT computation. Also, if you gift to your minor child, the income will usually be deemed to be your income as long as the child is under 18.

How is a Deed of Variation different?

If done correctly, a Deed of Variation will have the effect that for both CGT and IHT the gift you make is deemed to have taken place as at the deceased's date of death exactly as if they had written this in their will, and thereby your gifting incurs no IHT for you personally. For Income Tax purposes, however, the change only takes effect as at the date of the Deed, so any income arising before that date will still be treated as belonging to the original recipient.

Why might you want to do this?

As well as avoiding the charge to IHT (and possibly CGT), there are other good reasons such as:

- To include a beneficiary who was excluded from the will or intestacy provisions;

- To take advantage of an unused nil rate band or an exemption which the original dispositions ignored;

- To distribute the assets in a tax-efficient way to where/who they are most needed.

Of course, there are various conditions and options:

- Must be made within 2 years of the death;

- Must clearly identify the part of the estate being varied, and who is to benefit from the variation;

- Must be signed by all the beneficiaries who are 'giving up' a benefit;

- Must include a statement, in a prescribed form, of whether the beneficiaries intend the variation to be effective for IHT and/or CGT purposes.

And:

- Can only vary dispositions on death, not lifetime dispositions;

- Can only be carried out by the person who controls the inherited assets that it is wished to vary (i.e. you cannot insist on another beneficiary entering into a variation if they do not wish to do so);

- Can apply to dispositions under a will or under intestacy;

- The new beneficiary can be anyone. It is not restricted to those mentioned in the original will, or those who benefit on intestacy because they are related to the deceased. You can also for example benefit a charity or other organisation.

- Can effect a posthumous severance of a joint tenancy;

- Cannot otherwise be used to vary assets that are not within the deceased's estate;

- Can create a trust of the varied assets;

- Cannot be used to exercise trustee's powers posthumously;

- Cannot be retrospective for SDLT (or Income Tax).

Although HMRC indicates that they will accept a variation in any written form as long as it complies with requirements, it is usual for a formal deed to be prepared. It is not strictly necessary for the executors or administrators of the estate to be parties to the deed unless the effect is that more IHT is payable; however it is usual for them to be parties so that they are aware of the effect for distribution purposes and can also ensure that the deed is presented to HMRC.

The deed must be presented to HMRC within 6 months of being executed if the statement of intent for it to apply for IHT purposes is to be effective. In most circumstances you will want the deed to apply for CGT purposes as well (taking into account the rule that for CGT any gain up to the date of death is wiped out). So you would need the deed to state that it takes effect for CGT.

However, there could be circumstances where you don't want this to happen. For example, if the asset has risen or fallen significantly in value since the date of death, then you may want the beneficiary under the deed of variation to be deemed to acquire it at the value as at the date of the deed, not at the date of death. In this case the deed needs to state that it does not take effect for CGT. However, if you follow this route, then do bear in mind that the person who is giving up the benefit to which they were entitled may be making a chargeable disposition for CGT; so, as always; it's important to do the maths first.

There have been various indications prior to past Budgets that Deeds of Variation are to be discontinued. This has never come into being yet but that does not mean that it never will!

SECTION 11:
MANAGING YOUR PROPERTY FOR INHERITANCE (PART 2) – TRUSTS

Trusts are often, but not exclusively, used as a tool for Inheritance Tax planning, with strategies that can utilise some of the IHT exemptions and reliefs.

#49. What is a trust?

A trust is a legal device where the legal owners (the *trustees*) hold an asset (including property) for the benefit of others (the *beneficiaries*) who may include themselves.

There are important advantages to trusts, such as:

- Enabling several people to benefit from same assets;

- Giving flexibility in long-term decisions as to who should benefit;

- Facilitating tax planning and mitigation.

There are also some benefits to putting your incorporated investment business into a trust. This puts 100% of the value of the company immediately outside the estate for IHT purposes. As director of the company, you also retain control of the company and as 'settlor' (i.e. donor) of the trust you can appoint the trustees and have the power to change them, provided that the trust document is suitably drafted to give you these powers (they don't come into force automatically).

For most trusts, however, it is important to understand that putting personal assets into any trust usually means giving up a measure of control to the trustees as you are no longer the owner of the assets. Also, it is generally not tax-efficient for you or your spouse to be a beneficiary of the trust.

However, you may retain some influence:

- You can retain the power of appointment of new trustees;

- You can provide the trustees with an 'expression of wishes' setting out how you would like them to exercise their trustee powers.

DISCRETIONARY TRUSTS AND RELEVANT PROPERTY TRUSTS

Now known as one type of Relevant Property Trust, the old term of 'discretionary' explained these rather better. They are trusts where the trustees have discretion to use the assets for specified beneficiaries or for specified purposes. IHT is charged on lifetime gifts into discretionary trusts (unless within the nil rate band). This is what is known as a Chargeable Lifetime Transfer and is not a PET.

Taxation of discretionary trusts

Please refer to *PETs and Discretionary Trusts, Section 10, and Tax Treatment of Trusts*, below.

#50. Mechanics of Trust Law

SOME DEFINITIONS:

- Settlor: The person who puts the assets into the trust.

- Life tenant: The person with the immediate right to income or the use of the trust property. The interest need not be for the whole of life but could be for a stated period.

  Where the life tenant gifts their interest into a trust, or where the life or limited interest comes to an end (which for IHT is a deemed transfer of the property supporting the life interest), then they are also the 'settlor' for this purpose.

- Trust corporation: A special type of company complying with Rule 30 Public Trustee Rules 1912 empowered to act as trustee.

- Vested interest: The beneficiary is of full age and entitled to the benefit.

- Contingent interest: The beneficiary only becomes entitled on the happening of a certain event, e.g. reaching a specified age or on the death of another beneficiary.

TYPES OF TRUSTS

Bare trusts

This is a basic trust held in the name of a trustee(s) but giving to the beneficiary full right to the capital and assets as well as to any income they generate. Reasons for this might include the beneficiary being of minority age, or because there are more than four people entitled to a share in a property (but only four names are allowed go onto the legal title). Transfers into a bare trust are exempt from IHT providing the transferor survives another seven years.

Interest in possession trusts

This type of trust gives the beneficiary entitlement to trust income as it is generated, but not to the capital. This is referred to as their 'interest in possession'. There is no IHT for as long as the assets stay in the trust and remain the 'interest' of the beneficiary. Once the interest in possession ceases for whatever reason, the trust decides what happens to the capital.

It is also possible for the trust to give the trustees power to advance capital to the beneficiary or even for the beneficiary to have the right to apply to the trustees for capital to be advanced. The tax treatment of either of these courses of action will depend upon the way in which the trust is drafted.

Discretionary trusts (Relevant Property Trusts)

In these trusts, the assets are held by the trustees with discretion to use for specified beneficiaries or specified purposes. IHT is chargeable on lifetime gifts into the trust (unless within the nil rate band).

Accumulation trusts

This is any kind of trust where the trustees are either instructed to or have the power to accumulate all or part of the income and add it to the capital (instead of distributing it to the beneficiaries). This accumulation will continue either for a specific period or until an event such as the beneficiary reaching a set age. Income from the trust will be taxed within the trust at the trust's rate of income tax. Other taxation may arise depending on the underlying type of trust (e.g. discretionary trust).

N.B. In the past a popular type of trust for providing for a child's education was the 'Accumulation and Maintenance Trust'. This stopped in 2006.

Settlor-interest trusts

This is a trust where the settlor of their spouse or civil partner is able to benefit from the trust, irrespective of whether they actually do so. They include trusts set up so that the trust property can revert to the settlor. This category of trust can include possession trusts, accumulation trusts and discretionary trusts. The settlor is liable for income tax arising from the trust's income whether or not it is paid to the settlor, and tax is paid from the trust's income.

Parental trusts

This is where a trust is set up by parents for children under the age of 18 who have never been married or in a civil partnership. It is not a trust type in its own right as it will be either a bare trust, an IIP, an accumulation trust or a discretionary trust. Income tax is paid by the trustees but comes from the settlor who must also show it as having been paid on his or her self-assessment tax return. N.B. This type of trust may be of particular interest to some readers and you can read more about it further below.

Non-resident trusts

These are trusts where the trustees are not resident in the UK for tax purposes. The tax rules are very complicated and you will need specialist advice.

HOW IS A TRUST CREATED?

A trust can be created through two methods:

1. deed or declaration of trust: and

2. operation of law.

Deed or Declaration

This is the document that designates the terms of the trust. If it is 'signed as a deed' then it is technically a deed; and if it's not actually a deed, then the terms are only enforceable if there is 'consideration'. 'Consideration' means that there a benefit offered on both sides, but it's a big topic and has been the subject of a number of cases. So, if in doubt, make sure it's a deed!

You can use Income Tax Form 17 to vary the proportions in which you own the beneficial interest in a property, providing you hold the legal title in joint names.

Operation of law

This is where a trust is automatically created as a result of the way property is held. For example:

- **Joint ownership of property:** This is in fact a trust. The legal title is always a joint tenancy, but the beneficial interest may be tenancy-in-common.

- **Property passing on death:** The estate passes to the executors on trust to deal with it according to the will or intestacy.

- **Resulting trusts:** Uncertainty or a change of circumstances can give rise to a trust. For example, it sometimes happens that a settlor transfers property to the intended trustee, but the trust fails for some reason (maybe because it hasn't been properly defined as to duration or certainty of beneficiaries). The effect would be that the trustee holds the legal title but on trust for the settlor himself (as a bare trust). The trustee holds the legal title of the property on trust. The beneficial or equitable ownership is retained by the settlor.

'Presumed resulting trusts' can also arise where there is doubt about whether or not a voluntary disposition (a gift) was intended (for example someone might contribute informally towards the purchase of a property by another person). This depends very much upon the circumstances and the evidence available evidence, but the presumption would usually be that, in the absence of evidence, no gift was intended. If so, then the owner of the property would be holding the title upon resulting trust for both contributors to the price. (This is a generalization as in some circumstances other legal presumptions could come into play – the point to note is that you need to document what you intend to do)

TRUSTEES' RESPONSIBILITIES

Trustees have legal responsibilities, including:

- That trustee decisions are unanimous unless there is a power to have a majority decision;

- A duty to act in best interests of the beneficiaries

- A duty to abide by the terms of the trust

- Statutory obligations, e.g. Trustee Act 2000

- A duty to take appropriate professional advice (unless the trustees themselves have amongst their number the necessary expertise)

- Tax responsibilities - see below.

#51. Tax treatment of trusts

We touched on this when we compared different types of trusts, but here are more comprehensive details for the three most common types of trust:

Bare trusts

- All interests are vested (i.e. all beneficiaries are fully entitled);

- Beneficiary pays income tax on his entitlement as if it were held in own name;

- No IHT on lifetime gift of assets into trust if settlor survives 7 years;

- No tax consequences on vesting of legal title in beneficiary;

- Beneficiary is charged CGT on any disposal by trustees;

- Beneficiary can give away his interest during lifetime or on death and this will be a disposal for CGT and IHT.

Interest in possession trusts (IIP)

- Beneficiary pays income tax on any income generated from his entitlement;

- No IHT on lifetime gift of assets into trust if settlor survives 7 years (i.e. it is a PET);

- Beneficiary can transfer IIP to a third party who then retains interest for that beneficiary's lifetime. Note that from 5 October 2008 IHT may apply plus 10-yearly IHT charge;

- Cessation of interest in possession is treated as a *disposal of supporting capital* for IHT, and for CGT is it is a qualifying IIP (but without charge if this is on death of life tenant).

Discretionary Trusts (Relevant Property Trusts)

- IHT is charged when trustees vest property to a beneficiary (referred to as 'exit charge') to a maximum of 5.85%

- 10-yearly IHT charge (maximum 6% of value of assets in the trust where these exceed nil-rate band)

- Nil-rate band trusts (i.e. transfer within the settlor's individual nil rate for IHT) are very tax-efficient;

- Income tax is charged on trustees (38.1% to 45% and note lower trustees' annual allowance) unless the property has been 'appointed'. The term 'appointed' means that the trustees have decided to pass the assets to one or of the beneficiaries. This could be either a direct transfer or the trustees could themselves set up another trust vehicle. This could be the type of trust where the beneficiary is entitled to the income but not the capital (an 'interest in possession trust') and in this case the income tax would be charged on the person receiving the income (at their personal rate of income tax.

- As with most trusts, CGT is chargeable to the trustees on disposal of assets to a third party (and subject to trustee's annual CGT exemption) and is payable out of trust assets.

#52. Parental trusts for minors and other options

There may be many reasons why someone might want to protect assets and income for children of a minority age. Here we consider some of the options.

Parental trusts for minors are not a type of trust in their own right; they will be one of the following types of trust:

- Interest in possession trusts – where the child may be entitled to all the income;

- Accumulation trusts – where trustees can retain and accumulate income on behalf of the child;

- Discretionary trusts – where trustees can make payments at their discretion to the child.

The settlor must be one of the child's parents (not grandparents), and the child must be under the age 18 and have never been married or in a civil partnership.

With parental trusts for minors, the child's income from the trust is deemed to be the income of the settlor for Income Tax purposes.

There are alternatives to creating a specific trust, such as:

- Holding properties as tenants-in-common and gifting an interest to child – no real advantage for income tax, but long-term CGT and IHT advantages;

- Incorporating the property portfolio and creating different classes of shares ('alphabet' shares) with some passed to the children. Different dividends can be declared on different classes of shares to keep children's income to a minimum

In both of these cases, where the children are minors, the parents can hold as 'bare trustees' (i.e. the legal title is held by parents, but the shares belong to child), or as trustees of an accumulation or discretionary trust. Here is how the latter could work for tax:

1. Incorporate property portfolio and create discretionary trust for children;

2. Create alphabet shares and gift some of the Class B shares into the trust year by year staying within the CGT annual exemption (£11,7000 each for tax year 2018/19);

3. Whilst children are minors, restrict dividends on Class B shares;

4. Vest shares in children at say 18 or 21. This will mean one 10-year charge for IHT (maximum 6%) plus an exit charge on vesting (maximum 5.85%).

Another alternative is to use exempt lifetime gifts that can be made tax-free (and also by the grandparents). Remember though that income arising from gifts to children by parents is deemed to be income of the parents.

Points to consider

Assuming it's a discretionary or accumulation trust, then be aware that:

- Gifts into discretionary trusts are not PETs, so if you go over your nil-rate band you will be paying IHT;

- Every 10 years there's a periodic charge no more than 6% of the value of the property then in the trust;

- Every time property leaves the trust (to be paid to a beneficiary or for their benefit) there's a charge to IHT but no more than 5.85% of the value transferred.

Two parental trust for minors case studies

1. Setting up the trust to prevent incurring IHT

Sometimes a parent might want to set up a trust in order to avoid paying IHT should they die while the child is still of minority age or has not yet reached a particular age. Here's a simple example:

Let's say you set up a £150,000 discretionary trust when your child is just two, and this will continue for 19 years until the child reaches 21 at which point the trust assets will pass to the child (and the trust provisions allow you to decide to remove some of it within the period to pay for education or other costs).

Here are the tax charges that will be incurred:

- At year 10 there will be the periodic ten-year charge for the whole amount: 6% of £150,000 = £9,000

- Just after this you decide to vest £100,000 from the trust: exit charge of 5.85% = £5,850

- The other £50,000 stays in the trust for the remaining nine years and is then distributed: another exit charge at 5.85% = £2,925.

The total tax amounts to £17,775, compared to the IHT liability of £60,000 had you not set up the trust.

Total saving: £42,225.

Also, CGT holdover relief is usually available when assets leave the trust.

Of course, this is a generic example, based on the maximum tax rates applicable, and each scenario would need to be reviewed and a tax calculation made.

2. Here is a more complicated example where a parent with a terminal illness wants to secure maintenance funds for her minority-age son.

First some background:

As we will see, making this kind of provision is not straightforward, but there is a useful legal precedent in the case of McKelvey v HMRC 2008. This case established that lifetime gifts in favour of a dependent relative for his/her care or maintenance could be ignored for IHT purposes (set out in s.11(3) IHTA 1984).

In this landmark case, the deceased, Ms McKelvey, had known that she was terminally ill and, before she died, wanted to make provision for her blind, elderly mother. She gave her mother properties to allow her to fund her nursing care. The Special Commissioners held that the majority of the transfer was not a transfer for value under s11(3) IHTA.

Regarding the case study below, this subsection of the IHTA identifies qualifying dispositions for maintenance as including anything which it would be normal for the person making it to provide - e.g. holidays, pocket money, music lessons, a car, driving lessons, presents – and judged by the parent's standard of living (if the provision is made for a child).

Now to the case study:

Amy is 45 and has been told that she has maybe three months to live. She is separated from her husband (but they are still married). She owns a property and has a significant amount of assets in her own name. Her husband is wealthy so there is little chance of him making a successful claim against her estate.

They have a 16-year-old son, Tom, who may go to university. Amy wants the whole of her estate to pass to Tom. This is fine - it can be in trust until Tom is 21 or even older. However, any of the estate beyond the Nil Rate Band will suffer IHT at 40%.

Amy could make use of s.11 if she makes a lifetime transfer. If she does this as a simple gift then, although legal title cannot vest in Tom whilst he is a minor it will be held as a bare trust until his 18th birthday. However, does Amy think that Tom will be financially mature enough to manage large amounts of money? One alternative is to use a trust.

I mentioned s.11 IHTA 1984 earlier as ignoring IHT on expenditure incurred for family maintenance. To come within the terms of s.11 IHTA, the trust would have to be worded so that Tom becomes entitled to the funds *either* at the end of the year in which he reaches 18 *or* when he ceases full-time education. Amy may still feel that this is not the perfect solution, but to defer vesting to a later date when Tom may no longer be regarded as a dependent is likely to take the gift outside the terms of s.11.

To comply with s.11 Amy will also need to consider what would constitute maintenance. This means working out what Tom would need for university fees, accommodation and necessities, such as food and clothing, and try to maintain him at the standard of living appropriate to her dependent. As this will be tested by HMRC it could complicate the administration of the estate when Amy dies (as there will be no reason for HMRC to examine the s.11 gift before then).

Another complication is what happens to the fund if Tom dies before 18 or completing full-time education. Although he wasn't to get control of the fund until he reached that age, this gift is not 'contingent' upon him doing so. In other words, the trust cannot say 'if he reaches the age of… etc.' because if it does it may not comply with s.11 (again, because it is then possible that Tom may not need the gift for his maintenance). So, even though he is not in control of the fund, it is still technically a vested interest; and if he dies the fund will pass to his heirs. As he cannot make a valid will until he is 18, if he dies under that age (or does not make a will) then the fund will pass to his father as the person entitled to the estate under the rules relating to succession.

It's also worth noting that in order for the gift to be within s.11 the transferee must be a dependent. The situation might be different if Amy and her husband had divorced as Tom might not satisfy the definition of her dependent (this would be a matter of the financial settlement on the divorce).

Another possibility is that Amy could leave the money to Tom in her will with the instruction to create either a bereaved minor trust or an 18-25 trust (see below). However, whilst this would arrive at the same practical solution of providing for Tom's education, the sum would be in Amy's estate and attract IHT. The taxation benefits of these types of trust, created on death, relate to the lack of IHT during the trust and when the property leaves the trust. On the other hand the s.11 provisions for lifetime gifts (if successful) take the gift out of the IHT calculation altogether. You can read more about this under Trusts for Bereaved Minors, below.

#53. Some additional notes on trusts and trustee rates of tax

1. You might come across these terms when discussing trusts with an advisor:

   - **Inter vivos or life-time trusts:** Set up by settlor during his or her life with assets gifted into the trust;

   - **Will trusts**: set up by the will of the settlor (or in some cases arising out of the rules for the division of the estate on intestacy);

   You can also set up a lifetime trust (and gift a fairly nominal amount into it as trust capital) and then gift into the trust by will. This has no particular advantage for CGT but in practical terms it avoids creating a complex set of trust provisions in the will and, if you need to change your will, at least you don't have to re-think the trust provisions, only whether you still want to gift the same amount into the trust.

2. The Finance Act 2006 made significant changes to Inheritance Tax treatment of trusts:

   - All lifetime trusts set up on or after 22 March 2006 are now treated as Relevant Property Trusts (RPTs)

   - The only trusts set up on or after 22 March 2006 which can now be treated as a qualifying IIPs are those set up under a will or trusts for disabled persons. This is a trust set up by a lifetime settlement or by will to benefit a pre-determined class of beneficiaries, essentially a discretionary trust.

3. Some trusts are of mixed type or evolve from one type to another, and each part of such a trust is taxed according to the taxation rules for that type. For example, you might set up a trust for the life span of person A that will then pass to A's children or grandchildren in shares or proportions decided by the trustees. This would be an Interest

in Possession Trust followed by a Discretionary Trust. And if the trustees had the power to accumulate income for a minor beneficiary and exercised that power this would make that part of the trust an accumulation trust.

Trustee rates of tax

It should be noted that the rates of tax for trustees are higher than for ordinary individuals:

- First £1,000 of income taxed at 20% then the rate jumps to 45%. Dividend income is taxed at £38.1%;

- Trustees annual exemption for CGT is £5,650;

- Trustees CGT rate is 28% on residential property and 20% on other chargeable assets;

- There is no personal income tax allowance and no nil-rate band for IHT.

Trustees' tax responsibilities

Trustees are responsible for:

- Registering the trust with HMRC (by 5 October after tax year of set up, or when it starts to make income or capital gains if later);

- Reporting and paying tax on behalf of the trust;

- Nominating one as principle acting trustee where there is more than one trustee;

- Submitting tax return by 31 January after each tax year (unless HMRC advises this is not necessary e.g. where this is a bare trust);

- Providing information to each beneficiary (Form R185) on income and tax deducted;

- Filing a report for IHT where applicable;

- Reporting to HMRC any changes in the trust.

The above has been only a very brief review of some of the types of trusts you may encounter. You might also come across:

- **Trusts for vulnerable beneficiaries:** Also known as 'disabled trusts', these are for beneficiaries who are eligible for certain disability-related benefits or are incapable of managing their own affairs in line with the Mental Health Act 1983. As from 2013, all the income must go to the benefit of the beneficiary (except £3000 or 3% of the assets per annum). Capital is not taken into account as this is essentially a discretionary trust (but receives more favourable tax treatment for IHT).

- **Trusts for bereaved minors:** These are created by will (or arise on intestacy) for the benefit of the deceased's own children or stepchildren, to inherit if they attain the age of 18 (sometimes the trust defers inheritance to 25, known as an 18-25 trust). They may not include gifts from grandparents. Income tax is payable by the trust, but the main benefit is with IHT; even if the value of the trust exceeds the nil rate band, there will be no IHT on a distribution at age 18 nor a periodic ten-yearly charge. The exception is for an 18-25 trust where there may be an IHT charge if the fund exceeds the nil rate band.

In conclusion, trusts are complex in relation to tax law, but they are still very useful tools for tax-mitigation. However, this is an area full of traps for the unwary, so do take detailed professional advice on all implications before deciding to set up trusts.

SECTION 12: MANAGING YOUR PROPERTY FOR INHERITANCE (PART 3) – CASE STUDY

#54. Inheritance Case Study – Kerry and Steve

Even with the best tax planning possible, tax is a self-levelllng device – if you make a saving in one area, you probably have to decide to accept less of a saving in another. The particular challenge with inheritance tax is that you're not thinking just about your own position but sometimes, as in this case study, about three different generations of one family. Trying to make decisions that will provide positive outcomes for all three is not easy. Let's see how our protagonists Kerry and Steve manage it.

Background:

- Kerry is 40 years old, with 25 years to retirement;

- She is married with three young children;

- She has a 25-year £100,000 mortgage with 19 years remaining;

- She runs an unincorporated retail business (stationery);

- She also owns and rents out 8 properties (all with mortgages).

Her profit and loss looks like this:

Turnover	100,000
Costs	(60,000)
Pre-tax profit	40,000
Tax	9,633
Profits after tax	30,367

And if her turnover were to increase and her profit to rise to £75,000, her tax bill would rise by an amount determined by her business structure at the time to:

Sole trader:	£22,763, or
Partnership:	£15,976, or
Incorporated:	£14,250.

The family and its wealth:

- Kerry has one sister and both her parents are still alive;

- Kerry's parents have liquid assets (excluding their home, valued at £400,000) of around £300,000, including pensions and investments of that deliver annual income of £35,000;

- Kerry's husband Steve has a brother and a sister and both parents still alive;

- Steve's parents have liquid assets (excluding their home, valued at £800,000) of around £500,000, including pensions and investments of that deliver annual income of £50,000

The possible IHT scenario:

How much IHT will each of Kerry and Steve face when both sets of parents have died?

The big question is whether the main residences are sold, the proceeds becoming part of the estates, or whether they are passed on to Kerry and Steve as main residences, thereby attracting the enhanced nil rate band (an additional £150,000 for tax year 2019/20). Let's compare the differences.

First of all Kerry:

The anticipated IHT position on Kerry's parents' death (assuming everything passed first to the surviving parent on first death):

- Total estate passing to Kerry and her sister   £700,000

- IHT nil-rate band   £650,000
  (surviving spouse taking over unused nil-rate band of first to die)

- **IHT at 40% on remaining £50,000-£20,000**

But - if the main residence is left to Kerry and her sister (or grandchildren), the enhanced nil rate band available on the second death is now £950,000, so there is **no IHT to pay.**

Now Steve:

The anticipated IHT position on Steve's parents' death (assuming everything passed first to the surviving parent on first death):

- Total estate passing to Steve and siblings   £1,300,000

- IHT nil-rate band   £650,000
  (surviving spouse taking over unused nil-rate band of first to die)

- **IHT at 40% on remaining £650,000-£260,000**

But - if main residence left to Steve and his siblings (or grandchildren), the enhanced nil-rate band available on second death is now £950,000, so there is now £140,000 IHT to pay.

What could go wrong?

Clearly there is major financial benefit in the homes being passed on as main residences. However, there are two dangers in this scenario, one concerning the income each set of parents takes from investments, and the other arising from possible late-in-life care needs. Let's examine these first and then consider what Kerry, Steve and their respective parents might do to mitigate these.

- Either set of parents might have at some point ceased to use up their annual income, saving it up instead, so the surplus would be added to capital and bear tax at 40% on the second death.

- They might have to go into residential care and once they no longer live in their own home the main residence increase in nil-rate band is no longer available. However, the costs of residential care will reduce their capital and may take the estates below the IHT thresholds.

Is it possible to safeguard against care fees eroding the estate?

The basic principle is that the state will assess your available assets and you will have to pay for state-provided or state-financed care according to your means. If you give away assets in order to reduce your available means, you will probably be found out and assessed as if you still owned the assets. If you intend to off-load some of your assets by life-time gifts, do it at a point where you can demonstrate that:

(a)   your lifestyle will not be affected by not having these assets; and

(b)   your state of health is such that it is unlikely that you will need to go into care in the near future.

A better alternative is to consider taking out a care fees plan from a specialist provider. The earlier you do this the better. And with regard to your residence, you cannot be required to sell this to pay for your care if one of you is still living in the property. However if the partner remaining in the home and living independently does sell (e.g. to downsize) then there is a risk is that the share of the surplus proceeds belonging to the partner receiving care will be taken into account in any assessment.

And there is one further option:

Splitting the assets

Before the enhanced nil rate band option was made available, a popular tax-planning device was to split the assets between the spouses (especially the family home) and for each spouse to leave the nil-rated amount to the next generation either outright or in the form of a trust.

This still has a place in tax-planning, although the ability to use both nil-rate bands on the second death makes this less important. However, it still has a role in safeguarding assets against care fees.

How to use this:

- Split the assets in two and each of you leave your assets by will into a discretionary trust for the benefit of your spouse, children, grandchildren and any other beneficiaries;

- The survivor of you will have no entitlement as of right to those assets, so they cannot be included in an assessment for care fees.

So, with all this in mind, let's return to Kerry and Steve:

Possible strategies for Kerry's parents

- It looks as if there is unlikely to be much of an IHT issue as long as the survivor still owns the family home at their death;

- Off-loading any assets now will depend very much on what they can afford;

- If they have surplus income then they can make gifts out of normal income as this will not affect the IHT;

- They could consider IHT-exempt gifts on marriage (for grandchildren in due course) or covered by the annual exemption of £3,000;

- Anything they can off-load will reduce the amount eligible for assessment if either has to go into residential care but bear in mind the precautions to avoid any gifts being taken into account.

Possible strategies for Steve's parents

- All the above apply, but there is likely to be a substantial IHT charge on the death of the survivor;

- Steve's parents therefore need to think about how they can pass on their wealth during their lifetimes to save tax on their deaths;

- The earlier the tax-planning is done the better;

Some other strategies for Steve's parents:

- Creating a trust for the benefit of grandchildren: used to be called an 'accumulation and maintenance trust' with advantageous tax treatment - now simply 'accumulation trusts' with similar tax treatment to discretionary trusts;

- Creating a tenancy-in-common of the property and passing a share to children and grandchildren. This will not achieve an IHT saving until they cease to live in it, but could remove the value from the calculation for care fees;

- School fees provision - either in a trust or through a specialist policy;

- Life-time gifts as potentially exempt transfers (or nil-rate transfers if into a discretionary trust).

Finally, there is a simple way to help Steve pay the IHT their estate incurs - taking out a life policy written in trust, and therefore outside the estate, for the benefit of Steve to use for paying the IHT.

N.B. Decisions should never be made solely on the criterion of saving tax. I've known many people come up with great schemes for reducing tax (especially IHT) but in doing so they often overlook what they desire from their lifestyle. There is also the risk of things turning out other than how they had imagined, for example, leaving property to a child who then divorces his partner or dies, leaving the asset in the hands of the spouse with whom they may not get on (this is especially a problem with any scheme involving the family home).

Finally – how can Kerry and Steve pass on some of their inheritance to their own children?

Whether or not their parents take up any of the strategies I've looked at, it looks as if Kerry and Steve will each inherit around £350,000 (assuming the estate is divided equally between siblings).

This makes quite a difference to their total joint assets, so what might they consider as a long-term strategy with regard to their passing on some of this to their own children?

Key considerations for Kerry and Steve:

- The income of an asset gifted for a minor child's benefit by the parent will be deemed the income of the parent for income tax purposes (unless the annual income is under £100). N.B. this does not apply where the gift is to grandchildren;

- Capital Gains Tax may arise on the disposal of assets into a trust - but gains then arise within the trust and CGT is paid by the trustees on those gains (if there is a disposal - including vesting an asset in the name of a beneficiary).

Also:

- A gift to a child or into some types of trust is a potentially exempt transfer for Inheritance Tax (drops out of the computation if the donor survives for 7 years). Gifts into a discretionary trust are not potentially exempt but no IHT payable if the gift is within the nil-rate band;

- IHT is payable when an asset leaves the trust and every 10 years if this is a discretionary trust.

So, Kerry and Steve could:

- Gift assets that have low income but potential for capital growth;

- Manage a discretionary trust with regard to the 10-year anniversaries. It usually works out as more tax-efficient to have assets leave the trust just before rather than just after an anniversary;

Generally, As far as IHT is concerned, the rates of tax for lifetime gifts, assets leaving the trust, and the 10-year periodic charge are much less than the 40% that will be payable if they retained the assets until their deaths.

SECTION 13: HOW TO GET THE BEST FROM YOUR PROPERTY TAX EXPERT

+The best outcomes in business come from informed collaboration between the business owner and their expert advisers. So, whilst I hope that this book provides some really useful backbone to the vast topic of property tax, there will definitely be times when you must consult an expert. I hope that this short section will help you to choose which expert to consult and give you a flavour of the benefits you can expect.

#55. Who are the experts and how can they help?

It is a good idea to get together a team of experts that you can call on individually for advice as and when property opportunities arise. You may well need to have more than one of each type of adviser, depending upon the size of your portfolio.

So, how do you select your team?

The most important criterion is that each professional is capable of fulfilling the role of 'trusted professional adviser'. This means exactly what it says, someone who has the necessary professional knowledge and experience and whose opinions and ideas you trust. So, it's not all about the level of professional ability and nothing else (although of course that's important); you also need to feel 'comfortable' with your adviser. By that I mean you need to choose an adviser whose aims and ideals are reasonably in tune with your own, and who is able to explain the advice to you in a way which you can understand (without blinding you with jargon).

I'll now introduce some of the power team members and their roles.

Estate agents and lettings agents

As we're looking primarily at property, you'll almost certainly be dealing with these.

Estate agency is now a fairly highly regulated profession (which wasn't always the case), so you should have no problem in checking the accreditation of any estate agency practice. One point that I find is often overlooked is that the estate agent is the agent of the seller (or landlord), not the buyer. So, if you're using an estate agent to sell or let your property, they should be making your interests the priority.

It follows of course that the agent (being agent for the seller) isn't acting for you if you're the buyer. I find many buyers tend to assume that the agent is somehow acting for them too. You can of course appoint your own agent (as buyer) if you feel that professional advice is needed, for example in negotiating.

To get the best out of the service, make sure your agent knows what your aims and objectives are - don't just assume that these are obvious.

For example, are you looking for a quick sale or the maximum price? Maybe you need a tenant who is likely to want to stay in the property for a reasonable time, or a short-term let whilst you organise the long-term plans for the property.

It should go without saying that you also need to check the agent's terms and conditions of business, so that there are no unpleasant surprises. One area you might want to check is your own liability if the agent fails to find a buyer and you want to sell elsewhere.

What about if you are the buyer? Well, in order to carry out his role, clearly the seller's agent needs to interact with the other interested parties. Under the current legislation, the agent is obliged to ensure that property details and clear and complete and not misleading in any way. That's quite a high threshold. However, it stops short of pointing out any defects or disadvantages, so it's up to you to make your own investigations, (or appoint someone to do this for you).

Surveyors and valuers

You're also likely to need the services of a surveyor from time to time.

I think the key point here is to make sure that you know what service you'll be getting. A surveyor will belong to the RICS or one of the other professional organisations, depending upon the individual specialism (e.g. building surveyors, quantity surveyors, rating surveyors etc).

One misconception is that a mortgage inspection and valuation is a sort of low-cost survey for the buyer. If you're getting a mortgage, then the lender will instruct a surveyor to carry out an inspection. The sole purpose of this is to reassure the intended mortgagee that the property is of sufficient value to cover the amount being loaned, and also that there are no issues which could present a problem on future sale. In other words, they are safeguarding their proposed investment - and the surveyor is acting for them, not for you.

Of course, the mortgage valuation report may well provide you with some reassurance about what you are buying and, in the case of a modern property, you may well feel that this is sufficient. But it doesn't take the place of a structural survey.

In all other cases (including a full structural survey) the surveyor will be acting for you, so it is essential that you discuss and agree with the surveyor exactly what his report will cover. You'll use a surveyor not only when you're buying or leasing a property, but also if you're converting or refurbishing. The survey may, in addition, require the expertise of a structural engineer or other specialist, depending on the type of property, the geographical location (for example, when building in the Fens, my local area, it's common for piling to be necessary), and on what you actually want to do.

A word about the role of quantity surveyors if you're a developer using a building contractor: It may be worth getting a quantity surveyor's report on the quotation and specification. The builder may have given what appears to be an extremely competitive quote, but can it be done for the money and still provide the builder with a reasonable profit margin? If not, then there's a risk of one or both of two outcomes: 1) the builder may try to cut corners and therefore costs, so you end up with less than you expected, or 2) the builder may go out of business, leaving you with a half-completed project, which is likely to cost more, proportionately, to complete. I've seen this happen on a number of occasions

Architects and town planners

If you're building or converting, you'll certainly need architectural services. I'd say this is an area in which it is vital to choose advisers whose vision really chimes with your own. So how do you go about finding such an adviser?

Apart from the obvious precaution of checking professional qualifications, I'd say the best method is to look at recently completed projects by the same architect; get a feel for his or her 'style' and, if possible, speak to the clients, to see how they think the project went. No adviser should object to a prospective client asking about previous assignments; in fact, I welcome such enquiries, as I consider testimonials from satisfied clients to be one of the best advertisements of my services.

You are looking for someone who can take you own vision and make it happen. Of course, you'll expect ideas and suggestions from your architect, but what you want to avoid is an imposition of a 'house style' or the architect's own vision if this doesn't fit in with yours. They are after all supposed to be acting on your instructions. That said, in line with most creative professions, architects are likely to develop what I've called a 'house style' (for which they may well be noted) but you'll be able to see if this fits in with your vision by looking at their previous work.

Turning to town planners, this is a service that may to a large extent be provided by your architect, if you're using one. However, generally speaking, I'd caution against using an architect and use a good town planner, as they are worth their weight in gold. The same considerations apply, but here you'll be relying on their planning expertise and their knowledge of the local planning authority to get your project through the planning process with a minimum of fuss and expense.

Builders and contractors

I've included these because many of the same considerations apply, for example looking at previous projects undertaken and checking any accreditations. You should also check their accounts to gauge whether they can handle your size of project. Getting references is a good idea.

There's nothing wrong, by the way, in taking word of mouth recommendations as a starting point for choosing any adviser or contractor, as long as you follow this up with your own checks. In fact, this can save you a lot of time, especially if the recommendation comes from another trusted adviser!

I can't emphasise too strongly however the need to check the terms and conditions of the contract. In the case of a building contract (even if it's just a quotation for some work with a few standard terms and conditions attached) the main points to look for are:

- Exactly what work will be carried out
- Experience of your type of project
- Quality standards
- 'Snagging' procedures
- Payment terms-especially if stage payments are involved

- Use of industry standard JCT contracts

- Guarantees and warranties

- Insurance cover for the build cost

- Remedies if things go wrong, including provision for mediation and/or arbitration as an alternative to court action.

Solicitors

Along with accountants, this is a profession that many regard as a 'necessary evil', and lawyers are often seen as creating difficulties and delays in what may appear to be a fairly simple process.

Leaving aside for the moment the lawyer's role in litigation, it's important to appreciate what a solicitor is actually supposed to do when acting for you on a land transaction or on a contract. The solicitor is there to advise you on what the terms actually are and, even more importantly, to safeguard you from possibly unforeseen consequences. So, it's actually his job to say 'What if...?' The question does not indicate that your solicitor lacks knowledge of commercial realities.

So, if your solicitor seems to be nit-picking, do bear in mind that this is for your benefit. If you want to overrule the recommendations, then that is your privilege as client, as long as you understand the risks involved.

The considerations involved in choosing a solicitor are much the same as with choosing any professional adviser. It may be more difficult, because of client confidentiality, to see examples of the solicitor's previous work. One thing I do feel is particularly important is to ensure that you choose someone you are comfortable with and who can explain things to you in a way you can understand. Legal concepts are not always easy for the layman to follow, but you shouldn't have to put up with legal jargon so, if you don't follow something, then ask.

It's rare these days for the same individual solicitor to provide all the services you may need. The law is now too complex to allow for a detailed understanding of more than one or two specialisms. For example, an expert in, say, commercial contract law may have a broad understanding of the law of property transactions, but is very unlikely to be an expert in the details of land law, or what is known as 'administrative law' which governs for example bodies such as local authorities. To offer the best service, a good solicitor will call in help as necessary, either in-house if the firm is large enough, or by recommendation to another solicitor or other professional (including referring complex issues to a barrister).

This is not a sign of lack of knowledge. I would be a little suspicious of a solicitor who claimed to be an expert on a number of different areas of law.

If you are unfortunate enough to become involved in litigation, then the skill-set involved is rather different to that required for property transactions. You may well need the services of a barrister. And of course these days it is possible to instruct a barrister direct -assuming you know which barrister to choose.

So my advice is to find a solicitor who can offer a service covering your main needs, and who can explain the legal concepts and consequences to you -and accept that there may be times when it's necessary to call on the services of another lawyer or professional, so that you can have the best service.

Financial advisers

This term can cover a number of different areas. Perhaps the most obvious one is the independent financial adviser ('IFA'), but it also covers chartered financial planners, investment advisers, pensions specialists, insurance brokers and anyone who offers financial advice.

Since the first Financial Services Act in 1986, the financial services industry has become ever more highly regulated, and most of this sector is regulated, directly or indirectly, through the Financial Conduct Authority.

You'll probably come across IFAs in connection with your personal financial planning. With any type of financial advice, the main point to check is how the adviser is regulated and whether they are independent or tied to any one financial provider. This should be perfectly clear and, if it isn't, then I suggest you use someone else.

An independent adviser will review the whole financial market to source products suitable to your needs, whereas a 'tied' adviser will offer only the products from a specific adviser. This does not mean that you shouldn't use a tied adviser, as they are under the same obligation to check that a suggested product meets your needs, but you need to be aware of the distinction. These days, with so much information available online, many investors will have a reasonably good awareness of the range of products that are out there.

Apart from that, the same considerations apply as with choosing any professional adviser, as I've already mentioned.

Last but by no means least...

Accountants and Tax Advisers

The first point to note it that anyone can call themselves an accountant; it's not a protected term. However, there are a number of different regulatory bodies (with members who may have particular specialisms) and I suggest you always use a regulated accountant. That way you'll have the reassurance that your accountant has undertaken appropriate training, is obliged to comply with regulations and, if anything goes wrong, you can at least make a complaint to the regulator.

The regulatory bodies you're most likely to come across for 'general' accountancy and tax planning are the Institute of Chartered Accountants in England and Wales ('ICAEW) and the Association of Chartered Certified Accountants ('ACCA'). My firm is regulated by both these bodies. You may also come across the Association of Accounting Technicians ('AAT').

The considerations when choosing an accountant and tax adviser are really the same as the ones I've outlined above. However here are a few points that you should consider, some of them with particular reference to clients how are property investors or developers:

- Can the accountant demonstrate expertise in your business sector?

- Does the accountant offer a 'fixed fee' basis for their charges?

- Does the accountant offer a money-back guarantee if you can show that the service has not been what you could reasonably expect?

- Is the accountant   ' property-invested' i.e. in the property market themselves?

- Is the accountant credible and recognised in their professional niche?

All of these apply to my firm. Let me tell you a bit about how I operate.

#56. About my business

In my professional capacity as a tax specialist with 19 years' experience in the accounting profession, I have evolved what you might call my *client avatar* – the profile of my typical property investor client:

- A business that is already established, with no more than 4 or 5 business owners and ideally with turnover of at least £500,000;

- A serious commitment to improving their business;

- A property developer or a landlord with a minimum of five buy-to-let properties;

- A fierce desire to work with a professional adviser who can offer value-based advice.

And how do I help these clients?

As outlined in the Welcome, I always strongly advocate fully legal, non-aggressive tax planning. Drawing on all of the opportunities discussed in this book, it is possible to make intelligent and ethical decisions that improve both your tax liability and your business itself. On the other hand, I do also help clients to enter into discussion with HMRC where there is ambiguity or conflict – tax law can never account for every single unique business situation, and as I've explained many times during the book, a tax case in the courts often comes down to interpreting the nuances of tax law, not just stating the facts - so challenging the status quo need not be adversarial or bullish, just good business practice. The landmark case below is a good illustration of this.

Case study: Rice vs HMRC

Many business owners at some point or another decide to make a fundamental change to their business – perhaps, for example, the sector or the nature of what they sell, or changing from sole trader to a limited company. When this happens, it can also completely change the position regarding tax liabilities or reliefs – and it can certainly be of interest to HMRC. This case shows how we helped a client to contest HMRC's interpretation of the impact of business changes and saved the client considerable money in the process.

Now, the particular circumstances surrounding changes in business operations – the decisions that are made and the reasons behind them – can sometimes be as important in a tax dispute as the bare financial facts and figures, so we'll start by looking at some background (from before we were brought in to help Mr Rice).

Case background

Mr Rice was a car dealer, operating as a sole trader from a site in the centre of Peterborough, and selling high-performance sports cars. Several incidents of vandalism persuaded Mr Rice in May 2005 that trading from these premises was simply too risky. At the time he and his wife lived in a country property on the outskirts of a village several miles outside Peterborough. The property had an extensive area of land with it and Mr Rice understood from the planning authority that he would be permitted to sell cars from this property.

In the event, this proved rather more problematical than expected as the planning authority declined to allow any advertisement or directions board in the village (or on the main road) and only the smallest business signage at the property itself. Effectively there would be nothing to indicate to the casual traveller past the village that there was a motor-trader operating there at all.

However, Mr Rice had also decided that instead of selling high-performance cars he would specialize in family cars. As the buyers of these more mainstream vehicles were likely to research their options and even buy blind on line, Mr Rice was confident he could be sufficiently accessible to the marketplace.

Mr Rice's business model had clearly changed significantly, but his accountant at the time had not advised that closing accounts should be prepared up to the date on which he ceased trading from the city centre premises.

The unexpected tax bill

Mr Rice personally owned the original city-centre premises, and he now sought to sell these, but it took rather longer than he had anticipated. The premises represented a personal asset used in a business and would normally be liable for capital gains tax on their disposal. However, if he sold them within three years, as a sole trader he could claim Entrepreneur's Relief (ER) on any capital gain arising (being the associated disposal of a material asset used in the business). Fortunately for Mr Rice, exchange of contracts (which is the operative date) took place on 29 April 2008, only a few days before the three-year deadline and his accountant duly advised him that he could claim ER on the capital gain (reducing the rate of tax to a flat 10%).

However, they had both overlooked another important condition for claiming ER: for sole traders it is essential that there should be a cessation of the business. With no closing accounts for the city-centre operation, HMRC would not accept that the original business had ceased trading, nor that, if it had, that this took place in May 2005 as claimed – and therefore Mr Rice had not shown that the sale of the city premises had been an associated disposal within the required three years to qualify for ER. As a result, HMRC presented him with a massive CGT bill of almost £50,000, almost double the original tax demand.

To be fair to Mr Rice's accountant, at the time the claim for ER was made this relief had only just reached the statute book, so perhaps he could be excused for a degree of unfamiliarity with the ramifications. An appeal was lodged and it subsequently transpired that the accountant had written a number of letters (apparently without prior client approval of the content) to HMRC seeking to convince them that it was unfair to deprive the taxpayer of the relief. When the initial letters failed to impress, I regret to say that the accountant resorted to abuse - never a good idea.

It was at this point that Mr Rice's IFA suggested he should consult us for advice.

Our challenge

We reviewed the paperwork available (which at that stage did not include all the correspondence between HMRC and the accountant) and interviewed the client for further details of exactly what had happened. Our first step was to contact HMRC and request internal review but unsurprisingly there was no change in their standpoint. We therefore had to evaluate the chances of success before the First Tier Tribunal.

Amongst our team there were varying points of view. On the one hand, Mr Rice was a motor trader before and a motor trader afterwards so the HMRC argument that there had not been any cessation might be difficult to refute. The absence of cessation accounts for the city-centre business was clearly a stumbling block. On the other hand, my colleague with a legal background spoke at length with Mr Rice and felt that the change in his modus operandi, from high-performance to family vehicles could constitute the ceasing of one business and the commencement of another. This argument was supported by the way that planning restrictions had obliged Mr Rice to run his business and especially the consequent change to the business driver from forecourt display to internet traffic.

So, the main objective was to convince HMRC that there had in fact been a cessation. If we could succeed in that, we would also need to provide evidence that the cessation had occurred in May 2005 (putting the disposal of premises within the 3-year window), as HMRC had decided that, if there was a cessation, it had been earlier than this. Mr Rice agreed that the appeal to the Tribunal should go ahead and further that this should be entirely handled by ourselves.

The outcome

I'm pleased to say that this was a resounding success! Sometimes the key to managing taxation efficiently is to be able to form a cogent argument, and I consider that my colleague's skill in this area was largely responsible for convincing the Tribunal judge of the merits of our client's case.

The main point was establishing that there had indeed been a cessation, based on the evidence of change of location, change of type of product, change of method of attracting business, and client's intentions. None of these would have been likely to be sufficient alone, but my colleague succeeded in building up a case on the cumulative effect. I should say here that the preparation of cessation accounts would not necessarily have been conclusive evidence, but it would have helped! Mr Rice's evidence however was that, although he had made his previous accountant fully aware of the situation, the accountant had never suggested that cessation accounts should be prepared.

Having established this crucial point, the next hurdle was to establish the date of the cessation (another point where cessation accounts would have been valuable). In the absence of documentary evidence, it was fortunate that Mr Rice was able to fix the earliest date as being May 2005 by virtue of linking this to his wife's serious illness. We were also able to obtain proof from the local authority of the date on which empty relief from business rates was granted and again although this does not prove that the business ceased, when coupled with the other factors it suggested that this had been the case.

The Tribunal therefore found that, on the balance of probabilities, Mr Rice's account of events was correct and therefore that the change in business was capable of being a new business and that the former business had in fact ceased. As to date of cessation, it was accepted that other events in Mr Rice's life, which could be dated and which were likely to be accurately remembered by him, were sufficient to support the contentions as to the date of cessation. The Tribunal therefore found in Mr Rice's favour and thus his tax bill for CGT on the gain on selling the premises was reduced by over £25,000.

The HMRC representative on the day was, I understand, very far from pleased but as far as we were concerned it was ' a job well done'. HMRC could only have appealed against the decision made by the First Tier Tribunal if they could have demonstrated an 'error of law'. Mr Rice is now our client and has incorporated his business on our advice.

APPENDIX

The items here in the Appendix cover a wide range of themes arising from the book's main topics. They fall under three main headings – some basic personal tax issues, HMRC and Companies House, and additional property issues (relevant to landlords if not directly relating to tax). Finally, I include the fundamental principles that govern how accountants like myself must work.

If you think something here may be relevant to you but are not sure, my advice is to read it anyway, just in case.

#57. Some basic personal tax issues

UNDERSTANDING INCOME TAX, NATIONAL INSURANCE AND PAYE SCHEMES

Personal Income Tax

As an individual, your personal income tax is based on all of your income, from whatever source, which has arisen during the tax year from 6 April to the following 5 April. The overall calculation includes any income where tax has been deducted at source (usually salary or other remuneration where this is paid under a PAYE Scheme).

The basic rule is that income is taxable in the tax year in which it is paid. However it is also possible that your annual income for income tax purposes may include income which you haven't yet received. For example, you may have an investment for a term of say three years, with interest calculated at either the anniversary date or another set date. If this interest is added to the capital, then it is still deemed 'paid' even if you can't access it without penalty, and so it should be included in your tax return for that year.

This is the basic principle for personal tax, but let's now look at some specifics you might encounter through your business.

Rental income: Let's say you are entitled to rental income but your tenant doesn't pay; in this case then you would still include all the income *receivable* (whether paid or not). You deal with the cash shortfall separately by writing it off and claiming bad debt relief. The situation might be different if your property is a furnished holiday let as this is capable of being classed as a trade. So your income from this source would be the net profits of that trade. It really is a case of knowing the rules that apply to specific sources of income, so do ask your accountant!

Partnerships and LLPs: Your share of the profits from a partnership or an LLP is deemed to be your personal income. The partnership must file its own tax return (and, in the case of an LLP, file accounts and returns at Companies House), but is not responsible for paying the tax – that falls to you. Your share must be included on your personal tax return.

Limited companies: By contrast, the tax treatment of your income from a limited company will depend upon whether you receive a salary (as a director or officer) or dividends as a shareholder. Anything received by way of salary will suffer deduction at source under PAYE (see below for where this applies). Dividends will be taxed as dividend income, applying the Dividend Allowance, just like dividends from any other company.

Trusts: What about income to which you are entitled under a trust? It depends on the type of trust. If you have an *immediate* right to income from the trust, then the income counts as your own income and will be paid to you without deduction of tax. You must therefore include this in your personal tax return and pay tax on this as part of your personal income. For other types of trust, such as discretionary trusts, the trustees will deduct tax at source and issue a certificate (R185) showing the amount you have received and the amount of tax deducted. Should your personal tax situation mean that you would not have been liable to pay some or all of this tax, then you can claim it back via your own tax return.

Now let's return to the tax calculation itself.

Having collated all this information, your total income is added together and any allowances applied. The principal allowances will be the personal allowance for the year (£12,500 for tax year 2019/20) and the Dividend Allowance against any dividend income (see below). There may be other allowances which I've discussed previously. The resulting figure is the basis for your tax computation at basic rate, higher rate or additional rate tax.

From that figure, you subtract any tax that has been deducted already. This may be PAYE tax deducted by the employer from your salary (or by the pension provider for any pension income) or tax deducted by the trustees for trust income, as explained above.

Then there may be adjustments to be made, for example where you have received benefits from your company which are taxable in your hands. The company, as employer, is required to file a Form P11D with HMRC showing what benefits-in-kind directors and higher paid employees have received. There are exempt thresholds for different benefits and the rules are quite complex

Finally, whatever remains is your income tax liability for the year. You must file a Self-Assessment Tax Return by 31 January after the end of each tax year (unless HMRC have told you that this is not necessary) and pay any tax due. In addition, you are required to make two payments on account of your next year's tax liability, one on 31 January in that tax year and the other on 31 July after the end of that tax year. This will be based upon the previous year's liability but if you believe that this will be significantly different then there is provision to request an adjustment.

It is also possible of course to make interim payments on account of tax to HMRC at any time and many taxpayers do so in order to minimize the impact of a heavy liability on 31 January.

The annual Self-Assessment Tax Return also requires you to disclose any chargeable gains occurring during the year of assessment, so any Capital Gains Tax will also be payable by 31 January after the end of the year in which the gain occurs. You do not need to report any gains which are covered by your annual allowance for CGT in the year.

All this will change, to some extent, when Making Tax Digital (MTD) is implemented for personal income tax. At the time of writing no details of the proposals are available but it is anticipated that these will be similar to the MTD regime for VAT (which I discussed in Section 4). It has also been proposed that the timing for both reporting and accounting for CGT should be accelerated.

N.B. Inheritance Tax reporting follows a different course to income tax, with chargeable transactions being reported as they occur. There is currently no requirement for reporting Potentially Exempt Transfers.

The reporting requirements for limited companies are different. Every company apart from dormant companies (those who have no assets and have no current contracts) must file an assessment for Corporation Tax within twelve months of the company year end. However the deadline for paying any Corporation Tax due is only nine months after the year end.

National Insurance Contributions

Unlike income tax, NI is not assessed on the basis of total income, but on the income from each individual employment or self-employment. So, in theory, it's quite possible for an individual to have two or more jobs, none of which reach the threshold for NI, and therefore to pay no NI. However, where several different jobs are involved, it is quite likely that HMRC will seek to argue that the reality is that the taxpayer is in fact self-employed and should therefore be paying NI on his or her total income from 'employment' under the self-employed regime (see below).

If you have a written contract of employment for each post, this will help to establish that in each case you are an employee. But do bear in mind that HMRC will look at the substance of your activities, so if what you actually do in your role is more akin to a self-employed role, then HMRC may reach the conclusion that you are not an employee. HMRC's criteria includes whether and how far you can choose your hours of work, whether you can substitute someone other than yourself to do the work, whether and to what extent you have to work under instruction (or whether you just 'deliver the job'), and whether you have to provide your own tools and any specialist clothing or equipment.

If you have two separate jobs but with the same employer (or with an associated business), your employer will usually calculate your NI on the total income from both jobs. However there is a mechanism for you to make a claim for a rebate if this results in your paying more NI than you would if this were to be calculated as two separate employments.

I know this may all seem rather odd when compared with the cumulative approach to income tax. The reality is that the NIC system is simply not geared up to the situation where an individual may have two or more different jobs and be below the Lower Earnings Limit (see below) in one or more of them. When Real Time Information (RTI) was implemented for PAYE/NIC reporting, it was suggested that NIC should be aligned with PAYE as a calculation based on total remuneration, but no changes have yet taken place.

Just as with income tax, if you receive benefits in kind, these may be subject to NIC. However, (and good news for employees), NIC (Class 1A) is payable only by the *employers*, not by the employees. As with income tax, there are various exemptions and thresholds and, to make it even more complicated, some benefits are taxable but not subject to NIC! There is also Class 1B NIC which is like Class 1A but paid under what is known as a PAYE Settlement Agreement. This allows the employer to make one annual payment to cover all the tax and National Insurance due on small or irregular taxable expenses or benefits for employees.

What if you don't pay NIC?

As you can see, it may well be theoretically possible for an individual to arrange matters so that they pay minimal NIC or no NIC at all! Is this necessarily a good thing?

To answer that question we need to look at the different classes of contribution and see how they apply (the capital letters in the third column are explained below the table):

CLASS	PAYABLE BY	RATE 2019/20
Class 1	Employees who earn more than £166 but not more than £962 per week (£719 to £4,167 per month) and are under State Pension age. Employer must deduct from wages or salary	12% (but 2% for NI No. J & Z)
Class 1 (higher earners)	Employees who earn more than £962 per week (£4,167 per month) and are under State Pension age. Payable on excess and deducted from wages or salary.	2%
Class 1A or 1B	Employers pay these calculated on the expenses or benefits of their employees (see above)	
Class 2	Self-employed people who earn at least £6,365 a year, but not: • examiners, moderators, invigilators and people who set exam questions • people who run businesses involving land or property • ministers of religion who do not receive a salary or stipend • people who make investments for themselves or others - but not as a business and without getting a fee or commission	£3 per week
Class 3	Voluntary contributions - payable by anyone who does not have to pay any other class of contribution, or who wishes to repair their contribution record (see below)	No mandatory rate

Class 4	Self-employed people who earn over £8,632 a year	9% on profits up to £50,000 2% on profits over £50,000
Employers' NIC ('secondary contribution')	Payable by employers on that part of the employees' remuneration above £166 per week or £972 per month (excluding benefits which are liable to Class 1A or 1B). This still applies where employee is over State Pension Age	13.8% but for employees with NI No H, M or Z, only on excess over £962 per week (£4,167 per month)

All rates and thresholds are for the tax year 2019/20 and may be altered for subsequent tax years.

NI category letters (in the third column above) are the final letter in your NI Number. 'J' and 'Z' are employees who are deferring NI because they are already paying it in another employment (Z is for under 21). 'H' is for apprentices under 25 and 'M' for employees under 21. The standard letter is 'A' and 'C' is for employees who have reached State Pension Age.

It is not possible to defer paying Class 4 NI, even if you also have employment which means you are paying Class 1 NI.

There are some other rules applying to company directors and landlords running a property business.

Company directors are classed as employees and are liable to pay employee's NI on annual income (including bonuses, but not counting dividends) of over £8,632. A director's NI is worked out annually because a director is deemed to be working every day of the year!

The company must pay employer's NI and Class 1A or 1B on benefits even if the director is a sole director running a company with no other employees.

Landlord's must pay Class 2 NIC if the profits are over £5,965 a year and what you do counts as running a business, for example if all the following apply:

- being a landlord is your main job;
- you rent out more than one property;
- you're buying new properties to rent out.

What do you get from your NI contributions?

Your National Insurance Contribution record dictates your entitlement to State Retirement Pension and also to certain State benefits, including Contribution-based Job-Seekers Allowance, Contribution-based Employment and Support Allowance, Maternity Allowance and Bereavement Support Allowance. So if your circumstances mean that you are not liable to pay NI you may well want to consider making voluntary payments in order to secure your entitlement, particularly in relation to your State Retirement Pension.

You may have gaps in your contribution record, for example because you were unemployed but did not claim benefits, or your earnings were low, or you were self-employed but had low profits, or you were in one of the self-employed categories that exempted you from paying Class 2 NI. You can obtain a statement of your record (and how it affects your pension entitlement) by writing to:

National Insurance contributions and Employers Office
HM Revenue and Customs
BX9 1AN

Alternatively, you can get details of your contribution record by applying online.

If you find that you have not made sufficient contributions, or you are approaching State Retirement Age and can see that your remaining anticipated contributions will not entitle you to the maximum pension, you should be able to 'repair' your record by making voluntary contributions. It is really important to check this in good time so that you maximise your State Pension entitlement.

Unfortunately making voluntary contributions will not help you with entitlement to Contribution-based Job-Seekers Allowance, Contribution-based Employment and Support Allowance, Maternity Allowance and Bereavement Support Allowance.

PAYE Schemes

When should employers run a PAYE (Pay as Your Earn) scheme?

PAYE tax and NIC for employees is deducted through the payroll and therefore, if you have any employees (including directors) who are liable for deductions, you must set up a PAYE Scheme with HMRC. You will also use this to calculate the employers' NIC (including Class 1A and 1B).

I know it's tempting for businesses with a number of workers who only work 'as needed' to class these as 'casual workers', but the HMRC definition of a casual worker is actually quite strict. It only applies to someone taken on for a period of not more than one week and not taken on again in the same tax year. And even for casual workers, if their remuneration exceeds the various thresholds they still need to have a deduction calculation sheet in place and any deductions made and accounted for to HMRC.

I've spoken above about the thresholds for NI and when an employee is liable to have NIC deducted at source. However there is yet another threshold, the Lower Earnings Limit ('LEL') which for tax year 2019/20 is £118 per week, £512 per month or £6,136 per year. The significance of the LEL is that, although the employee won't start actually paying NI (at 12%) until earnings reach the 'Primary Threshold' of £166 per week etc., it is the LEL which governs entitlement to NI benefits.

So, if you have any employees who reach the LEL, you must run a PAYE Scheme.

Then other reason for the PAYE Scheme is to arrange deduction of PAYE income tax which, as I've explained, is assessed on a cumulative basis across the individual employee's total income. You'll do this by applying the Tax Code for each employee which HMRC will issue to you as the employer. The employee's tax code will be calculated in relation to the personal allowance and any other allowances to which the employee is entitled. Whatever the employee earns above this amount will suffer tax. If the employee has (or has had) income on which tax has not been paid, these sums will be deducted from the personal allowance and the resulting figure divided by 10 (to give a three or four digit number) will be the tax code (plus a letter which will be 'L' for people who have only one job).

You **must** apply this code. For a new employee you can work this out based on their P45 (as long as this is within the same tax year). If you don't have this and you don't yet have a tax code for an employee (because they've just started a new job after a break, or previously been self-employed) then you apply the emergency tax code if this is their only job, and if not you should apply basic rate tax (BR code).

PAYE works on the assumption that every time an employee receives a payment, then he or she will continue to be paid at the same rate throughout the year. So as the personal allowance for the current tax year 2019/20 is £12,500, the system will assume that, for an employee paid monthly, 1/12 of the allowance (£1,047.66) is set against each salary payment. The tax code will be 1250 plus a letter. The application of the code to the monthly income will result in the employee paying tax (at whatever rate he is assessable) on the portion of his monthly income not covered by his tax allowance.

If the emergency tax code is applied, this will be the standard tax code (1250 in the current tax year) but followed by the letter W1 (weekly pay), M1 (monthly pay) or X. The effect will be that only 1/52 or 1/12 of the tax allowance will be applied each payment, with no account being taken of the deductions record for the earlier part of the tax year.

So for example, if an individual worked from April to June (3 months) under PAYE and then did not work from July to September, he would have 9 months allowance to apply to the employment from October to March (6 months). The application of an emergency tax code means that, until the correct tax code is applied, his deductions will still only allow for £1047.66 to be tax free (£1250 divided by 12) whereas the tax-free amount for each of those six months should be £1,562.50.

In the absence of an in-date P45, the emergency tax code must be applied until a new tax code is issued by HMRC. At that point the application of the updated tax code to the next salary payment will result in any over-deducted amounts being repaid via the payroll.

If on the other hand the employee states, in response to enquiry, that this is not his only job, then unless and until a tax code for the employment with you arrives, the correct course is to apply BR rate. This means that no allowances are take into account and all income from the employment is taxed at basic rate. The application of the correct tax code will result in the repayment (in that week or month) of any over-deduction of tax as a result of applying the BR code in the meantime

It may be that none of your employees earn more than the Personal Allowance for Income Tax or reach the LEL in their employment with **you**, but what if any of your employees have a second job? In order for HMRC to assess their liability for Income Tax overall, they need to be registered as an employee. So you, as employer must set up a PAYE scheme if any of your employees tell you that they have a second job. The same applies if you give any of your employees a benefit, to enable HMRC to assess whether this affects the Income Tax or National Insurance position.

This only a brief outline of how the PAYE system works. Most, if not all, employers use a computerised payroll system and with the advent of Real Time Information, payroll details are required to be provided to HMRC almost contemporaneously.

As you will see, on the face of it you do not have to run a PAYE Scheme unless you have employees who earn a sum that is within the Personal Allowance for Income Tax and below the LEL for NIC, or who have another job. However you could still have employees who are on basic rate tax (for whatever reason) or who have a tax code which is non-standard and which shows that their pay from you should suffer deduction of Income Tax. If you have employees and are not registered for a PAYE Scheme, you will need to confirm to HMRC from time to time whether you have any employees and that none of them are subject to deductions.

You will also of course need to keep the appropriate records to determine whether or not you have any employees who are subject to auto-enrolment for a workplace pension.

PERSONAL SAVINGS ALLOWANCE, DIVIDENDS AND ISAS

Personal Savings Allowance (PSA): Introduced on 6 April 2016, the PSA allows basic-rate taxpayers to earn tax-free income from savings of up to £1,000 a year in savings free of income tax. For higher-rate taxpayers, this reduces to a maximum of £500. Additional rate taxpayers do not receive a PSA and must pay tax on any savings income they receive on savings outside an ISA account (see below).

Be aware that since the introduction of the PSA, banks and building societies have stopped deducting 20% tax from bank interest, so it is now paid gross. So, if you exceed the PSA, then you will have to pay the tax on the excess interest, either through your tax code or by declaring it on your Self-Assessment Return.

The PSA does not include ISAs since these are tax-free anyway. It's also completely separate from the Dividend Allowance, which means that individuals receive their first £2,000 in dividends tax-free, but any dividends above this amount will be charged at 7.5% for basic rate taxpayers, 32.5% for higher rate taxpayers and 38.1% for additional rate taxpayers.

The PSA applies to savings income from the following sources:

- Interest from bank and building society accounts;

- Interest from accounts with providers such as credit unions and National Savings and Investments;

- Interest distributions (not dividend) from authorised unit trusts, investment trusts and OEICs (open ended investment companies);

- Income from corporate bonds and gilts (government bonds);

- Purchased life annuity payments.

It does not apply to loan-based schemes and equity-based investments (dividends).

There are other schemes for helping to boost your tax-free assets:

Starting Rate for Savings: There is a special starting rate for savings and this is 10% for tax year 2019/20 and applies to income from savings up to £5,000. This is quite separate from your Personal Allowance and from the Personal Savings Allowance described above. To give you an example, if you have income of £18,500 in tax year 2019/20, and £6,000 of this is from savings with the balance from employment, then your Income Tax will be £500. The Personal Allowance (£12,500) will cover your income from employment, and the PSA will cover £1,000 of your savings. The balance of £5,000 savings will be taxed at 10% under the Starting Rate for Savings.

If on the other hand your income from savings was only £3,000, then again £1,000 would be covered by the PSA and 10% of the remainder would be taxed at 10% (£200). However your income from employment would be £15,500, of which £3,000 would be above the Personal Allowance for Income Tax, and this would bear tax at 20% (£600) so your total Income Tax bill (ignoring any other allowances that may apply) would be £800.

Individual Savings Accounts (ISAs): You can invest £20,000 per year in either a Cash ISA or a Stocks and Shares ISA, or you can divide this between both types. There is no Income Tax on the interest or dividends you receive from an ISA and any profits from investments are free of Capital Gains Tax. Stocks and Shares ISAs tend to be better for long-term investment (to iron out peaks and troughs in the market.

Some ISA providers now offer a flexible facility which will let you withdraw and replace money from your ISA, provided it is done within the same tax year.

Lifetime ISAs, available to people between the ages of 18 and 40, let you save up to £4,000 per year and get a government bonus of 25% (up to £1,000).

Junior ISAs: Family and friends can put up to £4,368 into the account on behalf of the child in the 2019-20 tax year and the threshold will be increased in line with the Consumer Prices Index each tax year. There's no Income Tax or Capital Gains Tax to pay on the interest or investment gains.

Junior ISAs are available to any child under 18 living in the UK who doesn't qualify for a Child Trust Fund. No new Child Trust Funds can be opened now, but existing ones may be transferred to Junior ISAs.

National Savings and Investments (NS&I): These offer Cash ISAs and Premium Savings Bonds (you won't get interest on Premium bonds but any prizes are tax free). They are considered safe as they are backed by the government.

Pension savings: Depending on the type of pension scheme you have, tax relief either reduces your tax bill or increases the amount paid into your scheme. Where tax relief increases the amount paid in, you get the relief even if you're a non-taxpayer.

Your pension fund grows tax-free and when you retire (or reach the required age even if you don't retire), you can usually take up to 25% of your pension fund as a tax-free lump sum, with the regular pension income taxed along with the rest of your income.

LOSS OF CHILD BENEFIT

High Income Child Benefit Charge was introduced in 2013. Under this scheme, if you and your partner each earn less than £50,000 a year, you will receive the full amount of Child Benefit without having to pay any of it back.

However, if either you or your partner earns between £50,000 and £60,000 a year before tax, you'll have to pay a portion of your Child Benefit back in extra Income Tax. The tax is 1% of the amount of child benefit for each £100 of income on a sliding scale between £50,000 and £60,000. For those earning more than £60,000 the charge is 100%

The basis is your adjusted net income. This is your total taxable income (i.e. basic salary plus benefits you get from your job, rental income etc), minus things such as pension contributions and gift-aided donations to charity. Any contributions made into a company or personal pension scheme will reduce the final amount of adjusted net income.

How does repayment work?

You will still get paid the full amount of Child Benefit each month (or each week, if you're paid weekly). However, whichever one of you has the higher income, will have to make the repayment in the form of Income Tax. You will need to fill in a Self-Assessment tax return so HMRC can calculate the extra Income Tax you'll have to pay.

#58. HMRC and Companies House

Your key dates for HMRC and Companies House

Individuals and Sole Traders	
Personal Self-Assessment Tax Return - Income Tax and Capital Gains-filing and payment of tax due	31st October after end of tax year for paper returns. 30th December after end of tax year if you wish any adjustment to be collected through Tax Code 31st January after end of tax year for online returns (no adjustment through Tax Code)
Payments on account for current year's Self-Assessment Income Tax	31st January and 31st July
Deadline to notify chargeability of Income Tax/Capital Gains Tax (new source e.g. new self-employment)	5th October after end of tax year in which this occurred
Making Tax Digital Regime	Projected start date April 2020
Partnerships (including LLPs)	
Partnership Tax Return (with annual accounts for partnership year ending within tax year)	31st October after end of tax year for paper returns. 31st January after end of tax year for online returns
Individual partners' personal tax returns	31st October after end of tax year for paper returns. 30th December after end of tax year if you wish any adjustment to be collected through Tax Code 31st January after end of tax year for online returns (no adjustment through Tax Code)
Making Tax Digital Regime	Projected start date April 2020

Limited Companies	
Corporation Tax Return (with annual accounts)	12 months after end of the accounting period (usually your financial year)
Payment of Corporation Tax (or notification to HMRC that no tax is due)	9 months and 1 day after the end of your accounting period
CT61 Return (income tax deducted from payments other than PAYE) and payment	14th day of month after end of each three-monthly period
Filing Annual Accounts at Companies House	21 months after date of incorporation and then 9 months after end of each accounting period
Filing Confirmation Statement at Companies House	First statement within 12 months of incorporation. Thereafter not more than 12 months to elapse between filings.
Filing special (shareholder) resolutions at Companies House	Within 15 days of event
Filing other changes not requiring special resolution e.g. change of directors' details	Usually within 14 days of event
LLPs	
Filing Annual Accounts at Companies House	21 months after date of incorporation (if accounts cover a period in excess of 12 months). Otherwise 9 months after end of each accounting period
Filing Confirmation Statement at Companies House	First statement within 14 days of first anniversary of incorporation. Thereafter not more than 12 months to elapse between filings.
Filing changes in LLP e.g. members, registered address	14 days from event
CT61 Return (income tax deducted from payments other than PAYE) and payment	14th day of month after end of each three-monthly period (with letter stating LLP status)
Also see requirements under PARTNERSHIPS	

PAYE/NIC/CIS	
Monthly deadline for postal payments	19th day of next month
Monthly deadline for electronic payments	22nd day of next month
Quarterly deadlines (if paying quarterly)	As monthly dates in month after end of quarter
Notifying HMRC that no payment is due	19th day of month after month in which no tax due
File P35 Employer Annual Return and P14 End of Year Summary for employees	19th May after end of tax year
Issue P60 to all employees employed during tax year	31st May after end of tax year
Deadline for PAYE settlement agreement	5th July after end of tax year
Submit P11D forms online to HMRC for benefits in kind (with copy to employees) and P11Db for Class 1A NIC due	6th July after end of tax year
VAT	
Deadline for quarterly returns and payment of VAT due	Last day of month following end of quarter
Making Tax Digital Regime	Commences April 2019 - no change to VAT deadlines

Understanding HMRC's perspective

I have mentioned several times in the book that tax issues often come down to interpretation rather than simply to hard facts. So, in this section we consider the nuanced viewpoint that HMRC might take in any dispute.

The HMRC website contains a wealth of information and it is tempting to think that as long as you can read through this with a reasonable degree of understanding, then all you need to do is make sure your affairs are arranged in accordance with this. But beware: I'm not suggesting that the information is necessarily inaccurate, but:

• It is a statement of HMRC's interpretation of the law;

- It is often an outline only and, as they say, 'the devil's in the detail';

- It is usually a statement of what has already been established - not what could be successfully argued (in your favour!)

To understand what this means, you need to appreciate that the tax regime in the UK is incredibly fragmented. It would be great if we had a unified and codified system, in which the rules and requirements for each type of tax all matched up. But the fact is   - we don't. So we need to look at the legal system that might come into play.

The UK's general legal system consists of:

- Statute law;

- Common law; and

- Case law.

Now statute is fairly easy to understand: it is what's set out in statutes and statutory instruments, approved and passed by the Parliament of the day. Some areas of law are entirely governed by statute, because they've come into being at a time after written legislation became the norm. A good example is Company Law, since limited companies are entirely created by and governed by the various Companies Acts. Another example is modern Data Protection and Intellectual Property Law.

I'm not of course a professional lawyer, but my understanding is that areas of the law which are older, such as criminal law and contract law, have a body of law known as common law. What this means is that it is not codified in the same way as, say, the American constitution.

Whether a legal issue arises from statute or from common law, the interpretation is affected by case law and the doctrine of precedent. Now, where a case is brought before the courts and a decision made, the judgement binds subsequent cases on that point, unless the case is taken to a higher court such as the Court of Appeal, which can overturn a judgement made in a lower court. The whole of the judgement is not necessarily binding; it's the part which sets out the reasons for the decision (known to lawyers as the *ratio decidendi* or 'the ratio'). You sometimes find that, in a judgement which may appear to the layman to be of very similar facts, the wording will explain why the judge thinks that the ratio is in fact different. This is known as 'distinguishing' the case from another case. Cases that decide a particularly important issue, or where the decision breaks new ground or differs from what has gone before, are known as 'leading cases' or 'landmark decisions'.

Enough of my attempt at legal explanations, although I hope this illustrates the importance of interpretation in dealing with tax issues. For all the reasons I've given, interpreting the tax laws and the HMRC practice requires a bit more than reading through the information on the HMRC website. What I would normally do is:

- Look at the views of HMRC first (because it's very useful to know what their view might be);

- Research available case law and tax legislation;

- Look at whether the issue is clear-cut or not. If it isn't, formulate the arguments in favour (as well as trying to address the arguments against)

- In appropriate cases, consider whether or not the issues are effectively breaking new ground i.e. it's a situation that isn't actually covered by the tax laws as yet.

This is what my legal colleague calls 'formulating a cogent argument' and it's surprising how difficult this can be to achieve. It is however essential in putting a case to HMRC, especially if it's likely to end up before the First Tier Tribunal (or even higher). Clearly in these cases it may well be necessary to seek counsel's opinion or for a barrister to represent you (especially if the case goes to the High Court).

What I haven't mentioned is that HMRC themselves issue statements of practice. These are valuable in that they tell you what HMRC are already prepared to accept. Although these do not have the force of law, if you can find one which supports your contentions, then it is after all rather difficult for HMRC to backtrack from their own published statements.

In the field of tax-mitigation strategies in particular, HMRC operates what they term Disclosure of Tax Avoidance Schemes ('DOTAS'). The idea is that the promoters of tax-avoidance schemes are required to notify these to HMRC in order to allow HMRC to review them and monitor their operation. The rules were broadened considerably in February 2016 as follows:

- Under DOTAS a scheme promoter is required to disclose the main elements of the scheme to HMRC;

- Special rules apply where disclosure is not made by a promoter, in those cases a scheme user must make disclosure;

- HMRC will then issue the scheme with a DOTAS number;

- A scheme user will have to notify HMRC that it is using the scheme by inserting the number in its tax return;

- HMRC will monitor the scheme's use and, if necessary, promote legislation to terminate it;

- Financial penalties are levied on those who fail to comply with the regime;

- If an obligation to disclose exists, notification must be made within 5 days of the arrangements first being made available.

Is this a good thing from the tax-payer's point of view? Well it does at least take some of the risk away, as the scheme is already on the HMRC radar and consequently you (or your advisers) should be aware of any restrictions that HMRC is looking to impose. Like it or not, you are obliged to notify HMRC when using a scheme with a DOTAS number. If on the other hand you are using an untried and 'one-off' strategy, then the risk is that this may open a tax enquiry that may ultimately lead to a case before the Tribunal.

GAAR and TAAR in detail

These acronyms stand for General Anti-Abuse Rules and Targeted Anti-Abuse Rules. GAAR was introduced by the Finance Act 2013.

Let's look at GAAR first.

It's based on the concept that the levying of tax is the principal mechanism by which the state pays for the services and facilities that it provides for its citizens, and that all taxpayers should pay their fair share. It therefore rejects the approach taken by the Courts in a number of old cases to the effect that taxpayers are free to use their ingenuity to reduce their tax bills by any lawful means, however contrived those means might be and however far the tax consequences might differ from the real economic position.

Needless to say, there are a number of leading cases relating to the application of GAAR.

The primary policy objective of GAAR is to deter taxpayers from entering into abusive arrangements, and to deter would-be promoters from promoting such arrangements. There may be tax avoidance arrangements that are challenged by HMRC using other parts of the tax code, but if they are not abusive they are not within the scope of GAAR.

If a taxpayer goes ahead with an abusive arrangement, then GAAR operates to counteract the abusive tax advantage that he or she is trying to achieve.

The counteraction that GAAR permits will be a tax adjustment that is just and reasonable in all the circumstances. The appropriate tax adjustment is not necessarily the one that raises the most tax.

It is recognised that, under the UK's tax code, in many circumstances there are different courses of action that a taxpayer can quite properly choose between. There are safeguards aimed at ensuring that any reasonable choice of a course of action is kept outside the target area of GAAR.

Using statutory incentives and reliefs to support business activity and investment in a straightforward way (for example Business Relief, Enterprise Investment Scheme (EIS), Capital Allowances, Patent Box) is also not caught by GAAR. However, where taxpayers set out to exploit some loophole in the tax laws, for example, by entering into contrived arrangements to obtain a relief but suffering no equivalent economic risk, they will fall into the target area of GAAR.

Since GAAR is designed to counteract the tax advantage which the abusive arrangements would otherwise achieve, it will usually be necessary to determine whether the arrangements would achieve their tax avoiding purpose under the rest of the tax code (that is, the non-GAAR tax rules), before considering whether the arrangements are 'abusive' within the meaning of GAAR. However, there may be some arrangements which appear to be so clearly abusive that it would be appropriate for HMRC to invoke GAAR without first determining whether the arrangements would achieve their intended tax result under the rest of the tax rules.

It is therefore not possible for a taxpayer to object to the use of GAAR simply because all other means available to HMRC to tackle what HMRC considers an abusive arrangement have not been used.

There are many statutory provisions relating to the taxes covered by GAAR that set out specific anti-avoidance rules. Some of these are known as targeted anti-avoidance rules (TAARs), while others may take the form of less explicit anti-avoidance protection. For example, the Finance Act 2016 introduced a new TAAR to prevent "phoenixism" – broadly where solvent companies are liquidated so that shareholders dispose of their shares to realise a Capital Gains Tax charge rather than paying income tax on the profits that would otherwise be distributed.

In many cases the existing (non-GAAR) tax rules will be effective in defeating abusive tax arrangements, and so in such cases HMRC will not need to rely on GAAR. However, there may be cases where abusive schemes would succeed in the absence of GAAR, in which case HMRC will seek to rely on GAAR.

GAAR applies with effect from 17 July 2013 to:

- Income Tax;

- Capital Gains Tax;

- Inheritance Tax;

- Corporation Tax;

- Any amount chargeable as if it were Corporation Tax (or treated as if it were Corporation Tax - such as a Controlled Foreign Company (CFC) charge - Bank Levy - Oil Supplementary Charge and Tonnage Tax);

- Petroleum Revenue Tax;

- Stamp Duty Land Tax;

- Annual Tax on Enveloped Dwellings;

- Diverted Profits Tax which was introduced with effect from 1 April 2015;

- Apprenticeship Levy with effect from 15 September 2016;

- National Insurance Contributions by extension under s s10 National Insurance Contributions Act 2014.

GAAR only comes into operation when the course of action taken by the taxpayer aims to achieve a favourable tax result that Parliament did not anticipate when it introduced the tax rules in question and, critically, where that course of action cannot reasonably be regarded as reasonable on the part of the taxpayer. As you will see below, the double use of the concept of reasonableness is deliberate in this case.

Taxpayer safeguards include:

- requiring HMRC to establish that the arrangements are abusive (it is not up to the taxpayer to show that the arrangements are non-abusive);

- applying a 'double reasonableness' test. This requires HMRC to show that the arrangements 'cannot reasonably be regarded as a reasonable course of action'. It recognises that there are some arrangements which some people would regard as a reasonable course of action while others would not. The 'double reasonableness' test sets a high threshold by asking whether it would be reasonable to hold the view that the arrangement was a reasonable course of action. The arrangement is treated as abusive only if it would not be reasonable to hold such a view;

- Allowing the Court or Tribunal to take into account any relevant material as to the purpose of the legislation that it is suggested the taxpayer has abused, or as to the sort of transactions which had become established practice at the time when the arrangements were entered into;

- Requiring HMRC to obtain the opinion of an independent advisory panel as to whether an arrangement constituted a reasonable course of action, before HMRC can finally apply GAAR.

GAAR does not provide for a clearance system of its own, but there are many provisions in the tax legislation applying to the taxes covered by GAAR that do include provision for a taxpayer to apply for a clearance in respect of a particular transaction.

Applications may be made for either statutory or non-statutory clearance. However, HMRC is not permitted to advise on alternative courses which would not trigger TAAR or GAAR, and, with regard to non-statutory clearance, recently it has become apparent that clearance may well not be issued if either the taxpayer or a competent professional adviser could make the decision themselves. In many cases it is necessary to demonstrate a bona fide commercial reason for the proposed transactions.

In an earlier section I referred briefly to DOTAS. This is a regime which was originally designed to enable HMRC to recognise the various types of tax avoidance schemes by requesting the promoters make a disclosure. HMRC would then review and, if necessary, amend legislation to block any scheme that was considered aggressive and unfair.

Changes to regulations, from February 2016, have significantly broadened the DOTAS rules, which may well capture more standard tax planning strategies.

I strongly recommend that, before taking any action, you consult a professional adviser about the application of GAAR, TAAR and DOTAS and also, where appropriate, seek HMRC clearance before proceeding.

#59. Additional property landlord issues

How to avoid remortgaging

If you're seeking to restructure your property business, then if the legal ownership of the properties (that is, the name on the title) is to be transferred and those properties are mortgaged, you cannot do so without the mortgagee's consent. There is no legal reason why title to a property cannot be transferred subject to a mortgage, but the reality is, in my experience, that the lenders will usually insist on a new mortgage, which means more costs.

However, there are some strategies that may avoid this (but as they are largely untested, always seek advice):

1. You could transfer what is known as the beneficial interest in the property but not the legal title. In other words, the name on the title remains yours but you are now holding it upon trust for you and X (or indeed X alone or X & Y). If properties are in a sole name, one way to reduce the tax burden is to transfer the interest into a partnership between, say, husband and wife. No CGT is payable but SDLT would be payable depending on the value of the property/s.

Transferring the beneficial interest only into joint names (without disturbing the legal title) is an attractive idea, but you may still be under an obligation to obtain the consent of the mortgagee (or at least notify the mortgagee). There's no general requirement by law but quite possibly a clause in the terms and conditions of the loan. So what might be the consequences?

If you tell the mortgagee, they are likely to require you to re-mortgage (possibly on less advantageous terms). If you don't tell them, and there is relevant condition, then you will be in breach that could cause problems if this comes to light.

There is however a theoretical way around this by allowing the partnership to manage the properties, collect the rent and pay the mortgages, with the profits divided between the partners in the profit-sharing ratio for taxation purposes. So what is happening is that the partners are sharing the partnership profits in the ratio agreed between them, as opposed to the income from a specific property or properties being shared between the beneficial owners, (which must follow the beneficial property-owning proportions).

Result - no remortgage, possibly no SDLT and no expensive transfers. But beware - this is a complex tax-mitigation structure and expert advice on the drafting of the partnership agreement is essential.

2. I have also considered a structure whereby an individual A forms an LLP with the other member being a limited company with the shareholding also owned by A. The proposal is that A then allows his portfolio of properties to be utilised by the LLP (collecting the rents, paying the mortgages and also managing the properties) with all or most of the profits of the LLP passing (by agreement) to the limited company. It would be preferable for the legal title of the properties not to pass to the LLP as this will incur refinancing costs and SDLT.

Deposits for residential lets

In 2013, rules came into force requiring the landlord of most residential lets to pay any tenant's deposit into one of the three official schemes. In 2015 these was extended to apply even where the tenants had been in occupation prior to that date.

The penalty for not doing so is a fine that is potentially unlimited but is typically three times the deposit.

What you can deduct from the deposit must be set out in the tenancy agreement but may be covered by wording such as 'deductions from your deposit can be made for breaches of your tenancy agreement'. What you can deduct includes:

- unpaid rent;

- damage to the property (but not ordinary wear and tear);

- missing items;

- cleaning costs.

You cannot include unpaid utility bills or the cost of re-letting.

Failure to return the deposit, or making unlawful deductions, will entitle the tenant to take you to court.

From June 2019, the Tenant Fees Act makes it illegal for landlords and agents to charge tenants for referencing, inventories and 'admin' fees. The Act also:

- Limits tenancy deposits to five weeks' rent;

- Limits holding deposits to one week's rent;

- Bans any other payments (except contractual default penalties).

This will be enforced by a fine of up to £5,000 for the first infringement and fines of up to £30,000 for any subsequent infringement and this may also lead to criminal proceedings.

Houses in Multiple Occupation (HMO)

The definition of an HMO includes:

1. An entire flat or house that you let to three or more tenants;

2. Bedsits that you let singly and where the tenants share facilities of a kitchen, bathroom and toilet;

3. Separate flats (which include studio flats) let singly where the tenants share some facilities;

4. A building that is entirely converted into flats which doesn't meet the current regulations (the 1991 Building Regulations) and where a third of the flats are let on short-term tenancies.

The tenants must use it as their only, or main, residence and the property should be used solely, or mainly, to accommodate tenants. This includes students.

If the HMO has three or more habitable storeys and is occupied by five or more people in at least two households, then you need to register with the local authority for an HMO licence. Failure to do so is a criminal offence carrying an unlimited fine and conviction may mean that you are unable to operate or manage an HMO in the future.

Selective Licensing: Even if you're not operating an HMO, the local authority may designate residential areas for selective licensing. The effect is that any property in the private rented sector must be licensed. It's a licence per property, not per landlord.

Generally, the same rules apply when granting a Selective Licence as with an HMO licence. The main differences are:

1. It is mandatory to take up references for a prospective tenant before letting a property subject to Selective Licensing;

2. Unlike HMOs the licence authority does not have to consider suitability for letting or amenity standards when granting a selective licence. However, the licence holder must still be a fit and proper person.

As with HMOs, it's a criminal offence to let in a designated area without a licence and this carries an unlimited fine.

There are some exemptions and temporary exemptions to the requirements.

Ground rents and rentcharges

Ground rents

In connection with ground rents, I should just point out that, at the time of writing there are proposals to outlaw the creation of new leases which reserve a ground rent, or at least severely restrict the amount of ground rent that can be charged.

There have been many stories recently about the lease-owners who escalate their ground rents exponentially to the massive disadvantage of the leaseholders. At the time of writing there are proposals to outlaw the creation of any new leases that do this.

The reason why this has been such a well-used strategy is the mechanism of valuation of the ground rent at intervals during the long leasehold term. This can be quite difficult as, unlike ordinary rent reviews, it does not relate to open market value. As a consequence, many leases have adopted the easy option of saying that the ground rent simply doubles at specified intervals.

However, this means the increase is exponential, seeing a ground rent of, say, £250 a year go up to £2,000 after three sequential increases. An interval might be 20 years (although this is quite a short interval in ground rent terms but certainly not unknown in recent cases), so someone buying a 250 year lease at a point when 50 years have expired, will find that ten years later the annual ground rent moves from £1,000 to £2,000. Worse still, the prospect of further increases can make the property unsaleable, or unmortgageable.

Of course, the way in which the ground rent operates must be clearly set out in the lease, so any buyer ought to be well aware of the situation before purchasing, but I guess that when you buy a long leasehold even 20 years seems a very long way away.

Long leaseholds are now most commonly found for apartments, but there is no reason why they should not apply to houses as well (and historically in some parts of the country this was quite common). I believe there have been recent cases of houses that one might expect to be sold as freeholds being sold as long leaseholds in order for the developer to retain an income stream by way of ground rent - especially as, unlike a service charge, the freeholder/landlord usually has no obligations to meet. It's also the case that failure to pay the ground rent (even if this is a nominal sum) has the probably unintended result of allowing the landlord to seek possession of the property under the Housing Act 1988 and there have been instances of companies buying up ground rents with this in mind.

Whatever the reasons, it looks as if the days of lucrative ground rents are numbered.

How does this affect companies?

Companies are liable to pay higher rate SDLT on the purchase of residential properties (or a major interest therein) at a figure or more than £40,000 if all of certain conditions are satisfied. One of these is that the property is not subject to a lease with at least 21 years unexpired, so higher rate SDLT could be avoided by creating leases of a longer length.

There is also the distinct possibility that HMRC would seek to treat the new leases as linked transactions, which would mean that all the new leases would be treated for SDLT purposes as if they were a single transaction.

However, another crucial issue in the creation of leases either without a premium or at a less than commercial rent is Section 53 Finance Act 2003.

This applies to any transaction between a vendor (individual or company) and a company connected to them, when the company is the purchaser. The chargeable consideration for SDLT purposes will be not less than the market value at the effective date, not the actual value of the consideration for the transaction. This will apply to the grant of a lease as well as to a sale because the section itself uses the word 'transaction'.

So an otherwise attractive strategy using the grant of the lease by the freeholder to a company, as a way of retaining an income by way of ground rent, or as a first step to avoiding higher rate SDLT on the subsequent transfer of the freehold, may be caught by section 53 if the grantor of the lease is connected to the company. The resultant SDLT charged on the deemed value is likely to outweigh the advantages.

However, if the transactions are between companies in the same group (75% ownership for this purpose) then 100% SDLT group relief may be claimed. I have outlined earlier how this would apply.

Rentcharges

Also known as 'chief rents', these are charges which relate to freehold properties (not to leaseholds) and are sums payable (usually annually) to a third party who usually has no legal interest in the property. The 'rentowner' is the individual (or entity) to whom the sums are payable.

Since the Rentcharges Act 1977 no new rentcharges or chief rents can be created. However you may come across these if you acquire older properties, since the original idea of rentcharges was that a landowner could release land for development whilst still retaining an income stream. The Rentcharges Act brings to an end any existing rentcharges after a period of 60 years from the date on which they were first payable or 60 years from the date of the Act, whichever is the later, so in another 20 years (22 June 2037 to be precise) these will no longer exist.

Under the Act you can apply to redeem a rentcharge (i.e. pay a single lump sum to settle it, which is a matter of valuation) or of course negotiate a settlement with the rentowner.

However there are also 'estate rentcharges' and these are an exception to the 1977 Act. Typically these are rentcharges which has been imposed to enforce the observance of covenants on the property (for example an obligation to contribute towards a joint feature such as a boundary wall or a shared access), or towards the maintenance of a communal feature in a newbuild development.

There is no statutory right to redeem an estate rentcharge and so usually the only way to terminate it is by negotiation with the rentowner. This may prove difficult if the purpose is the maintenance of a communal feature which is shared by a number of properties.

Why do rentcharges matter?

Just as with ground rents, they are a liability attaching to the property and although on the face of it they may appear to be a relatively insignificant obligation there are a number of pitfalls:

- They may be subject to regular, exponential increase (as with ground rents)

- If they are not a quantified sum, there is no mechanism for challenging the amount

- Penalties for non-payment can be severe, including court action for recovery

- There is a statutory right for the rentowner, if the rentcharge is unpaid for 40 days, to grant a lease over the property to raise money to pay the rentcharge, with the lease continuing for its full term even if the rentcharge is paid.

- There is a statutory right (and possibly an express right) of re-entry for the rentowner until the rentcharge is paid

Ordinary rentcharges are more common in certain areas of the country, but estate rentcharges can crop up anywhere where there has been development of a private estate. So, as with groundrents, the golden rule is to ensure that you read the small print relating to any rentcharges that apply, especially if they are estate rentcharges. Not only may you suffer the consequences of non-payment, but the mere existence of the rentcharge (especially an estate rentcharge) may make it difficult, expensive of impossible to mortgage the property and the property may therefore be almost unsaleable.

#60. Institute of Chartered Accountants in England and Wales – fundamental principles

As a chartered accountant, I am obliged to adhere to the ethical and professional standards and guidelines of the profession. In particular, I list below the Fundamental Principles as set out by the Institute of Chartered Accountants in England and Wales.

Integrity: To be straightforward and honest in all professional and business relationships.

Objectivity: Not to allow conflict of interest or undue influence of others to override professional or business judgements.

Professional competence and due care: To maintain professional knowledge and skill at the level required to ensure that a client or employer receives competent professional service based on current developments in practice, legislation and techniques and act diligently and in accordance with applicable technical and professional standards.

Confidentiality: To respect the confidentiality of information acquired as a result of professional and business relationships and, therefore, not disclose any such information to third parties without proper and specific authority, unless there is a legal or professional right or duty to disclose, nor use the information for the personal advantage of the member or third parties.

Professional behaviour: To comply with relevant laws and regulations and avoid any action that discredits the profession.

GLOSSARY OF TERMS AND ACRONYMS

AIA

Annual Investment Allowance

Alphabet Shares

A system of issuing different classes of shares (e.g. Class A, Class B ......) to allow for different rates of dividends to be declared for each class

ATED

Annual Tax on Enveloped Dwellings

Business Asset Rollover Relief

A system which allows a trading business to roll over the capital gain on the disposal of land, buildings, fixed plant and machinery into the purchase of new business assets, deferring the CGT until the disposal of the new assets

Business Holdover Relief

A relief correctly known as Gift Holdover Relief which now applies only to the gift of business assets of a sole trader, partner or by your personal company or shares in your personal company. The CGT is 'held over' and paid by the transferee on disposal of the assets

Capital Allowances

Allowances on the purchase of plant, equipment or machinery by a limited company for the purpose of calculating Corporation Tax

CGT

Capital Gains Tax charged on the net gain realised on the disposal by sale or gift of chargeable assets (cash gifts are exempt)

Close Company

A limited company controlled by five or fewer 'participators' (anyone entitled to a share or interest in capital or income) or by any number of participators if they are all directors

CLT

Chargeable Lifetime Transfer for IHT (any lifetime gift that is not exempt nor a PET). This will bear IHT (but the rate will be 0% if within the nil rate band)

Companies House (Registrar of Companies)

The regulatory body for registration of limited companies and LLPs, including details of directors, shareholders, accounts, major company decisions and other compliance. Register of information is open to the public, so most companies file abbreviated accounts only.

EIS

Enterprise Investment Scheme providing tax relief to new investors in a company

EMIs

Enterprise Management Incentive Scheme offering shares options to employees of a limited company with favourable tax treatment

ER

Entrepreneurs' Relief (for Capital Gains Tax)

GAAR

General Anti-Abuse Rules, introduced by the Finance act 2013

GWR

Gift with reservation (in relation to IHT)

HMO

House in Multiple Occupation

IHT

Inheritance tax (a tax on lifetime gifts or on the assets passing on death). Some gifts are totally exempt e.g. gifts between spouses or civil partners

Inheritance Tax Agricultural Relief

Relief from IHT available on some agricultural assets (works by reducing the value for IHT by either 100% or 50%). Available for lifetime transfers or on death

Inheritance Tax Business Relief

Relief from IHT available on the ownership of a business or a share in a business (works by reducing the value for IHT by either 100% or 50%). Available for transfers on death, but relief may be claimed for estate in respect of lifetime transfers as long as the transferee has kept the business going

Inheritance Tax Nil Rate Band

The cumulative amount of chargeable lifetime transfers by an individual and the estate passing on death which is taxable at a nil rate (currently £325,000). This excludes any transfers that are exempt and any PETs where the donor has survived for seven years

Inheritance Tax Enhanced Nil Rate Band

An additional nil rate band available on death only on a property occupied by the deceased at any time which is passed to a lineal descendant

IR

Investors' Relief: Tax relief for external investors in unlisted trading companies who receive newly-issued shares which are held for at least three years

Intra-Group Relief (SDLT)

SDLT relief where property is transferred to, by or between companies in the same group. (Intra-group relief may also apply to other taxes)

Land Remediation Relief (LRR)

A scheme to encourage developers to put right contaminated land

LLP

Limited liability partnership

Loss Relief

A relief available where losses have been incurred in the taxpayer's trade, profession or vocation. This can be set against trading income for a previous or future year, with some restrictions as to how this is applied. Trading losses in limited companies can be set against Corporation Tax

MDR

Multiple Dwellings Relief (SDLT). Available where two or more residential properties are purchased in the same transaction

MTD

Making Tax Digital – An initiative by HMRC (already in force for VAT) which requires the majority of taxpayers to file their tax returns and supporting information via a digital platform. Expected to be implemented for Income Tax after April 2021 and subsequently for Corporation Tax

Personal Company

A definition for CGT purposes which means a limited company in which you have at least 5% of the ordinary shares, or of the voting rights, or you would be entitled to at least 5% of the assets on a winding up, or on a disposal of the company

PET

Potentially Exempt Transfer (for IHT). Any transfer that is not a chargeable lifetime transfer at the time of making it. This will become an exempt transfer if the donor survives for seven years

POA Tax

Pre-owned Assets Tax: An annual income tax charge imposed where taxpayers still benefit from assets that they previously owned (but are not deemed to have reserved a benefit for IHT purposes). Mainly refers to land and buildings

Research & Development (R & D) Tax Relief

A scheme to incentivize genuine innovation in science & technology (which may include working methods and practices if sufficiently innovative). Only available to limited companies and increases the amount allowed as tax-deductible on qualifying expenditure.

Replacement of Domestic Items Relief

An allowance for landlords of rented residential property to replace certain domestic items such as furniture and white goods. Replaced the former 'wear and tear allowance' from 6 April 2016

Sale and leaseback relief

An SDLT relief where property is transferred within the same group and then leased back.

SBA

Structural and Buildings Allowance, to encourage investment in new non-residential structures and buildings

SDLT

Stamp Duty Land Tax

SPV

Special Purpose Vehicle (a company or LLP)

TAAR

Targeted Anti-Abuse Rules, introduced by the Finance act 2013

TOGC

Transfer of a going concern (for VAT)

TOMS

Tour Operators Margin Scheme (for VAT)